MW00628804

More
Morning by Morning

Clara Payne

More
Morning by Morning

"Books for the Journey"
StoneGate Publishing Co., Inc.
Longview 2013

Stonegate Publishing Co., Inc.
P. O. Box 8321
Longview, TX 75607
www.stonegatebooks.com
StoneGateBooks@aol.com

I dedicate this book to my precious husband, Bill Payne. He is my best friend and prayer partner and is always loving, supportive and wonderfully fun to live with. He is my greatest fan and my severest critic. He is also head editor and is like living with a dictionary and encyclopedia. His fantastic memory and knowledge of history is a constant source of help.

Besides being the best husband in the world, he is also a great father, grandfather and great-grandfather to all our huge family. I thank the Lord daily for the blessing of a joyous marriage.

I also dedicate this book to the Lord God Almighty who gave me Bill and all my other countless blessings. Every good and perfect gift is from Him.

Contents

Introduction

It is hard for me to believe that it has been eight years since *Morning by Morning* – my first devotional book – was written. Many great things have happened since then with several marriages and births in our families. We are especially proud of eight more adorable great-grandchildren arriving safely. Bill and I have both celebrated 80th birthdays and are still thankful to be healthy. I had a very successful bilateral knee surgery and Bill had cataracts removed from both his eyes this year.

We bought a vacation home in Palm Springs, California, five years ago, so we now spend half the year there and half the year at home in Texas. Staying in California three months at a time, we have been blessed to find a great church, Victory Christian Center in nearby Rancho Mirage. We have made many good friends there and love the messages by Dr Jeff Walker, our pastor.

We have also been privileged to be part of establishing a weekly Bible Study beginning in our home and growing into a larger group now meeting at the church. It has been a privilege to sit under the anointed teaching of Rev. Gerie Martin, head of Loaves and Fishes Ministry. There have been many salvations, baptisms in the Holy Spirit, healings and deliverances. Bill and I have made lasting friendships with many of the members of the Wednesday Bible Study but we still miss our family and many dear friends in Texas and Louisiana while we are gone.

I will recap a little of my story so you will know some of the people that are mentioned in this book. I begin telling you about losing four beloved people in my life, my parents Grace and Julian Hurst, sister-in-law Jane Jo Hurst and first husband William Burke Patterson (Billy) in less than two years. Thus being widowed at age 38 with two daughters, Grace, 15 and Julianne (Julie), 13, and a two-year-old son, William (Burke) Patterson, Jr. But with all this tragedy and darkness, especially Billy's death, a glorious Light came into my life when I was born again a month after Billy died, around my 39th birthday. Knowing Jesus as my Lord and Savior changed my life! He has kept me close to Him from the very beginning, and He completely delivered me from fear. Glory to His name!

I immediately noticed a real hunger for the Word and began reading the Bible constantly. I was so surprised when the words started jumping off the pages giving me guidance and instruction. I began reading the Living Bible (that daughter Julie gave me) and then progressed to the New International (NIV) and New King James (NKJ). Many of the quotes will be from NKJ, but I will often note which translation including the Amplified and Message Bible.

After all my losses, the Lord blessed me with a precious new husband, Bill Payne, who had also been widowed and left with five much-loved children: Kathy, Brant, Lee, Jim and Tim. Also a Christian, Bill and his first wife Ann had been born again at 29 years old after realizing that all they needed to do was to simply fall on their knees and ask Jesus to come into their hearts.

Certainly we have had many problems through the last 40 years including trials in raising all these eight children, but we've had just as many victories. We truly love all our stepchildren and consider them as our very own. We have lost many loved ones including my brother, JG Hurst, daughter-in-law Debra Payne, Bill's parents, our beloved Nana and Granddaddy and our special dog, Tippy.

Several of the devotionals in this book will come from experiences learned from being the matriarch of this big family so you will read about many of them.

Here are the *Much Loved Children*: Kathy and husband Johnny Harville, Brant and Betsy, Grace and her husband Dennis LaMaster, Lee and wife Donna, Julie and husband Frank, Jim and dear friend David Bruyere, Tim, Burke and wife Laura.

Our extraordinary grandchildren and great-grandchildren are: Kathy and Johnny Harville, Emily and girls, Allie, Riley and Katie; Keller and sons Buddy and Brant; Molly and husband Will and baby Evie Walker; and Ellen and husband Jesse Llamas and sons, Christian and Isaac.

Others are Brant Payne, William Brant III (Will) and wife Amber and son, William Carson; Michael, Ann and husband Brooks Alvestad and children Bo and Aston; Austin Payne. Grace and Dennis LaMaster: Laura Grace and husband Jeff Whitworth and their children, Katherine, Drew and Caroline; Julie Katherine and her husband Chris Englerth and baby Clara Jane (am I proud of this name or what?), and a new baby due in 2013; Leslie Claire; Grace Elizabeth; John (Clark); Jane Anne and Scott William. Lee and Donna Payne: Lee Francis (L.F.); William Colin.

Julie and Frank Setzer: John William Crabtree; Clara Elizabeth (Beth) Crabtree and husband Kris Estep and children Emma and Ethan Burke; Evelyn Anne Crabtree (Anne). Burke and Laura Patterson: Mary Margaret and William (Payne).

I also must mention longtime friend and house manager: Billy Flowers.

And our darling dog Doc and his brother Happy who belongs to son Tim.

This second devotional book is also compiled of many of my teachings and journals through the years. Hopefully I have grown spiritually in the past years but in re-reading the devotionals, I wonder. It seems as though I still see many areas in my life that need working on. My prayer is that the readers will be blessed by the reading of my failures as well as successes. This time I have asked my family and friends to contribute their own devotionals. They have already blessed me and I am sure they will you, too.

Through the years, now over 40 since I was saved, I have been privileged to teach two weekly Bible Studies and have spoken at several women's meetings and conferences. I love to give my testimony telling of all the miracles the Lord has done in my life. In our life right now, Bill and I both are learning more and more about the great love the Lord has for us and the importance of receiving His love and grace, not being sin conscious but grace conscious. We often quote, "I am the righteousness of God in Christ." (1 Corinthians 1:30, 2 Corinthians 5:21)

My sincere prayer is that in reading this book people will come to know the great love our God has for them personally and how He yearns to have a closer relationship with each of them as they "grow in the grace and knowledge of the Lord and Savior Jesus Christ. To Him be the glory both now and forever" (2 Peter 3:18).

In His love,
Clara (Sister) Payne

Acknowledgements

Thanks to my editor-in-chief, sweet husband, Bill Payne and our daughter, Julie Setzer, editor, as well as the support of all my large family. And thanks to Rev. Melanie Hart for typing the entire book! She also put in countless hours shortening some Bible Study teachings that I had done through the years, as well as editing other parts of the book. Special thanks to Betsy White who photographed the back cover photo. And, of course, for all my dear contributors!

Contributors

Contributors: Julie Setzer, daughter; Grace LaMaster, daughter; Dennis LaMaster, son-in-law; Kathy Harville, daughter; Burke Patterson, son; Payne Patterson, grandson; Donna Payne, daughter-in-law; L.F. Payne, grandson; Will Payne, grandson; Anne Crabtree, granddaughter; Clark LaMaster, grandson; Dennis LaMaster, son-in-law; Grace Elizabeth LaMaster, granddaughter; Scott LaMaster, grandson; Jane Anne LaMaster, granddaughter; Leslie LaMaster, granddaughter; Beth Estep, granddaughter; Laura Whitworth, granddaughter; Molly & Will Walker, grandchildren; Julie Kathreine & Chris Englerth, grandchildren; Katherine & Drew Whitworth, great-grandchildren; Grace Anne & Ray Woodruff, niece and nephew; Rachel Rice, friend; Rev. Melanie Hart, friend, editor; Ashley Dufeu, friend; Susan Taylor, friend; Judy White, friend; Bob Lowry, friend; Delores Morris, friend; and Lincoln Wingerd.

More Morning By Morning

January 1st ~ Genesis

It is so wonderful beginning a New Year of reading the Bible through in one year. This year I have a New American Standard giant print that I love. It is so neat to start underlining favorite passages again. I begin with Genesis which, of course, means "beginning."

The first four words, IN THE BEGINNING GOD, jumped off the page. When I meditated on this first verse, I thought about everything in our lives beginning with God. It is no wonder that He calls us to put Him first before anything or anyone else. This sounds simplistic but we have to be constantly reminded of this truth because there are so many other things trying to push themselves to the head of the line before God and His rightful place: our families, our jobs, our friends, our church.

This made me think about how we hate it when we have been waiting a long time in a long line and someone pushes past us. Well, literally everything tries to push past the Lord and take first place in our hearts and minds, even good things!

Genesis 1:2 says, "And the earth was formless and void and darkness was over the surface of the deep and the Spirit of God was hovering over the surface of the waters." We, too, were formless, void and in darkness before the Spirit of the Lord hovered over us. Thank the Lord for His mercy. The God who created the heavens and the earth created us in His own image! (Genesis 1:27) How difficult that is to comprehend sometimes.

He blesses us even when we forget to give Him first

place, but we bless Him when we do. And then our lives are so much better.

Matthew 6:33 says, "Seek first His Kingdom and His righteousness and all these things will be added to you."

January 2nd ~ Letting Go of the Past

In Philippians 3:13, Paul is telling us to "forget those things that are behind." We all know we need to get rid of emotional wounds, but it is easier said than done. However, the truth is if we are bitter or resentful it is because we are allowing ourselves to remain that way. God will help us change if we only ask Him.

Unless we let go of the old, God will not bring in the new. We need to get on with our lives and keep our minds focused on all the good things that He has done for us and all that He is going to do.

When I was widowed at age 38, I was absolutely devastated and thought my life was completely over. Someone told me "a grateful heart has less room for grief" and also that I could either get "bitter or better." Of course I chose "better." Of course, I chose better and with the Lord's help I did gradually get better. Certainly I could never have dreamed of the fantastic future the Lord had in store for me: another much-loved husband and five more precious children. I wonder what would have happened if I had not chosen the "better way?" (No one would have wanted a bitter, self-pitying widow.)

Jesus asks in John 5:6, "Do you want to be made well?" Do you want to keep lying around feeling sorry for yourself? Let's not sit around by the pool for 38 years making excuses like the man at the pool of Bethesda, but let's get up and start moving on with our lives…walking by faith with a good, loving Father God. He has a wonderful future in store for each one of us.

January 3rd ~ God's Audible Voice

The first time I ever heard the Lord speak out loud was when I was a widow, very much wanting a new husband. I was at my mailbox in the front yard when I received a letter from my Hockaday Junior College roommate, Wanda Swaim Walker, who lived in Paris, Texas. She wrote to tell me the sad news that another Hockaday friend, Ann Bridges Payne, had died. And I immediately heard a voice saying, "That is your next husband," talking Bill, Ann's widower. Wow, I actually looked around to see who was speaking, but then quickly realized it was a message from God. But five children, Lord, surely we can do better than that? The thoughts were racing through my mind. But now I know that He did a fantastic job of bringing two families together for His glory. I adore my Bill and all our precious eight children.

The next time I heard the audible voice was going to Paris to see Bill when we were dating. I was driving over 80 miles per hour and heard a very clear voice say, "Slow down." I instantly obeyed and knew why I was warned when my right front tire had a huge blow out. If I had been going faster, I would have had a serious wreck.

At that time, I was a new Christian and had not really learned to hear the still small voice that comes to all believers. So He had to speak loudly so I would be sure to hear Him. The Holy Spirit is such a gentleman that He usually speaks very softly and mostly can be heard when we really listen and fellowship with Him. But He yearns to get His messages to us and will try any method of communication. Thanks be to God. "My sheep hear My voice and I know them and they follow Me" (John 10:27).

January 4th ~ Scary News, by Beth Estep, Granddaughter

When I was pregnant with my son Burke, I got a call

from the doctor with the results from my blood tests. There had been a chance that my son was going to be born with Down syndrome, which devastated me. After talking to my mother, one piece of advice she gave me was to open the Bible to any page and read the first verse I see. I do not remember the specific verse, but you can imagine my shock when the verse was about slaughtering sheep! I'm not sure what message God was trying to send me but He made me laugh. Needless to say, my MiMi sent me a list of very comforting verses. My favorite one was Psalm 34:4: "I sought the Lord and He heard me, and delivered me from all my fears."

My husband Kristopher and I went to see a more experienced doctor who performed a more advanced sonogram. From the results of that sonogram, the doctor increased the risks of the baby having Down.

We *sought the Lord* and He *heard us*, and He *delivered us* of *all our fears* and we did not spend one more minute worrying about our child. We KNEW he was going to be just fine.

Ethan Burke Estep was born January 1, 2010, a happy, healthy, strong, beautiful baby.

January 5th ~ Hymn #808, **written for my 80th birthday, January 5, 2012**

Look What the Lord Has Done For Me

Lyrics: Julie Englerth, Ashley Dufeu,
Laura Whitworth

Music: Julie Englerth, Chris Englerth,
Ashley Dufeu

Vocals: Dennis, Grace, Laura, Julie Katherine,
Leslie, Baby Grace, Jane, Anne, Scott and Chris

Instruments: Chris, Clark, Lincoln Wingred, Ashley Dufeu

Spoken Scripture: Katherine and Drew Whitworth

Verse 1
I once was caught in darkest Pit
My soul was lost, no hope for it
Until that day, that glorious hour
When God came down in Grace and Power

Chorus
Jesus' blood has ransomed me
He has redeemed my family
With His great Love He set me free
Look what the Lord has done for me

Verse 2
And as I've grown to trust Your name
Stand on Your word, and shout Your fame
I've seen the captive be released
I've traded fear for victory

Psalm 66:1
Katherine: Come and listen, all you who fear God
Drew: Let me tell you!
Katherine: What He has done for me.

Alle, Alleluia, Precious Jesus, glorified
Heaven's praise, I'll sing forever
Sons and Daughters by my side!

January 6th ~ He Loves Me, He Loves Me Not

Remember when we used to pull daisy petals to see if our new boyfriends loved us or not? If the last peel was "he loves me" then we were happy. How silly this seems today.

But silly as it seems, some act as though the Lord's love for us changes daily. If we've been good, then He will love us. But if we are bad, He does not. This line of thinking is just as silly as the daisy test.

This morning in my quiet time, I looked up and saw my digital clock read "808," my personal sign from the Lord when He wants to remind me of His love. (Growing up, 808 was my family's phone number and I called it collect every night when I was away at college.) I saw this 'love note' Is this the 808? from God and said to Him, "I know You love me, Lord."

He quickly asked me, "How do you KNOW I love you?" I answered, "Because the Bible tells me so." He replied, "Good answer, Sis, your knowledge of My love should always be based on My Word which is truth and never changes, not even on feelings or emotions. Although sometimes you will feel My presence, you must be convinced of My unchanging love at all times, whether you feel like it or not. It is not based on whether you are having good times, prayers answered or bad times and I seem far away; it's always the same. My love is the one sure, solid, constant thing in your life that you can always count on. It will never increase or decrease; it is unconditional and there all the time no matter what is going on around you. Be a grateful receiver of My love, accepting it, and embracing it. Remember, love never fails. I am Love and perfect love casts out all fear."

If you ever have any doubts about God's love for you, cast them down quickly and reread the books of John and 1 John and, of cou7rse, 1 Corinthians 13. Then meditate on Jesus' sacrifice for you. John 3:16 really shows God's magnificent love for each of us

January 7th ~ Palm Springs Bible Study

When Bill and I first began renting our vacation home in Palm Springs, I wanted to start a weekly Bible Study. I had two Bible studies going at home in Texas so I thought it would be easy to start one in California. So Bill drove me around in his golf cart and I put notes in the mailboxes of some of the neighbors, inviting them to come the following Wednesday morning at 10:30 for coffee and a time of fellowship in the Lord. I also gave them one of my devotional books so they could read it and tell I was not a flaky person, but a solid, mature Christian.

Well, not only did no one come, I had some ugly phone calls. One man cursed me, telling me to never come near his house again. One lady was so indignant I was afraid she might go to the police to complain. "How dare you!" was the theme of most of the calls.

The next year, after we had bought the same house, the Lord prompted me to call Rev. Gerie Martin who I knew to be an anointed teacher and ask her what she thought about starting a Bible Study in our home. She said the idea was definitely of God and she would be happy to teach it! We started the very next week! We were so pleased because 12 ladies came. We have seldom had less, and once we had 22, but we average around 15 each time.

What a perfect example of the difference in trying in our own strength and in doing it God's way. This reminds me of Moses getting ahead of God's timing and in his own strength killing an Egyptian he saw beating a Hebrew. After that, Moses had to flee to the desert until God was ready to deliver His people from their bondage. Then He enabled Moses to lead the entire nation out of slavery from the Egyptians. (Exodus 11:25)

January 8th ~ Mighty and Marvelous

Yes, God is mighty and marvelous. That phrase kept going through my mind as I was thinking how wonderful it was that the Bible Study, that began in our home two years ago in January with 12 people, had grown to over 30 people in two years. Bill and I were simply amazed when we returned to Palm Springs from Texas in January of this year and attended the Wednesday Bible study, now meeting at a large clubhouse in a gated community in Rancho Mirage. What a blessing!

Nothing is impossible with God. The group is still growing with new people each week. We have seen salvations, healings, baptisms, relationships restored, strong friendships begun and other exciting miracles. Gerie Martin, our anointed teacher, moves in all the gifts of the Spirit and we are expectant each week to see what the Lord is going to do through her; something new and exciting every time.

One of my favorite things to do is stay close to Jesus and participate in the communion service so you can imagine how pleased I was when Rev. Gerie announced we will be now partaking of the Eucharist once a month at the meetings. She allowed Bill and me to be the first to preside at the table this morning. Everyone was so thrilled to be sharing this special spiritual time together.

We are obeying the command to "study to show yourself approved." Also, we are commanded to not forsake the assembling of ourselves together. "For all scripture is given by inspiration from God, and is profitable for doctrine, for reproof, for correction, for instruction in righteousness, that the man of God may be complete, thoroughly equipped for every good work" (2 Timothy 3:16-17). This is Rev. Gerie's desire for her students that we be thoroughly equipped.

January 9th ~ True Christian

On Christian radio today I listened to the best definition of a true Christian I had ever heard. A true Christian is a person who trusts in Jesus the Christ. It's so simple, yet profound. We try to make it so difficult when really the Lord wants to make it easy for us to believe. The program I was listening to was a Q & A show where people were asking the difference between a carnal Christian and a true one. I loved the explanation - it witnessed to my spirit.

I grew up thinking I was a Christian because I went to

church and was baptized at age 11. I even taught Sunday School as an adult. But after a series of tragedies, I actually did fall on my knees and ask the Lord to take over my life because I could not make it without Him. And, of course, Jesus did and He changed my life completely. I realized I was born again after reading Hannah Whitehall Smith's *The Secret of a Happy Christian Life.* I even remember reading a testimony by a newly born again Christian who said she had never been around a real Christian before she had become a believer. She had had a privileged life and even attended the same denomination that I did so this statement was really shocking to me. I now understand that she meant a "true" Christian – one who lived trusting the Lord on a daily basis.

I am still learning to depend on Him completely. But I certainly know it is safer to trust Him. The best way I do this is by leaning on Him and looking to Him instead of any problems. Proverbs 3:5-6 says, "Trust in the Lord with all your heart and lean not on your own understanding; in all your ways acknowledge Him and He will direct your paths."

January 10th ~ Damascus Road

Wow! What a conversion Saul of Tarsus had! He was knocked off his horse and given a heavenly vision. He then made a firm decision to follow Jesus with all his heart. His name was changed to Paul and he became one of the most important figures of Christianity throughout all the ages. (Acts 9:3-6)

After this experience, Paul spent time being discipled by Christian leaders and developing the ministry God was entrusting to him. Afterwards, Paul preached diligently about Jesus Christ. Many were amazed that he converted to Christianity because they had known his zeal in persecuting Christians. Sometimes people are surprised about the changes that come in our lives, too.

That is why it is so important that everyone who has had a genuine encounter with Jesus make a real effort to share the love of Jesus with others and give testimony to how the Lord has changed their own lives for the better. So people can see the changes. I think the first thing they will notice is the new peace. The circumstances were no different, but the people were!

My personal conversion was not an actual "Damascus Road" experience, but to me it was just as life changing... when on my knees beside my bed I simply asked the Lord to take over my life as I could not manage it alone anymore. This was only about a month after my 39-year-old first husband had died while jogging. Although I was still grieving, at least now it was with hope.

I immediately began hungering to read my Bible and to tell everyone I met about the goodness of the Lord. "For I am not ashamed of the gospel of Christ, for it is the power of God to salvation for everyone who believes" (Romans 1:16).

January 11th ~ Revive

Last year I asked all the kids to tell me their favorite Psalm so I could put their name out by it. Grace's was the one I call the "Word Psalm,, Psalm 119, which is also the longest Psalm with 176 verses. Several years ago I did a study of the prayers in that Psalm and printed them out. I enjoy praying them occasionally.

In my new Giant Print New American Standard Bible (I had worn out a smaller print one in the 70's and 80's and had been in a New King James the last few years so the NAS seems brand new to me), as I was reading Psalm 119, I began noting how many times David asked the Lord to "revive" him. I looked in a Bible Dictionary to see exactly what "revive" meant. It means restoring to life or vigor or to make alive, to quicken. (This reminds me that when I was a new Christian in the 70's and would hear people pray

"Lord quicken Your Word to me," I would secretly chuckle as this sounded very strange to me.)

It was interesting to note that sometimes David prayed that the Lord would revive him according to His Word or His ordinances (verses 25, 107, 154). And then in verses 88 and 159, he just asked the Lord to revive him according to His loving-kindness. Well, certainly we can always trust His Word and indeed His loving-kindness. But I often forget that all His promises are true and I get off into worry and doubt, even doubting His loving-kindness that is always there for me.

Other action words that David used when he prayed to the Lord: redeem, strengthen, establish, sustain, uphold and teach. I say, "O, yes, me too, Lord." I really need the Lord to do all that in my life, also. And He will do it as I believe Him for it, ask Him and then do not doubt His Word that is settled forever in heaven. (Psalm 119:89)

January 12th ~ Giving

God loves a cheerful giver who's ready and willing to give! Our giving hearts come from Him, the Giver. He gave us His indescribable gift, His only Son, our precious Savior, Jesus. Our giving shows our love just like He showed His. Giving is a love language. When we give to Him, we are only giving back what is already His, because EVERYTHING we have comes from Him. Every good and perfect gift is from Him. (James 1:17)

I still remember admiring the gorgeous diamond bracelet Bill had just given me and thinking to myself, "Bill loves me so much to give me this marvelous gift." The Lord quickly said, "Who gave you Bill?" That's true, Lord.

God always gives back superabundantly more than we could desire or pray for; you simply can't out-give the Lord. In Malachi 3:10, we are commanded to give our tithes and also alms to the poor. Giving is a way to show our love for Him or others. Christ is our pattern for giving. He gave His all. As we give to God it shows our faith that He will provide for us. He is Jehovah Jireh, our Provider.

I heard an example about being openhanded: "Do you have a tightly closed fist or an open hand?" Then another question: "HAD YOU RATHER HOLD ON OR BE HELD?" Personally, I had rather trust the Lord.

January 13th ~ Prospering Souls, by Rev. Melanie Hart, Friend and Editor

"Beloved, I desire above all things that you prosper and be in good health even as your soul prospers" (3 John 1:2).

Soul prosperity is the greatest blessing outside of our spirits and many of us aren't even aware of it. The scripture in 3 John is a special key to physical and financial healing.

The soul is three dimensional: the mind, the will and the emotions. When the soul is prospering, the body and the finances will prosper. A rich, healthy, prospering soul will never be lodged in a weak, sickly body. The condition of the body always follows the condition of the soul.

How do you acquire a prospering soul? The blood of Jesus and the Word of God can wash your souls (mind, will and emotions), and give us courage to forgive those who have caused fear, shame, stress, hurt, rejection or great disappointments. Wounds on our soul can cause us to see life "through a glass darkly." Seeing through the wounds causes us to react to circumstances and the words of others instead of responding in faith and love.

As God brings a wound to our remembrance, we have the privilege of taking responsibility and repenting for receiving and holding on to those wounds. We then apply the blood of Jesus to the memory of the wound for the cleansing and atonement. And lastly, we have the Light of God Himself that works like a laser and removes the wound like removing a tumor. Light heals because Jesus is the Light of the world.

A prospering soul is a healed mind, will and emotions;

no longer disappointing God or others by old reactions, willful disobedience or wrong choices. You are becoming whole and free!

January 14th ~ Forgiveness

The Lord wanted me to write on a universal problem in the body of Christ. It is the sin that blocks our joy, prosperity, faith, healing and certainly our answers to prayer. The problem is UNFORGIVENESS!

This is the sin that also particularly blocks the flow of kingdom power. We simply cannot walk in unforgiveness and expect our prayers to be answered. And we all want kingdom power so we need to look at this major problem that we may not even think we have. We have opportunities to forgive every day, so we can never say that we have no unforgiveness in our hearts. (Matthew 18:21-35; Mark 11:22-26)

Jesus teaches us in the Lord's Prayer to pray for God's forgiveness. He says that we are forgiven AS we forgive others. (Matthew 6:9-15) Oh my, forgive as we are forgiven? Sounds like we need to daily set our will to walk in love and forgiveness. Both are our choices and He will help us after we make the choice.

We have been forgiven so much, how can we dare to keep from forgiving others? (Luke 17:3-5) The human capacity to forget God's gracious gift of forgiveness and allow smallness of soul to breed unforgiveness is soberly warned against. Jesus teaches how the spirit of unforgiveness exacts its toll on our bodies, minds and emotions. The "binding" power of unforgiveness is potentially dangerous to any of us. We actually bind ourselves to the people we don't forgive and this keeps God from working in our lives as well as theirs.

Every "kingdom" person is advised to sustain a forgiving heart toward others. Forgiveness is unlocking the door to set someone free and realizing you were the prisoner.

That is real forgiveness and the key to kingdom power.

January 15th ~ Sunday Dinner

It was always fairly hectic getting two little girls and myself ready for Sunday School and church. In those days, I cooked a big breakfast, too. Usually we would eat out for lunch, mostly at the cafeteria, although I really knew Billy would rather have eaten at home. So one Sunday morning I thought I would surprise him and put on a roast to cook while we were gone. I could not wait to tell him after church we did not have to go out. There was complete silence for a moment and then he said, "I turned off the oven thinking you had left it on by mistake." Of course, we had a big laugh over it and I didn't have to cook after all!

This reminds me of Proverbs 16:9 that says, "A man's heart plans his ways, but the Lord directs his steps." God always has a better idea and I have learned to trust Him to direct my steps. I have certainly learned that His is the better way, the way of abundance.

Proverbs 3:5-6 says, "Trust in the Lord with all your heart and lean not on your own understanding; in all your ways acknowledge Him and He will direct and make straight and plain your paths." It's so easy to do; just acknowledge, and then recognize His sovereignty in all our ways.

Direct - Hebrew "Yashar" — means to be and make straight, right, upright, pleasing, good. God will "straighten out" the path of His devoted, trusting servants. I love it. I sure have lots of people in my family that I would like God to "straighten out." Ha. How about me, myself and I?

Other significant words in the above passage are "ways" and "acknowledge." Ways means a road, a course, or a mode of action. Acknowledge - Hebrew "Yada" — suggests being fully aware of and in fellowship with Him. So, as we have direct, intimate contact with God, He promises to guide our paths toward fruitful and abundant lives.

January 16th ~ Lemon Tree

We have had such fun picking the fruit and eating from the grapefruit and lemon trees this winter in our backyard at our home in Palm Springs. We just picked a few at a time until someone told us we should harvest the entire tree so that there would be an abundant crop next year. My son Tim said he felt like a farmer when I bought a fruit picker – a basket on a pole with a claw to reach the highest fruit.

John 15 tells us about Jesus being the true vine and every branch may bear more fruit. Verse 5 says, "I am the vine, you are the branches. He who abides in Me, and I in him, bears much fruit; for without Me you can do nothing." And in Galatians 5:22-23 we read of the fruit of the Spirit which is love, joy, peace, longsuffering, kindness, goodness, faithfulness, gentleness, self-control."

And I keep singing to myself the old Peter, Paul and Mary hit, "Lemon Tree." It goes like this: "Lemon tree very pretty and the lemon flower is sweet, but the fruit of the poor lemon is impossible to eat." I began to think about the fact that lemon juice heightens the flavor of our food and drink but by itself is bitter. How true of us. We need to add our flavor to others instead of being loners that are sour. When we help others, we become fruitful and a blessing. In John 15:16, Jesus says, "You did not choose Me, but I chose you and appointed you that you should go and bear much fruit that your fruit should remain, that whatever you ask the Father in My name, He may give you."

January 17th ~ Who Are You?

Knowing who we are in Christ is to know what we have in Christ. We have the precious fruit of the Spirit: love, joy, peace, patience, kindness, goodness, faithfulness, mercy and self control. (Galatians 5:22-23) Every good thing that is in Christ Jesus is what we have, as well as who we are. In Christ we are regenerated, renewed and born again. This new creation is spiritually minded; the old nature is carnally minded. We can fellowship with God as His own, obey His will and serve Him.

He's already provided all we need because we are now His children. Philemon 1:6 says, "I pray that you may be active in sharing your faith, so that you will have a full understanding of every good thing we have in Christ."

We do not need to beg God for what we already have. Just need to acknowledge it. It is like trying to get in a chair we are already sitting in, if we keep begging Him for things He's already given us. (Ephesians 1:3) He's already provided all we need.

Of course, this does not mean we aren't supposed to ask God for anything. No, the Bible tells us to ask. But God does not want us to beg or worry. He wants us to ask Him for what we need and then believe that we have what we've asked for. Who we are is "worthy" to receive all that is necessary for life and godliness. (2 Peter 1:3) Sometimes I just plain forget to ask Him even though I know He is so ready to answer. Help me remember, Lord, because You make life so much easier doing it Your way.

Believing what the Word of God says about us is the key to being set free from all the lies of the enemy. Once we begin to consistently believe the Word instead of what we think, how we feel and what our circumstances are, we will begin to experience more victory in our lives.

January 18th ~ Abiding in the Vine

The word "abide" has a sense of permanency about it. (John 15:1-8) It doesn't mean to come in and go out. It refers to a place where you remain and dwell continually. Jesus didn't tell us to live in fellowship with Him one day and in the world the next. He was not talking about a temporary arrangement, but was instructing us to make that place of dependency and communion with Him our permanent home. We may stay in a hotel for a short while, but we abide in our homes.

The reason is so we can produce fruit in our lives. The moment a branch is broken off from the vine, it begins to die. There will be no sap flowing from the vine in to the branch. The same is true for us. When we become too busy to spend time with God in prayer and in His Word, we immediately begin to wither.

The word "wither" means to shrivel, to lose or cause to lose energy, force or freshness. That's a vivid picture of what happens to us when we aren't in vital contact and living union with the Lord. We still belong to Him. We still have His life within us, but His energy is not flowing though us. We won't produce anything.

Have you ever been to a church and heard an old dry sermon? It was dry because it did not flow from a heart that was making living contact with God. It's like the manna the children of Israel ate in the wilderness. It had to be fresh each day! And preachers aren't the only ones that dry up. Anyone that fails to abide in Jesus will be spiritually barren. He said straight out "without Me you can do nothing." (John 15:5b) "But we can do all things through Him who strengthens us" (Philippians 4:13).

Let this truth be written in your heart: "The Christian life is simple when you abide in Jesus through prayer and through the Word. When you don't, it's impossible."

January 19th ~ A Cold January Monday Morning

What fun I had talking with the Lord this morning. He really has my number. Since the temperature was in the low 20's and I had had a few cold symptoms from the night before, I had already decided to skip going to early morning exercise without even praying about it. Remembering the old saying "Feed a cold – starve a fever" I decided to forgo my usual routine of fasting Monday morning breakfast and planned to eat some of the good bread I had bought at the famous Collins Street Bakery in Corsicana, Texas.

The Lord immediately said, "I see you believe man's sayings as though they were written in stone, but pass over My promises that you walk in Divine health, always healed by My stripes." (1 Peter 2:24)

But Lord, You do say that I am to cooperate with my healing. Doesn't that mean to eat well and drink lots of liquids; stay in and don't go out to exercise in this cold weather and all the other old wives tales?

"O Sister, you are so hard to change, but I'm not giving up. You might as well begin to bend to My will. I let you get away with lots but remember I will not let you forever. I am molding you and making you into My own image and eventually you will have to change. Don't try to get ahead of Me though, just turn the volume up and listen for My voice and drown out that of the world's. You are tuned into My channel, but tend to turn the volume down when I tell you things you aren't too eager to hear. You can hear My leadings when you are listening closely as they are very clear. You are My special daughter and I am well pleased with you, so remember that and don't be afraid. Billy said to you often 'Act enthusiastic and you will be enthusiastic' so I am saying to you, 'Act young and you will feel young.' Don't think old thoughts, your youth is being renewed like the eagles' when you claim this promise. (Psalm 103:5) Bill's too. Hallelujah! Put down all sick thoughts, think healthy ones."

I excused myself by saying, "Well, You know me, God." He quickly replied, "I sure do! Better than you know yourself. Who do you think you are fooling with your excuses?" I give up, Lord. You win. Right as usual.

January 20th ~ Testimony by Dennis LaMaster, Son-in-law

Before I start "my story," I would like to share with you some of my experiences to set the stage. I am husband of one wife of 29 years, father of seven beautiful children, a modestly successful business owner and member of Longview Christian Fellowship for over 25 years. At 50 years old I see my life as a series of rescues and sovereign acts of the providence of God, and His various servants, in the form of family members, church members and many others used of God.

Through many indescribable dangers, toils and snares, I have managed to be able to tell you about the Grace of God and how He preserved me for His good pleasure. I am in debt to God and to the loved ones who have patiently waited on the Lord to bring me around to the fullness of God's purpose for my life.

After moving our troubled home around from California and landing in Texas, my parents were losing the battle to keep their marriage together. I ran away from my home in East Texas at 16 years old. I got in my car to go to school and instead I began driving west. I called my mother from New Mexico to tell her I was gone for good. She said she would be praying for me to come back. I had made up my mind to keep going and kept driving till my car broke down in Arizona. I had 80 dollars left in my pocket. I was very much alone.

My uncle from California drove through the night to come and rescue me and repair my car. My grandparents in Northern California asked me to stay with them for awhile. They were wonderful to me, encouraged my walk with God and showed me how to pray. They told me stories of the depression, of their roots in Oklahoma and their trip to California during the DUST BOWL. I managed to finish the 11th grade, made preparations to take my GED and go to a local community college.

But I was homesick for my roots in East Texas. My father sent a plane ticket. Grandpa sold my car for me and sent me the money after deducting my room and board. I was glad to get home. But the family unit was splintered forever. My parents never reconciled; a tragedy worth learning from. I determined that I would not be like my parents that whatever the cost I would work to maintain my family unit. It was a worthwhile goal but harder than I could have imagined.

A former pastor, now living in another town and realizing my home life was unstable, asked me to come and live with him as a son. I was proud to have a father figure who was willing to correct me. I knew I needed it.

Eventually I left the pastor's home to strike out on my own (once and for all) and try my hand at adult life. At 20 years old I thought I had graduated. I knew two things I had to have soon: a wife and a church.

I knew I needed a body of believers and I wanted a wife to show the world that I could right the wrongs of my parents. I sought these things with all my best efforts and the Lord blessed me in both. I struck GOLD on both counts. I met Grace Patterson and married her as soon as possible. Soon after we joined the church where we have been a vital part and raised our family. That is not to say all has been a bed of roses but God continues to bless us daily as we focus on Him. Especially with our seven wonderful children, two great son-in-laws and four fantastic grandchildren.

January 21st ~ "Off With Their Heads"

Can you believe that sovereigns actually had the power of life and death over their subjects? They could have someone beheaded or burned at the stake just because they felt like I that day. The charges were because of treason, which translated to mean that the person disagreed with them, especially about religion.

History has always been my favorite subject to study and I really enjoy the period of English history dealing with the Tudors. Between Henry VIII and his daughters Mary and Elizabeth 1, they killed many innocent people. Queen Mary, a devout Catholic, was called Bloody Mary because she burned hundreds for espousing Protestant beliefs. I just read a book about this period of time and am always shocked at their power to simply condemn a person to the London Tower and then death in a horrible fashion.

Guess what the Lord showed me? We have the same power. "Death and life are in the power of the tongue" (Proverbs 18:21). When we speak evil about someone, it is the same as speaking death to them or at the very least condemning them to the "Tower" or prison. This scripture and Verse 20 speak about us eating the fruit of our words. We have to eat our words? I guess we need to keep them sweet and not sour, good and not evil.

We need to talk about good things to be happy. If we murmur and gossip, we will eat the fruit of death. But if we speak life, we will eat the fruit of the Spirit.

Lord, I realize You are really trying to impress this truth on me as every devotional or scripture I have read lately seems to include an admonition about my mouth. Today it was Psalm 17:3, "I have purposed that my mouth shall not transgress." Alright, with Your help, Lord, I purpose to not transgress with my mouth and instead speak only words of life.

January 22nd ~ "Yes and Amen"

"All the promises of God are yes and amen unto the glory of God by us" (2 Corinthians 1:20). Our walk in the Spirit begins when we give a confident, intractable "divine yes" to all of God's promises. It means having unwavering confidence that the Lord will keep every promise in His book to us personally. It's saying, "Father, I have read Your promises and I say 'yes' to all of them. I believe Your Word to me." Amen, so be it. Let it be as You say, Lord.

Just say "yes." It sounds so simple and it is. The better you come to know God and His Word that is Truth, the more you are able to say "Yes and Amen." In other words, I agree with the promise and so I believe it will be fulfilled. Must be a settled, "Yes and Amen" and not a maybe.

I will never forget the day that I had a revelation as I

reread one of the many passages that say, "Thy Word is Truth." It hit me like a bolt of lightning; the Scripture IS TRUTH, the only real Truth. I can go to the bank with the promises of God because they are the Truth. God is not a man that He should lie. (Numbers 23:19)

Every time I claim a Scripture for my very own, I am saying "Yes and Amen" to it and I'm agreeing with God. I have been regularly praying the Word since the early 1970s and I have seen many of these promises manifest in my life and the lives of my family.

Once in desperation over a seemingly impossible situation with one of the children, I acted on the Word and actually threw the Bible down and stood on it. I told Father God that I believed His Word and needed Him to act on it quickly. Sometimes I believe so strongly that I see the answer by faith. I know that I know that I know that it is already done in the Spirit.

January 23rd ~ Thank God It's Friday, by Julie Setzer, Daughter

What's so great about Friday? In my world, Friday is the morning my prayer group meets. The seven to ten of us ladies gather at Denise's house at 5 a.m. in our pajamas to drink coffee and pray. How did it start and what's so great about it? I'll tell ya.

In January of 1997, my friend Kennette asked me if I would like to start praying together each Friday morning at 5 a.m. That was a no-brainer for me. "NO" was my answer. Why in the world would I WANT to get up in the middle of the night to drive to someone's house to pray? I can pray right here at home, at a decent hour, without a trip-taking!

But I knew as soon as I said no and walked away from her that it had been God doing the asking, not Kennette. I reconsidered and reluctantly said yes. I was hooked and committed by the end of our first prayer meeting. That's the how-it-started part, now for the what's-so-great-about-it part. For openers, God is there, literally. "For where two or three have gathered together in My name, I am there in their midst" (Matthew 18:20).

Secondly, Denise and Cliff's house is nice, quiet and smells good. The dress is casual, no makeup required and we get to drink coffee. The main draw is the Holy Spirit. We are reading *The Purpose Driven Life* book together and other devotionals then Ginger, our trustworthy list-keeper, reads the list of people to be lifted up in prayer. There are four lists, one for each Friday of the month: the healing list, salvation/deliverance list, leadership/military list, relationships/jobs list. We pray until 6:30 a.m., crying out to God on behalf of people for their special needs. We ask God to change our hearts to be willing and contrite, to line us up with His Word and His will. We cry out for mercy, wisdom, understanding, strength, compassion. We praise Him, telling Him how much we adore Him. We admit our faults and thank Him for the blessings.

How can I describe the bond that has developed between those of us who have gathered together through rain, snow, heat and darkness? How can I express what these women mean to me who have lifted up my children and other loved ones in prayer, cared about me, loved me unconditionally, put up with me, listened to me, helped me carry my burdens? We've cried, laughed and been touched by God together and touched by death and by life. We will be in heaven together. You'll recognize us; we'll be the ones in our pajamas.

January 24th ~ EVERLASTING ARMS

They are always there!! Praise God! His everlasting arms are always there for us to lean on, to catch us when we fall.

Deuteronomy 33:27 says, "The eternal God is your refuse and underneath are the EVERLASTING ARMS; He will thrust out the enemy from before you, and will say, 'Destroy!'"

Charles Spurgeon said, "God, the eternal God, is our support at all times, especially when we are sinking into deep trouble. There are seasons when we sink quite low – Dear child of God, even when you are at your lowest, UNDERNEATH ARE THE EVERLASTING ARMS."

Matthew Henry said, "However low the people of God are at any time brought, EVERLASTING ARMS ARE UNDERNEATH them to keep the spirit from fainting and the faith from failing, even when they are pressed above measure – EVERLASTING ARMS with which believers have been wonderfully sustained and kept cheerful in the worst of times. Divine grace is sufficient."

I think of the hymn, "Leaning on the Everlasting Arms."

"What a fellowship, what a joy divine, leaning on the everlasting arms; what a blessedness, what peace is mine, leaning on the everlasting arms."

Chorus: "Leaning, leaning, safe and secure from all alarms. Leaning on the everlasting arms."

"What have I to fear, what I have to dread, leaning on the everlasting arms, I have blessed peace with my Lord so near." Yes, He is always near for us to lean on. Praise His name!

January 25th ~ He's Got Your Back

Isaiah 53:5 says, "The chastisement of our peace was upon Him." John 14:27 says, "My peace I leave with you, My peace I give to you; not as the world gives do I give to you. Let not your hearts be troubled, neither be afraid." Because of Jesus we can have peace even in the midst of the storms of life. He bought our peace for us at such a terrible, terrible price that we should not take it lightly. We should not LET our hearts be troubled. He would have not commanded us to do that if we were not able to do it.

Think how very hard it was for Jesus to turn His back to be whipped. He made Himself so helpless when we know He could have called upon thousands of angels to help and put an end to His ordeal. He did it for us so that we could have peace all the time, not just every now and then, but every day in every way. I've heard some football players say, "I've got your back" meaning they are covering for you. Well, Jesus has always "got our backs" because He allowed His to be beaten for us. How good is that? He even holds us by the hand IF we will PUT our hands in His. I do that right now, Lord.

Back to Isaiah 53:1 that says, "Who has believed the report and to whom has the arm of the Lord been revealed?" To those of us who believe the report? I think so! I believe His arm is continually outstretched to us and we just need to take His hand and He will lift us up. (Jeremiah 32:17) Right now, Lord, I am believing that Your strong right arm has gained us the victory even in our most difficult needs because You've got our backs! Please reveal to all of those who need You so much that You are reaching out to them right now and all they have to do is turn around and grab hold and You will lift them up out of the miry clay – the pits. Nothing they have ever done is too bad for You to accept them into Your loving arms and cover their backs. Praise Your name!

January 26th ~ Manifold Troubles/Psalm 107

One of my favorite Psalms is Psalm 107. The heading in my Bible says, "The Lord Delivers Men From Manifold Troubles." Oh, He certainly does! I am amazed that even though the Israelites sinned and grieved the Lord, when they cried out to Him, He was faithful to deliver them. He shattered gates of bronze, cut bars of iron asunder, and caused storms to be still. He brought them out of darkness and the shadow of death. Yes, He saved them out of their distresses over and over.

Although there are several verses telling about how they cried out and He saved them, my favorite is Verse 20 that says, "He sent His Word and delivered them from their destructions." I have used this many times, sending His Word to people in distress and needing to be brought out of the pit of destruction.

Also to situations that were destructive - what a wonderful way to pray knowing we are in God's will when we send His Word. I love to couple it with Hebrews 4:12 that says, "For the Word of God is living and active, sharper than any two-edged sword and piercing as far as the division of soul and spirit, of both joints and marrow, and able to judge the thoughts and intentions of the heart." Isn't that marvelous? Knowing how powerful the Word of God is!

Back to the heading...Manifold Troubles, haven't we all had manifold troubles? Marilyn Hickey taught on that subject once and it has stuck with me. For manifold troubles we have God's manifold grace! (1 Peter 4:10) She held up both hands and putting the fingers together to show us that God has our troubles covered. How marvelous, how wonderful is our fabulous God.

January 27th ~ "If I Could Be With You"

The tune "If I could be with you one hour tonight" keeps going through my head. So I looked up the lyrics online. The chorus goes, "If I could be with you one hour tonight I would love you strong, I would love you long." Then a verse says, "I am so blue I don't know what to do, all day long I'm pining for you. I did wrong when I let you go away, for now I grieve for you night and day. I'm unhappy and dissatisfied but I'd be happy if I had you by my side."

These lyrics made me think of being with or not being with my precious Lord for at least an hour each day. When I do miss my early morning quiet times with Jesus, then all day long I am pining for Him and am unhappy and dissatisfied. And I would be happy if I had Him at my side.

The good thing is that I don't have to say "IF" because He is always by my side and I can commune with Him any time I want for an hour, or even much longer. The Lover of my soul is always available to be with me. Praise His name. It is my fault when I miss the pleasure of His company.

My family is familiar with my tendency to shorten words. I say things like I am "dissa, dissa" for being for being disappointed or dissatisfied. Or "boohoo" for when I am sad. Or "my cup, my cup" when I am delighted about something, meaning my cup is overflowing with blessings.

Well, I do feel "dissa, dissa" when I deny myself time alone with my Beloved. I just don't feel satisfied or complete. Song of Solomon 5:16 speaks of my Beloved, "His mouth is full of sweetness, and He is wholly desirable. This is my beloved and this is my friend, O daughters of Jerusalem." O yes, He is wholly desirable and I am always happy when I have Him by my side.

January 28th ~ Appointed and Anointed

How exciting to think we are not only appointed, but anointed! John 15:16 says, "You did not choose Me, but I chose you and appointed you that you would go and bear fruit and that your fruit would remain so that whatever you ask of the Father in My name He may give it to you."

Acts 10:38 says, "You know of Jesus of Nazareth, how God anointed Him with the Holy Spirit and with power, and He went about doing good and healing all who were oppressed by the devil, for God was with Him." God is with us, too, and we are now as Jesus was when He was here on the earth.

1 Peter 2:9 says, "But you are a chosen race, a royal priesthood, a holy nation, so that you may proclaim the praises of Him who has called you out of darkness and into His marvelous light." We are chosen and anointed as priests. I find these truths extremely awesome.

Years ago I was reading in Exodus 28 about the High Priest's garments and was especially impressed with the two onyx stones that were worn on the shoulders of the ephod (an ornamented vest) as memorial stones for the sons of Israel. The priest would have the names of the 12 tribes engraved on the stones on his chest when he would go into the holy place to pray. Since I believe in acting on the Word of God, I decided to type my family's names on a paper and hold it on my chest as I went to the Lord in prayer. I liked this idea so much that I took the names of the ladies in my Bible study and other friends to the Lord, also. I guess that is what intercession is – taking others to the Lord in trusting, believing prayer. (I need to do this again, soon.)

"You shall be to Me a kingdom of priests, a holy nation consecrated, set apart to the worship of God" (Amplified Bible, Exodus 19:6).

January 29th ~ Thanking God For His Favor

Remember the 10 lepers in Luke 17:11-19? They were all cleansed but the one who returned to thank Him was made completely whole. Jesus asked where the other nine were and said the one who thanked Him was made whole and did not have the side effects, scars or signs of ever having the disease!

Every time you see a manifestation of the favor of God, immediately say out loud, "That was the favor of God." Even if it is something very small like a parking place, we can give thanks to God by recognizing His hand of favor.

Then we will start recognizing the extraordinary and unusual acts in our lives. With a grateful heart, you will see it happening more and more in your life. This is an "attitude of gratitude" that gives glory to God and causes more favor. What we reap we will certainly sow. People who are grateful receive more of the miraculous than those who just take it for granted. There is a connection in consistently saying thank you and consistently seeing God's favor. The Word of God says the redeemed of the Lord shall say so! (Psalm 107:2) God expects me to say what He says.

Confess the favor of God when adverse things break loose and thank God ahead of time for what He is doing.

Job 10:12 says, "Thou hast granted me life and favor." Job declared this in the middle of his problems. He began with what he feared had come upon him and then he changed his mouth. He did get delivered and had restoration through repentance and thanksgiving.

Favor doesn't always happen automatically. We must believe it, thank Him for it and say it. "I will say of the Lord, He is my refuge." (Psalm 91)

Psalm 5:12 says, "For You, O Lord, will bless the righteous; with favor You will surround him as with a shield." The favor of God goes before us and prepares the way.

January 30th ~"His Eye Is On The Sparrow"

Civilla Durfee Martin wrote this favorite hymn for singer Ethel Waters after visiting a couple, both of whom were invalids. When asked how they maintained their cheerfulness and positive attitudes in spite of their affliction, the wife answered, "His eye is on the sparrow and I know He watches me." Her answer inspired the words of this famous song:

"Why should I feel discouraged, why should the shadows come, why should my heart be lonely and long for heaven and home, when Jesus is my portion? My constant friend is He. His eye is on the sparrow and I know He watches me.

"Let not your heart be troubled, His tender word I hear, and resting on His goodness, I lose my doubts and fears; though by the path He leadeth, but one step I may see. His eye is on the sparrow and I know He watches me.

"Whenever I am tempted, whenever clouds arise, when songs give place to sighing, when hope within me dies, I draw the closer to Him, from care He sets me free. His eye is on the sparrow and I know He watches me."

Matthew 10:29-31 says, "Are not two sparrows sold for a penny? Yet not one of them will fall to the ground outside your Father's care. And even the very hairs of your head are all numbered. So don't be afraid; you are worth more than many sparrows."

Our precious Lord does not want His children to live in fear and trembling. God's eye is not focused on war, terrorists or drastic weather changes. His greatest concern is His children and all their needs, hurts and struggles. He is in control of all the world events and soon we will see His hand in all of them, but in the meantime, He cares more about us and our sorrow and suffering.

January 31st ~ Valley of Berachah

After the Lord gave Jehoshaphat victory over all his enemies, he and his people assembled in the Valley of Berachah (which means blessing) where they blessed and thanked the Lord for the miracle deliverance. And it really was a miracle! We read the story in 2 Chronicles 20, one of my favorite chapters in the Old Testament. Judah had been invaded by Moab and Ammon and so King Jehoshaphat prayed to the Lord and listened for His answer. The instructions that he received from the prophet Jahaziel seemed rather strange. He were told, "Do not fear or be dismayed because of this great multitude, for the battle is not yours but God's."

Then they were told to go down against their enemies, station themselves, but not to fight. But instead they were to send out the singers and praisers ahead of their army, saying, "Give thanks to the Lord, for His loving-kindness is everlasting." When they began singing and praising, the Lord sent ambushes against the enemies, who destroyed one another. And then Jehoshaphat and his people took more spoil than they could carry; many valuable things. In fact, it took them three days to just gather it all together.

Talk about blessing from the Lord! No wonder they returned to Jerusalem rejoicing and praising the Lord. Verse 30 says, "So the kingdom of Jehoshaphat was at peace, for his God gave him rest on all sides." There are many good lessons for us to learn from Jehoshaphat when we are surrounded by enemies (problems and pressure). We are to pray, fear not, sing praises to the Lord and trust in Him as He brings the victory. Then we will have peace and rest on all sides in the Valley of Blessing.

February 1st ~ Showering God's Love

After you have received and believed God's love, it becomes natural for you to shower that love on others. Begin by really forgiving people who have wronged you. Don't just casually say, "Oh I forgive so and so." Rather, in prayer, take time to picture those people — one by one — in your mind. Lift them up before God and say, "Father, I turn the unloving feelings I've had toward these people over to You. I will not be bitter against them. Please surround them with Your love."

Imagine Jesus walking up behind that person and putting His big arms around him, bringing peace to his heart. Keep confessing, "I love that person as much as I love myself." Don't hurry through it. Take time to cleanse your soul. Spend extra time loving God and focus on forgiving people who have been especially hard cases in your life. Pray for them at night before you go to bed.

In addition, begin to practice being agreeable. Consciously endeavor to live and walk in harmony with those around you, especially your family, pastor and people at your church. The devil will work hardest to get you into strife with them because he knows when you're in agreement with them there is power. You activate the promise Jesus gave in Matthew 18:19 that says, "Again I say to you that if two of you agree on earth concerning anything that they ask, it will be done for them by My Father in heaven."[a]

Don't allow yourself to become accustomed to being angry. You cannot shower God's love on others with anger. Stop getting mad at your car, your computer, or traffic lights. When you let yourself get irritated at the physical things around you, you're actually practicing being angry, even if you aren't. Repent out loud. Say, "I judge myself for that in the Name of Jesus. I'm not full of anger; I'm full of the love of God."

It's amazing what that will do for you. The more you practice being agreeable and kind, the more love you will shower on others. However, the car and the computer may not really appreciate it as much as the people around you!

February 2nd ~ "Love Lifted Me"

"Love Lifted Me" is the hymn God brought to my remembrance. It goes like this, "I was sinking deep in sin, far from the peaceful shore, very deeply stained within, sinking to raise no more. BUT the Master of the sea heard my despairing cry, from the waters lifted me, now safe am I."

Chorus: "Love lifted me, love lifted me, when nothing else could help, love lifted me."

Sing the second verse, "Souls in danger look above, Jesus completely saves, He will lift you by His love, out of the angry waves. He's the Master of the sea, billows His will obey; He your Savior wants to be, be saved today."

This morning in my quiet time the Lord reminded me not to pray negative prayers. Instead, always pray positive prayers. Pray His goodness and mercy for each person no matter how awful he or she is behaving. Pray blessings for them. It's alright to pray for Holy Spirit conviction on them because God showed me that means a conviction of His love. Remember that it is the goodness of the Lord that leads to repentance (Romans 2:4b), not beating others over the head with a stick.

I heard Beth Moore say that when we try to change a person, we might be like Peter using his sword to lop off the ear of the servant of the high priest. But Jesus, in love, put it back on. Instead, love them into the Kingdom consisting of righteousness, peace and joy in the Holy Ghost. (Romans 14:17)

Also remember that where sin abounds, grace abounds much more. We may be hard on ourselves, but not on others. Don't criticize or judge even in our prayers which can become preachy if we aren't careful. Overcome evil with good. He reminded me to tell of His love to everyone I see, not condemnation, but love. (1 Corinthians 13:4-8) Jesus is our guide to staying in the "love walk".

Our job is to show His love and trust that love to lift our friends and loved ones out of the bondage of sin. Love lifted me and it will lift them, too.

February 3rd ~ Philippians 4 – The Joy Chapter

In looking at Philippians chapter 4, one of my favorite Bible chapters, Paul is instructing us about everything we need to live an overcoming Christian life. It begins with the admonition to stand fast and praise, and to rejoice always. Verses 6 and 7 are such important verses and the very first ones I memorized: "Be anxious for nothing, but in everything by prayer and supplication, with thanksgiving, let your requests be made known unto God and the peace of God which passes all understanding will keep your hearts and minds through Christ Jesus."

Recently, I was especially convicted of giving a "bad report" and the Lord told me to memorize and keep meditating on Verse 8 that says, "Finally brethren, whatsoever things are true, whatsoever things are noble, whatsoever things are just, whatsoever things are pure, whatsoever things are lovely, whatsoever things are of GOOD REPORT, if there is any virtue and if there is anything worthy of praise, meditate on these things." What a good example of how the Word teaches and corrects us. I am sure there will be times when I slip and give bad reports but maybe not so often. I really want to store this verse deep down in my heart.

In Verse 9, Paul reminds us to do these things that we have learned and the God of peace will be with us.

Then in Verse 13, he says, "I can do all things through Christ who strengthens me." Wow – all things? How about Verse 19 that says, "My God shall supply all your needs according to His riches in glory by Christ Jesus." I claim both of these verses often, for myself and for others.

The chapter ends with praise, "Now to our God and Father be glory forever and ever. Amen." Notice "our" God, not someone else's God, but ours! Hallelujah! And it closes with a prayer for believers both then and now, "The grace of the Lord Jesus Christ be with you all. Amen."

February 4th ~ Expectation of Good

A contrast between a cursed man and a blessed man is seen in Jeremiah 17:5-8: "Thus says the Lord: cursed is the man who trusts in man and makes flesh his strength, whose heart departs from the Lord. For he shall be like a shrub in the desert and shall not see when good comes, but shall inhabit the parched places in the wilderness, in a salt land which is not inhabited."

A cursed man cannot see good when it comes? The cursed man trusts in his own strength, while the blessed man trusts in the Lord. It is important to know that God does not curse a person, but he curses himself by turning away from the Lord.

The Word tells us, "Blessed is the man who trusts in the Lord and whose hope (expectation of good) is in the Lord. For he shall be like a tree planted by the waters, which spreads out its roots by the river and will not fear when heat comes; but its leaf will be green and will not be anxious in the year of drought, nor will cease from yielding fruit."

Another difference is seen in a person who has pride in his own self efforts and does not have a grateful heart. Whereas a blessed man realizes that all his blessings come from the Lord and he continually has a thankful heart.

I have known people who received a large monetary windfall and instead of being overwhelmed with gratitude, have immediately thought and worried about the taxes they would be paying, or how the amount would not quite cover their debt. O, my, talk about not "seeing good when it comes".

A cursed man is like a shrub and a blessed man like a tree. I want to be like a tree planted by the water of the Word, not being anxious or ceasing from yielding good fruit even in a year of drought, and always having an "expectation of good" as I hope in Jesus.

February 5th ~ King Jesus

A picture came into my mind of me running to Jesus and, like a small child, throwing my arms around His waist and holding on tight. Not the Jesus who we think of when He was walking on the earth, but King Jesus in all His royal robes. He was looking down at me with so much love that it was hard to take it all in. I thought of the brightness of His glory. I laid my head on His breast and felt His very heart-beat. How awesome that I could grab hold of the King of Kings and the Lord of Lords in His glorious splendor.

This made me think of Queen Esther appearing before King Ahasuerus and having to wait for him to grant her permission to approach his throne. In Esther 2, we read of all the regulations a virgin candidate to be the next queen was required to go through before she was allowed into the king's presence. There were twelve months of beautification to be completed and even then she was only able to go in to the king one time unless he summoned her again.

Esther found favor in the king's eyes and he proclaimed her to be his Queen. Even after that, she had to wait to be called and pray that he would extend his golden scepter to bid her enter his throne room. (Esther 5:2)

How blessed I feel that I can go freely into the throne of God and hug the King of Kings and the Lord of Lords. I can even sit on Father God's lap and feel His love. He is always holding out His scepter to me and to all of His children, with extravagant love.

Hebrews 4:16 says, "Therefore let us draw near with confidence to the throne of grace, so that we may receive mercy and find grace to help in time of need."

February 6th ~ Keys to the Kingdom

Matthew 16:19 says, "And I will give you the keys to the kingdom of heaven, and whatever you bind on earth will be bound in heaven, and whatever you loose on earth will be loosed in heaven."

Rev. Linda Young spoke to our Wednesday Bible Study and taught on using the keys that Jesus gave us. She said we all know we have them, but we don't always remember to use them. Sometimes, we even forget that we have them.

She asked the question, "Have you ever lost any keys?" Of course, we all have! In fact, I had just lost my car keys the day before! And all the time I was searching for them, they were right there on the passenger seat. This made me think that our keys to the Kingdom are there all the time, too. They are not lost, just not being used. Sometimes they are even getting rusty.

Keys are symbols of authority. Sometimes celebrities are given the keys to a city. But to think we have been given the keys to the Kingdom of heaven! This is hard to comprehend.

Jesus gave us power and authority over all our enemies and we just need to use it. Some of our enemies are of our own flesh like unforgiveness, offenses, addictions, fear, worry, negative thoughts and on and on. We have authority over those fleshly things in our lives that hold us back. Our bodies fight to take control, but we can actually speak to our bodies and command them to get in line with God's will. We pray in the Lord's Prayer, "Thy will be done on earth as it is in heaven." He gives us the keys to see this come to pass, daily.

All the miracles Jesus did were done by Him using the keys to the Kingdom to unlock healing, prosperity, peace, food and whatever was needed. Jesus openly and simply demonstrated Kingdom principles. He gave thanks, spoke, prayed and believed His Father would perform it and He did!

In Luke 8:10, He said, "The knowledge of the secrets of the Kingdom of God has been given to you." We have the keys alright, but most have no clue which doors they open or how to work the "deadbolt" to unlock the realm of the supernatural into our natural world. Just like Jesus did, we can, if we will only start using them.

February 7th ~ Reconciliation

I just heard Marilyn Hickey talk about Colossians 1:20, "And by Him (Jesus) to reconcile all things to Himself, by Him, whether things on earth or things in heaven, having made peace through the blood of His cross." Since I have always loved to hear about the importance of the blood of Jesus, I really listened as she stressed reconciliation by the blood.

Naturally I had read this many times, but had only thought about the fact that Jesus had reconciled us to God. But she said this also includes reconciliations here on earth, and not only vertical reconciliations but horizontal, too. I feel sure we can all think of people that we need to be reconciled with, whether a family member or a friend. It may be just a small strain between us or an all-out separation. Either way, it can be made peaceful by the blood of Jesus. How wonderful is that?

I have actually seen this truth come to pass in my own life when the Lord turned around a situation in a certain relationship. I read Proverbs 16:7, "When a man's ways please the Lord; He makes even his enemies to be a peace with him." We were able to be close friends again even after I had hurt the person deeply.

God wants us all to live in peace and love with each other and He makes it easy for us to live that way. Ephesians 2:14 says, "For He Himself is our peace, who has made both one, and has broken down the middle wall of separation."

If we have someone we are at odds with, let's pray Colossians 1:20 over the situation and see the Lord watch over His Word to perform it. (Jeremiah 1:12)

The blood of Jesus is so powerful that it speaks to any problem that we have.

February 8th ~ To Be Well Pleasing To Him

2 Corinthians 5:9 says, "Our goal is to be well-pleasing to Him." In the Amplified it says, "We are constantly ambitious and strive earnestly to be well-pleasing to Him." Of course the reference is to Jesus.

Do I really make that my aim, to be well-pleasing to Him? I hope so. I choose right now to strive earnestly to do just that. Whenever I make a decision, my first thought should be, "Will this please Jesus?"

Several things I know do NOT please Him: refusing to forgive someone, being angry, bitter, hateful, or rude. Or being caught up in self-pity or not trusting - even doubting His goodness or provision. It also does not please Him when we are envious or jealous of others. One of the things He hates most is pride and second may be a lying tongue.

Lately I have been hearing more and more teachings on walking in love. We would not have any of above-mentioned faults if we truly walked in love. I know it will certainly be pleasing to Him and we can't go wrong when whatever we do is done in love. But sometimes it is hard to know what love is in certain situations - tough love for example. (I have never been very good at that. I am not even sure I understand it and I know Bill doesn't, yet.)

There is a fine line to walk between showing mercy and confronting someone. I can do nothing without Him. Prayer is the answer to learning what love would do. He is always so much more willing to tell us than we are to ask. (James 1:5)

Even though Bill and I made many wrong decisions in raising our children particularly in their teens, I believe that the Lord has redeemed most of our mistakes because He saw our hearts were filled with love for them. We mostly erred on the side of mercy so this has surely helped all the children to have a better understanding of the grace of God. I hope so.

February 9th ~ Broken Pieces

When Bill and his first wife Ann were living in Fresno, California, he worked as Executive Vice President for the Pacific National Bank. The bank president and his wife – the Andersons – more or less adopted them as their children since they were far away from their Texas family. When the Andersons returned from a trip to Europe, Bill and Ann hurried over to see them to receive a gift they brought back from Europe for them. It was a lovely antique China cup and saucer that Mrs. Anderson knew Ann would love.

After a nice visit, as Bill was busy putting the three children in the car, he placed the cup and saucer on top of the car. You have probably already guessed the horror story. He forgot it and as he was driving out of the driveway, it fell off the car and broke into a jillion pieces. Mrs. Anderson was inconsolable as she had been so proud of giving them this treasure.

We've all had moments when we wished the earth would open and swallow us up, and this is certainly the way Bill felt. There are times when there is absolutely nothing we can do about what has happened, it is already done and that's that.

Sometimes we feel like that is the way it is, even with the more serious problems in our lives. It's true, often we cannot change the situation, but with God's help, we can change our attitudes about it and go on with our lives. Do as David did. He got up, washed his face, changed his clothes and went into the house of the Lord and worshiped. (2 Samuel 12:20)

It is always good to encourage ourselves in the Lord.

We read about David doing the same thing another time of tragedy in his life when all seemed to be lost and broken. His response was to fall to his knees and strengthen himself in the Lord, his God, asking for His help and the Lord gave him wisdom to handle the problem. (1 Samuel 30:6) God can put the broken pieces of our lives back together.

February 10th ~ Testimony by William & Molly Harville Walker, Grandchildren

Note: the following was taken from the Permian Basin Teen Challenge Newsletter.

William and Molly met and were married two years ago after going through Teen Challenge. Before going to Teen Challenge, they were living a life of complete hopelessness. When Molly entered Teen Challenge, she had lost everything and had nothing to live for.

"I am amazed at what God has done for me in the past two years," Molly said. "We both have been delivered from drugs and alcohol, but that is only a small part of what God has done for us."

Through Teen Challenge, Will and Molly were able to begin a relationship with Jesus. Molly also said, "I know we would never have had the chance if we had not gone through the program. Jesus showed me that no matter what I had done, He still loved me and His plan for my life had never changed. Only through His love was I able to change."

"God has also started working in my family by healing old hurts and restoring our relationship," Molly said. "Through the testimony of the change in my life, my sister has decided to come through the program. I am always amazed by how big my God is and how He chose me. I am now intake coordinator at Teen Challenge. My husband and I are both blessed to work for the ministry that saved both of our lives." (Will is office manager and leads Praise and Worship services.)

Author's Note: I really enjoyed being with Will's family

at their rehearsal dinner and wedding. They were lovely Christian people from Bastrop, Louisiana, and we had a great deal in common. One of the grandfathers said how thankful he was that Molly was from a nice Christian family, too, as they were not sure what she would be like having been in a place like Teen Challenge. We had to laugh as we had felt the same way about Will! God is so good.)

February 11th ~ God's Goodness and Love

Do we really know God loves us? And that He is a good God? Do you really believe in His goodness and mercy? Not just as a concept, but do you personally know it? I think that unless a person believes in the goodness of God, they will not be able to trust Him. If there is even a lingering doubt that God is mad at us, then we won't trust Him for His goodness. Or if we have the mistaken idea that we are not worthy of His blessings, then we have a problem trusting Him.

God is not mad at you. He loves you. Understanding this will change your life. The more we know God's goodness, the more we trust Him. The more we trust Him, the easier it is for us to put our lives into His hands. He is always endeavoring to help us. So we can relax and receive His blessings. Remember, the Bible even says His blessings will overtake us. (Deuteronomy 28)

I am convinced that God wants to give to all of us lavishly, without reserve, and pour His blessings upon us. He wants us to be blessed that everywhere we look we see the goodness of the Lord. God wants to bless us in every area of our lives. He wants to give us the desires of our hearts. Jesus came that we might have a life of abundance. (John 10:10)

I know it seems too good to be true, but that is not surprising. If you think about it, Jesus Himself seemed too good to be true. The fact that God sent Him to pay the price for all our sins, and the fact that He died so we could live by simple faith in Him, sounds too good to be true. But we all know it is true. Romans 8:32 says, "He that spared not His own Son, but delivered Him up for us all, how much more shall He not with Him also freely give us all things."

The revelation of God's goodness will help us have confidence and receive from Him whatever we need.

Glory be to God!

February 12th ~ Jesus Our Rest

Matthew 11:28-30 says, "Come unto Me all you who labor and are heavy laden and I will give you rest. Take My yoke and learn from Me for I am gentle and lowly in heart and you will find rest for your souls. For my yoke is easy and my burden is light." Jesus calls us to come to Him for rest.

In the Jewish tradition in Jesus' time, there were many rabbis, each with their own interpretation of the Scriptures. Choosing to study under a particular rabbi, you became his *talmid* (disciple) - one who not only wanted to learn what his teacher knew but who would imitate his lifestyle. This was called "taking the yoke" of the rabbi. (A yoke was an obligation or commitment.)

Jesus invited His *talmid* to take His yoke upon them because it was easy and light. Jesus walked with amazing lightness of heart, unencumbered by worry, unwounded by criticism, unfettered by greed or ambition and undeterred from His purpose. We also can learn to live like that.

Want to lighten your load? We must come to Him with the intent to learn and live as true disciples. Then He promised in John 8:32, "And you shall know the Truth and the Truth shall make you free."

Picture it: Jesus on the hillside, the crowd at His feet. Like other rabbis, He taught in parables, only His interpretation was very different. He spoke not of rule-keeping, but of a relationship. He corrected the Pharisees who made it hard to approach God. They thought, "Whatever it is, we are against it." Know some people like that?

You would think that after a lifetime of intense study of Scripture, the Pharisees would be the first to recognize and welcome Christ. But that wasn't the case. They were nit pickers devoted to religion and religious people. They emphasize behavior, rituals, traditions, forms, procedures, guilt. Relationship is about transformation of heart, character and grace. Jesus was the hardest on the Pharisees because they should have known better!

God offers an alternative: Jesus, our permanent resting place. (Hebrews 4:7-10) We were never meant to live a burdensome life. The One we follow came to bring us abundant life – life to the fullest. (John 10:10)

February 13th ~ Hairs on Your Head

Jesus told us His Father's eye is on the little sparrow and that He counts every hair on our head. That is how valuable we are to Him as His children. Eleanor Roosevelt once said, "God is too busy with world affairs to care about the details of life." WRONG! Not so!

We can stand strong because God is focused on our present struggles and He has promised to give us the strength to bear up under any and all trials. Remember nothing is spinning out from under His control. He is still the "Governor of all nations…Sovereign…King of Kings and Lord of Lords." (1Timothy 6:15) Nothing happens in the world without His knowledge and governance. How comforting that thought is.

Which brings me to the word "control" and its meaning: to keep under check, to restrain, to govern. The course of human events cannot be controlled by human wisdom and power. We often pray for God to be in control, to be sovereign in our situation, believing this will make everything right.

The devotional in Word for Today on the 13th was fantastic. Ephesians 5:18 talks about being filled with the Spirit;

being under the influence or control.

This is such a good explanation of control. The power He provides is controlled and channeled towards a life that's not possible by any other means. And that power is available to us today. Yea! You are His child and He cares about everything in your life.

Matthew 10:30 says, "But the very hairs of your head are numbered." Luke 21:18 says, "But not a hair of your head will perish."

February 14th ~ "Just My Bill"

Remember the old song, "Just My Bill"? It reminds me of how I still feel about my precious husband Bill, after almost 40 years. Since the word 'thrill' rhymes with Bill, that is a good way for me to begin speaking about him. Just seeing him thrills me, still.

I get up early in the morning to pray and, after about an hour, I listen for Bill to awaken. Although I am at the other end of the house, I am alert to hear what I call "sputtering" as he clears his throat and coughs. Then I am ready to turn on his coffee. I try to have the house warm, his newspaper ready for him and set out a glass of ice water and his meds. I am in tune with him in every way. I feel such excitement just waiting for him to come down the hall. It is easy to thank the Lord for him.

As I was expectantly waiting for Bill this morning, the Lord showed me that He felt the same way about me. He gets all excited about me coming to be with Him! It's too marvelous for words. Yes, I believe He does, but it is so amazing that it is hard to explain. He wants to have everything nice and ready for me, too. He sets a banqueting table of His love for me each day. (Song of Solomon 2:4) His banner over me is love. (He is Jehovah *Nissi.*)

When I know that my Jesus is waiting expectantly for me, it becomes even more important to be careful not to miss these special quiet times with Him even when sleeping an extra hour is very tempting. He says, "Come and sit with Me and I will give you rest" (Matthew 11:28).

February 15th ~ Same as Hitler by Rachel Rice, Friend

Isaiah 53:6 says, "All we like sheep have gone astray; we have turned every one, to his own way; and the Lord has laid on Him the iniquity of us all."

One again I was down on my closet floor asking His forgiveness. I had "done it again." I felt I was going around for the 'umpteenth' time with the same old besetting sins of hateful, hurtful words and actions. I was repenting with contrite heart, lots of tears and all my being when I heard God's sweet peace-filled voice saying, "You're the same as Hitler".

"What do you mean, I'm the same as Hitler, surely not?" I shuddered with that thought. "Yes," He said ever so gently, "but that's before you came to Me!" Stunned, I realized that Hitler's clay and my own old human clay were from the same big lump of fallen flesh. But, thank God, I'd made my own personal, choice for Jesus and changed my earthly status to that of His heavenly Kingdom! When you've got a mighty, delivering Savior, then you've really got a Deliverer and a Savior. His saving power stretches into eternity, covering all the bases for me, and "whosoever will."

Hallelujah! I've got my own transfer from human dirt to glory dust and do I like it here! No more groveling in soulful regrets or rejection. I have the release of joy and praise since I've learned the truth about His grace and permanent forgiveness, even though I'm still in process and quite imperfect. His love has no end this side of heaven! None!

I know I can run back at any time into his arms with a happy heart and tell my Father, "Thanks for Jesus, my Older Brother" who made that great exchange for me, His place for mine. I thank Him for my new long robe of righteousness, beautiful sandals of peace, surrounding belt of truth and His crowning helmet of complete salvation because "His burden is light and His yoke is easy." What a gift He's given in the Holy Spirit, who is our happy GPS - always with us, even if we come across any road with shadows of death or darkness. (Psalm 23)

It's a Kingdom choice. It's a New Covenant place of peace! No more prodigal Rachel, but a whole new one hidden with Him in Christ. If you've not gotten your own transfer yet, grab His and go on with me! Anyone who belongs to Christ has become a new person. The old life is gone; a new life has begun! (2 Corinthians 5:17)

February 16th ~ State of God's Grace

Psalm 31:15 says, "My times are in Your hands." How comforting a thought that is! The Lord corrected me and said, "Not a thought, but a truth." Wow! Am I ever blessed?

Psalm 31:19 says, "O how great is Your goodness which You have laid up for those who fear You, which You have prepared for those who trust in You in the presence of the sons of men."

Verse 20 says, "You shall hide them in the secret place of Your presence from the plots of men."

How great are all those truths?

I had also been meditating on Romans 5:12 that talks about standing in God's grace, "Standing firmly and safely into this grace - state of God's favor!" (Amplified) I love it. That is because we have been justified through faith in Jesus Christ!

Bill and I are now living in two states: Texas and California. Our home is still in Longview, but we spend about half of the year in our vacation home in Palm Springs. We are constantly amazed at the difference in the laws and customs. So it comforts me to know that we are always in the state of God's grace that never changes. Also, we have learned that we can fellowship with Christians in both places. We love both of our wonderful churches and we've even found a weekly Bible Study similar to the one at home in Texas.

So, let us be full of joy, now. Rejoicing that our times are in His hands and we are in the state of God's grace and favor, and rejoicing in the hope of the glory of God. We are justified by His blood and saved from wrath.

February 17th ~ Blessed, Blessed, Blessed

My close friend Betty Hurst has a dear housekeeper, Ann Davis. When you ask her how she is, she always answers, "I'm blessed, blessed, blessed." What a joy it is to hear her sweet reply. She radiates the love of Jesus.

In His Sermon on the Mount, in the Beatitudes, Jesus repeats the words "Blessed, blessed, blessed" in which I believe HeHe tells us of His desire for us to be blessed.

"Blessed" in the Amplified Bible has many definitions: "Happy, to be envied, and spiritually prosperous (that is with life, joy and satisfaction in God's favor and salvation, regardless of their outward conditions)." And "enviably happy" means with a happiness produced by experience of God's favor and especially conditioned by the revelation of His matchless grace. Or, "Happy, blithesome, joyous, spiritually prosperous." Or, "Fortunate and happy and spiritually prosperous (that is, in that state in which the born-again child of God enjoys His favor and salvation)." Or, "Enjoying enviable happiness." My gracious, that covers a lot of ground.

The old hymn says, "Count your blessings, name them one by one." A good idea for all of us. We are blessed to live in our great USA and all of us, no matter how poor we might be, are still richer than 90 percent of the world.

When the devil accuses us of having done wrong and tells us we do not deserve God's blessings, what should we do? We are to point everything back to Jesus, who qualifies us for all of God's blessings. We have a right to walk in all the blessings of God, not because we are good but because Jesus shed His blood and qualified us to have them.

Praise His name.

February 18th ~ Laundry

With seven children, our daughter Grace is a laundry expert. She always has several loads a day and changes washing machines almost yearly. Recently we were out eating prior to a school program when Scott, age six, spilled catsup on his nice clothes. Grace immediately whipped out a stick that looked like a magic marker and rubbed it on the spot and it miraculously went away. I was so impressed that I wanted to know all about it. It was an instant stain remover called "Tide to Go." Of course, I could not wait to buy my own and now carry it around with me.

An instant stain remover. Wow! Wish we could remove the stains caused from our sins as easily! Even after we are forgiven, we still bear the stains. Jesus' blood washes the sins away, but often the stains remain. We still bear the consequences and we have to forgive ourselves, too, in order to be completely and totally cleansed.

One of my favorite hymns is "Nothing But the Blood." How true. I am also reminded of the verses in Ephesians 5:25-27, "Christ so loved the church that He gave Himself up for her that He might sanctify and cleanse her with the washing of water by the Word, that He might present her to Himself a glorious church, not having spot or wrinkle or any such thing, but that she should be holy and without blemish."

Washing of the water of the Word; when we stay in the Word and let it teach and correct us, it helps us stay clean. "Without spot or blemish" is certainly my desire. I do wish I had a "Tide to Go" but I realize it isn't always that easy to stay free from sin. What can wash away our sins; nothing but the blood of Jesus.

Praise God for His blood.

February 19th ~ Humility

Bill's word for this past year has been "humility." He prays that our entire family would humble ourselves under the mighty hand of God; not being proud, arrogant, or haughty. I know he is right and this truth is straight from the Word.

Humility is the key to honor and favor. God resists the proud, but He gives grace to the humble. "Therefore, humble (denote, lower yourselves in your own estimation) yourself under the right hand of God that He may exalt you at the proper time" (1 Peter 5:5-6, Amplified). I love Him giving me grace when I am truly humble and cast all my cares on Him, instead of proudly trying to do everything in my own strength. (Verse 7)

The NAS suggests that in the Bible "humility" is usually an honest self appraisal, characterized by the knowledge that one is merely human and by the absence of pride. In the New Testament when Jesus applies the term to Himself, it refers to His attitude of service of others and His willingness to forego the rights and exaltation that is His rightful place as the Son of God.

Matthew 11:29 says, "Take My yoke upon you and learn from Me as I am gentle and 'humble' in heart, and you will find rest for your souls." Hopefully, we can learn to be more humble from Him.

Psalm 37 is one of my favorites and I especially love Verse 4 that promises if we delight ourselves in the Lord, He will give us the desires of our hearts. Well, I do delight myself in Him and believe He will give me every good and perfect gift. Verse 11 says, "The humble shall inherit the land and will delight themselves in abundant prosperity."

Glory! I like that one, too.

February 20th ~ Afraid to Ask Him?

It is interesting to read about the disciples misunderstanding something Jesus said, but were afraid to ask Him what He meant. (Mark 9:32) I started to be critical of them before I remembered that I am sometimes that way, too.

Although we are told in James 1:5, "But if any of you lacks wisdom, let him ask of God, who gives generously and without reproach."

Instead we spend a lot of time trying to figure out the answers to our problems ourselves, when all the time He is waiting to give us the wisdom that we need. All we have to do is ask, believing He will happily supply the direction desired.

First and foremost, He is telling us to take heed to what He's saying. When we purchase something, we understand the process of paying and receiving. When we pay attention to God, we need to expect to receive divine revelation in return. God constantly speaks to us and we need to stop and listen. He gives us instructions we need and the wisdom to live as 'overcomers' and not as victims.

The very first time I asked the Lord for wisdom, was whether to marry Bill. Since I was so blinded by my love for him, I wanted to be sure I was doing the right thing. It would mean uprooting my three children, moving them to Paris, Texas, and becoming a mother to Bill's five children! This was a tremendous decision and I desperately wanted God's will. He was so gracious to tell me to "Go" and to trust Him. What a witness this was to me as a new believer.

I know He answers our prayers for wisdom. We need never be afraid to ask. God is faithful to His Word.

February 21st ~ Be Available

God is not looking for ability, He is looking for availability. All He needs is faithfulness. It doesn't matter whether we are talented, God has all the ability we need. He uses the foolish things to confound the wise. (1 Corinthians 1:27)

The new birth is the great equalizer. It takes you out of your natural station in life (whether it be high or low) and puts you in the anointing of Jesus. It makes all His wisdom and ability available to you. As you make yourself available to Him, He will cause that ability to flow through you by anointing you to do whatever He wants you to do.

Colossians 2:6 says, "Just as you trusted Christ (the Anointed One and His Anointing) to save you, trust Him too for each day's problems; living in vital union with Him." (The Living Bible) In other words, depend on Him to help you through the things that you face in your life.

This thrills me to know that I don't have to have any special talents to be used by God. I just have to be faithful, yield myself to Him, and stay in living contact with Him.

What encouragement!

God wants us to cultivate an attitude of dependency. This has been easy for me because I was a dependent person in the natural. I know this is harder for independent people; especially men, because they are told from childhood to be in control. Our inadequacy actually helps us to depend more on the Lord.

Self-sufficiency is a drawback. Sometimes our talents and intellect must be given up to God and then let Him give them back as He desires. He will use our past experiences and gifts, but our cry should be, "I can do all things THROUGH CHRIST" and not through myself.

February 22nd ~ Sheep

The Bible often uses the relationship of sheep to their shepherd to depict our relationship to God. When God compares us to sheep, it is not a compliment. Real sheep are not those cute, fluffy creatures we see in the Hallmark store. They are smelly, dirty animals and they are DUMB. Jesus knew we were all like sheep and would go astray and would need a shepherd. Following the ways of the world and the ways of empty religion, we would become wearied and lose heart

Matthew 9:36 says, "But when He saw the multitudes,

He was moved with compassion for them, because they were weary and scattered, like sheep without a shepherd." A shepherd on the Judean hillside would join other shepherds at night and build a stone wall around their sheep to protect them from wild animals. Encamped at the door of the sheepfold, they would take turns keeping watch. In the morning each shepherd would go to the door of the fold and call his flock. As stupid as sheep are, there is one thing they know - their shepherd's voice.

Sheep will see green grass on a dangerous ledge, jump down to eat it and not be able to get back up. The shepherd then waits till the sheep gets very weak and hungry, then lassos him and pulls him up. If the sheep is not weak and helpless, he might try to get away and fall off the ledge. It is only when he is at the end of himself that the shepherd can rescue him. Sound familiar?

"My sheep listen to My voice and they follow Me," Jesus said. Can you hear His voice over the noise of your life? Do you recognize it? Or have you mistaken another voice for His and been led astray into a life 'crammed full' of the world?

Whenever we wander from our resting place (Jesus) we become prey. School, church, work, family, media - they will all eat away at our time, our values, our resources, until they have devoured us. This breaks God's heart, for He loves us and longs to show compassion. When Jesus calls us to Himself and we recognize His voice, we have a choice to obey or to stubbornly stay where we are.

Help us, Lord.

February 23rd ~ God Loving Me

What? I thought this was about me loving God, not about God loving me! Oh, but it is about Him loving you. 1 John 4:10 says, "In this is love, not that we loved God, but that He loved us and sent His Son to be the propitiation for our sins." In other words, the cycle of love begins with God.

His love for us is what ignites within us a love for Him and for others. Receiving His love is what enables us to walk in our personal assignments and dreams.

Think about that! The creative principle of the heavens, the very love of God Himself, has been imparted into your spirit and you have been authorized to love others with it. When you begin to believe it, you activate within yourself the most powerful force on earth. You'll not only love God with all your heart, soul, mind and strength, but you'll start loving and praying for the meanest people you know. You'll be so full of love, it will begin to overflow.

So the important thing is to know how much God loves you. Do you really believe that? Most believers don't. John 17:23 says, "I in them and You in Me; that they may be made perfect in one, and that the world may know that You have sent Me and have loved them as You loved Me."

God loves you and me as much as He loves Jesus! Wow! This is very hard for us to comprehend. Old religious thinking tries to stop us from believing this. Begin saying aloud: "God loves me just as much as He loves Jesus." Joy will fill your soul!

Keep saying it and thanking God for it until the truth of it begins to saturate your heart. Father, thank You for loving me so much. Thank You for giving Your own Son for me that I might not perish. I receive that love, now. Amen.

February 24th ~ A Sense of Humor

Many years ago, Bill and I attended a Marriage Encounter weekend and gained much insight on marriage in general and ours in particular. One of the questions that we were asked to meditate on in our 'quiet times' together was, "What is the quality you most appreciate in your spouse?" We were to write our answers in our notebooks and then compare them. So we were delighted to see that we had written the same things: our sense of humor and we were fun to be with!

What a blessing - a gift from God - the ability to see humor in every situation. I truly feel for people who don't have this gift. I remember an occasion when Billy was in college at Texas Tech and several of us were sitting around a table talking, telling jokes and laughing. One of Billy's friends looked straight at me and asked, "Would you please tell me what was funny about that joke that made you all laugh so hard?" For once I was speechless as I found it hard to explain why it tickled us all. He said he realized he did not have a sense of humor and so could never quite "get it" when we all laughed. How sad was that?

God likes to laugh, too. Psalm 2:4, 37:13, 59:8 are a few examples. Since we are made in His image, naturally we get our sense of humor from Him. My opinion is that some people just take life too seriously. God meant us to enjoy and have fun in life. He gave us all things richly to enJOY. (1Timothy 6:17) And JOY is a fruit of the Spirit.

A wife asked her husband, "What is it about me you appreciate the most; my gorgeous body or my beautiful face?" He thought a minute and then said, "I believe it is your sense of humor." Sounds like something my Bill would say to me. Thankfully I could laugh!

February 25th ~ Useful to God

I want to be useful, but the usefulness of my life is God's concern, not mine. I need to trust Him to show me what He would have me do after I worship Him. That always comes first. When I try to be useful to Him, I always fail. He will direct my steps. He decides whether to use me and how to use me. All I have to do is focus on Him. "But who are you, a mere man, to criticize and contradict and answer back to God? Will what is formed say to him that formed it, 'Why have you made me thus?'" (Romans 9:20, Amplified).

I may want to be a cup; a cup is so useful. But God may intend for me to be a saucer, which also has its uses. Furthermore, if God wants to set me on a shelf and leave me there, that's His prerogative. "Let patience have her perfect work, that you may be perfect, entire, wanting nothing" (James 1:4.)

Our ambition to be used by God leads us into all kinds of dangerous traps, such as separating out what is and isn't useful to the kingdom. Pride of usefulness also causes us to judge others. "But Martha was distracted by all the preparations that had to be made, and she came up to Him and said, 'Lord, don't you care that my sister has left me to do all the work by myself? Tell her to help me'" (Luke 10:40).

There will always be needs in our world. Our natural impulse is to run toward the needs. Don't run, unless God tells you. We are not the Living Water; He is. If we run ourselves ragged helping the needy, we can sometimes become spiritually impoverished. It is a mistake to be preoccupied with our own usefulness instead of being preoccupied with God.

If we focus on our faithfulness to God, usefulness will follow. Then we become more like Jesus. And the more we become like Jesus, the better equipped we are to be useful to God.

February 26th ~ God Works With the Word by Judy White, Friend

Isaiah 55:11 (Amplified) says, "So shall My Word be that goes forth out of My mouth; it shall not return to Me void, without producing any effect, useless, but it shall accomplish that which I please, and it shall prosper in the thing for which I sent it."

1. The nature of the Word is miraculous.
    a. Jesus is the Word (John 1:14)
    b. The Word is a living thing. (Hebrews 4:12-13)
    c. We are born again by the Word. (1 Peter 1:23)
    d. We are healed and set free. (Psalm 107:20)
    e. God watches over His Word. (Jeremiah 1:12)

f. The angels harken to God's Word. (Psalm 103:20)

2. The miracle action of the Word is released in two ways:
   a. Through the words of our mouths (Romans 10:8, Mark 11:23, 2 Corinthians 4:13)
   b. Through actions (James 1:22, 2:17-22)

3. People stop the miracle action of the Word by fear, doubt and unbelief. (Matthew 14:27-31, Luke 12:22-32, Hebrews 4:2, Mark 6:5-6)

The Anointed Word

1. The Word is the power of God unto salvation. (Romans 1:16)
2. God has exalted His Word above His name. (Psalm 138:2)
3. The Word is full of authority and power. (Luke 4:32)
4. Signs and miracles accompany the Word. (Mark 16:20)
5. No Word from God is without power. (Luke 1:37)
6. There is Self-fulfilling power in the Word. (Isaiah 61:11)

The Word will work all the time for anyone who will stand and believe it. Remember as you work with God's Word, the Lord will work with His Word, confirming it with signs following. It is no respecter of persons. God's power and ability are not manifested until the demand is placed upon His power.

February 27th ~ Are You Watering Your Camels?

Author's note: Samantha Landy, well-known author and speaker, taught this lesson at a 'Walk In the Light' Bible Study in Rancho Mirage, California.

Genesis 24:10-27 is the story of Rebekah, and Abraham's servant, Eleazer. Verse 19 says, "When she had given him a drink, she said, 'I'll draw water for your camels, too, until they have had enough to drink."' Talk about a commitment! Camels are about eight feet tall and they usually drink eight to ten gallons of water at a time and more if they have been on a long journey. Their journey had taken months as it was about 800 miles.

There were 10 camels so that meant 80 to 100 gallons of water and a jug only held three gallons. That meant 33 trips for each camel, 333 trips to the well to draw water! Rebekah, having been around camels her whole life, knew what she was getting into and she didn't quit until it was done. Rebekah in Hebrew means "captivating" and she sounds more than that to me. Eleazer prayed a very specific prayer and Rebekah was the fulfillment of that prayer.

Today we will liken the camels to the issues, difficulties, and problems we face in our lives. Are we hanging in there and watering them with the water of the Word? Let's look at some of the attributes of a camel and see how often they line up with the problems (camels) in our own lives.

Camels are impatient, stubborn, demanding and they often fight for position. (After riding one in Israel, I want to add that they are also smelly.)

What can we do to water our own camels? How about choosing to let the Holy Spirit help us walk through our days with joy and commitment? A happy person is not a person with a certain set of circumstances, rather a person with a certain set of attitudes.

February 28th ~ "God Love!"

When Grace, my daughter, was about two and a half years old, I told her that Aunt Fonny was coming to see her from Crockett, Texas. Grace immediately said, "And she will say 'God Love'." How wonderful to be known even by a small child for such wonderful words.

That definitely was Aunt Fonny's favorite saying, but I did not realize that Grace had noticed it. (She was actually not my aunt, but was my mother's first cousin and I had always called her aunt. She was a gracious Southern lady who I loved dearly.)

Her son Bob was two days younger than me and we were very close when we were growing up. We often visited back and forth. His daddy was the Chevrolet dealer in Crockett and mine was the Ford dealer in Longview so we spent lots of time arguing about which car was the best and who sold the most. We tactfully decided that there were more Chevrolets in Crockett and more Fords in Longview.

Mother was born in Crockett, had lots of family and friends there, and I loved visiting with them. Since Aunt Fonny only had two sons, I was her special 'daughter.' When I took the train to go see her, she often had parties for me. She was very interested in nutrition (my family was not) and would have unfamiliar foods that I was not too fond of. She laughed once when she served fresh peas and I exclaimed, "Peas, how sweet!"

I have many, many more precious memories of her and what a blessing she was to my life. She really believed that God loved us all and helped also me to know it. What a wonderful expression: "God Love" is a prayer like "God bless," and also a statement of truth. 1 John 4:16b says, "God is love, and he who abides in love abides in God, and God in him."

February 29th ~ "Only Trust Him"

As usual in my morning "quiet" time, I was singing out of my old hymnal. (It had belonged to my grandfather John Henry Hurst and was signed with a beautiful signature – my daddy could write great, too. What happened to me? I think they put more emphasis on penmanship in their school days.)

Anyway, one of the hymns for today was "Only Trust Him" and as I was singing, the Holy Spirit whispered to my spirit, "Do you trust Me? Really trust Me? Seems to Me like you have been letting fear creep in, even this morning when you read something else about earthquakes. Don't you think I would protect you and Bill, if there was one? Don't you know I am always with you to see that you are safe? And what is this fear you seem to have of having a stoke? Or dementia? You have My promises that you walk in Divine health and I bore all your sicknesses and diseases upon the cross. And what about Psalm 91 that you claim every day? Do you believe it or not? It is my solemn word on the matter so trust and do not fear. I have not given you a spirit of fear, but of power and love and a sound mind (1 Timothy 1:7) so you must see that fear is not of Me, so cast out even a tiny bit that tries to come on you. Only trust Me - and I will surely give you rest. I have saved you thus far and I will lead you on."

I was also reminded that there is no fear in love and perfect love casts out fear. (1 John 4:18) And since God is love, there is no fear in Him and His love is perfect.

The hymn goes on to say, "For Jesus shed His precious blood, rich blessings to bestow; so plunge in today into the crimson flood that washes white as snow."

Glory be to God!

March 1st ~ Battle of Jericho

Joshua told the Israelites to be silent, not to speak a word when they marched around Jericho. (Joshua 6:10) How hard was that for 40,000 men to keep silence? No noise - nothing to proceed from their mouth for seven days!

There is a big lesson for us in this. Because of their murmuring and unbelief, the Israelites had to wander in the wilderness for 40 years. So Joshua is telling them to keep total silence now, so they will not speak fear, doubt or unbelief. When we are facing great challenges we, too, need to keep our lips from speaking unbelieving words. Words can bind up or set free, hence the order to keep silent. Exodus 14:14 says, "God will fight the battle for you. And you? You just keep your mouths shut." (Message Bible)

Isaiah 30:15 says, "In quietness and confidence shall be your strength." The best example of all is Jesus who opened not His mouth when He was led as a lamb to the slaughter. (Isaiah 53:7)

We cannot help everything we see or hear. But if we refuse to speak doubt and fear, our hearts will be inclined to remember what God can do, instead of what we cannot see. The Israelites were able to SEE the salvation of the Lord following their shout of triumph when the walls of Jericho fell down flat before them. (Joshua 6:20) Our walls will fall down flat before us, too, when we trust God to act in our behalf. How hard it is for us to obey His command to keep quiet; especially for me - a world-class talker. (Once when I introduced Bill to a friend with the preface that she talked more than anyone I knew - he really hurt my feelings when he claimed she did not talk as much as I did!)

Proverbs 30:32 says, "Put your hand on your mouth." Good advice to me personally. And I pray with David from Psalm 141:3, "Set a guard O Lord, over my mouth; keep watch over the door of my lips."

March 2nd ~ Never Give Up by Julie Setzer, Daughter

Hebrews 12 says, "Therefore, since we are surrounded by such a great cloud of witnesses, let us throw off everything that hinders and the sin that so easily entangles, and let us run with perseverance the race marked out for us. Let us fix our eyes on Jesus, the author and perfector of our faith, who for the joy set before Him endured the cross, scorning its shame, and sat down at the right hand of the throne of God. Consider Him who endured such opposition from sinful men, so that you will not grow weary and lose heart."

Here's what I've watched my mother go through - the death of her beloved sister-in-law, parents, first husband, brother, daughter-in-law, three sets of parents-in-law; the addiction of first one family member after another to alcohol; the disappointments that go hand in hand with watching your children and grandchildren make poor choices that are too numerous and personal to list here; raising a blended family and cancer.

Here's the number of times I've seen my mother depressed or discouraged: 0. Here's the number of times I've seen my mother exasperated or frustrated: 0. Here's the number of times I've seen my mother in a bad mood: 0.

Is my mother superhuman? Is she void of emotion? No. What my mother is, however, is a dependent child of God. She depends on God as the Source of her stability, strength, security, happiness. My mother got saved when I was 12 years old, shortly after my daddy died. I watched her transform into a completely new person. Hmmm…isn't that funny? Does that sound familiar to any of us?

2 Corinthians 5:17 says, "Therefore, if anyone is in Christ, he is a new creation; the old has gone, the new has come!" She went from being scared of her own shadow, to scared of nothing. She went from depending on all her family members to baby her and meet her every need to relying on God completely. She went from being a slave to her circumstances to not even considering her circumstances.

My mother taught me by example what it means to smile when you don't feel like it, have hope when you're sad, believe when it seems stupid, rest in God that He's truly taking care of the things that concern us and to never give up. My mother prayed me and many others into the Kingdom. My mother has given me the greatest gift a mother can give. She has given me her Faith.

March 3rd ~ Blessed Beyond Measure

His mercies really are new each day. Great is His faithfulness. (Lamentations 3:22-23) Just this week we got another tremendous prayer answer to a seemingly impossible situation. The second breakthrough in a month! Wow! What a mighty God we swerve. He really does answer prayers;

even those that we have prayed for many years without seeing the answer.

Eight of the Love Overflowing board members were at my house this week for prayer and we were discussing that even those prayers we prayed 20 or more years ago are still out here and we can believe that God will watch over His Word to perform it. (Jeremiah 1:12) That very afternoon we received our wonderful miracle, fulfilling a promise that I had claimed faithfully, "The seed of the righteous is delivered" (Proverbs 11:21).

I was reading Gloria Copeland's book *Blessed Beyond Measure* and I know what she means about experiencing the extraordinary goodness of God. She stresses that it is up to us to receive these blessings and he first step to receiving begins when you discover and embrace God's goodness and kindness towards you.

God loves us all and is not mad at us. In fact, understanding and believing the goodness of God is the very foundation for our faith. The more we trust Him, the more we are able to place our lives in His loving hands. The Bible is full of verses about the goodness of God. One of my favorites is Psalm 27:13, "I would have despaired if I had not believed I would see the goodness of the Lord in the land of the living." When everything looks hopeless, we can hold on to that promise. I believe and receive the goodness of the Lord in every area of my life and my family's right now. Amen, so be it.

March 4th ~ Tasteless Salt

Matthew 5:13 says, "You are the salt of the earth, but if the salt has become tasteless, how can it be made salty again? It is no good for anything, except to be thrown out and trampled underfoot by men."

I think the Lord was trying to tell me something when I heard a teaching about the importance of our being salt. And then in reading Pastor Deci Connelly's book *Lessons from the Red*, she has a chapter titled "Pass the Salt." (She is an associate pastor at our church in Rancho Mirage, California.)

The teacher said something I am still digesting – "we are called to be salt, not sugar." Am I being too sweet and not truthful enough when I know someone or something is wrong; or about what is really sin in a person's life? In not telling my Bible Study friends the hard lessons instead of majoring on all the good stuff? In other words, am I sugar coating the Word of God? Much food for thought.

It's amazing how Jesus calls US to be the salt of the earth. We are to provide the flavor of God to others. One of the translations said flavorless instead of tasteless. I don't want to be either tasteless or flavorless. We have nothing to offer the world if we don't stay filled up with Jesus. When we are filled up with Him, we are able to share Him with others – like 'passing the salt.'

Please show me, Lord, how to be flavorful and still be salty enough to make others thirsty for You.

March 5th ~ Abraham and Lot

Abraham brought his nephew Lot with him when he left Ur of the Chaldeans to go to wherever the Lord would lead him. They became very successful and had so many flocks and herds that the land was not able to support them both. So Abraham said to Lot, please let there be no strife between us (good family advice), so you choose the land you desire. And Lot chose the plain of Jordan that was well-watered like a garden (before the Lord destroyed Sodom and Gomorrah).

We read in Genesis 14 that four kings went to war with the kings of Sodom and Gomorrah and kidnapped Lot and his goods. When Abraham heard this news, he armed 318 of his servants and went to rescue his nephew from the much larger force.

These four kinds represent four of the primary spirits

that try to kidnap our family members, keeping them from the Lord:

1. King of Elam - Elam meaning to bind up; like putting them in a straight jacket causing every thought and action to be bound.
2. King of nations, Tidal - to make afraid, causing terror and making them feel unworthy.
3. King of Shinar - representing darkness causing them to be unable to see the light of God's Word.
4. King of Ellasar - lion-like; bringing a spirit of confusion because of a lion-like roar temporarily paralyzing his prey and making it difficult to hear for the roar in their minds. (Satan comes like a roaring lion according to 1 Peter 5:8. But Jesus is the Lion of the tribe of Judah.)

Abraham rescued Lot and all he had. He won using a natural sword, but we win our family with the sword of the Spirit, the Word of God.

March 6th ~ Experiment

Daughter-in-law Laura Patterson was upset when she realized that her eight- year-old-son Payne had filled his bathwater with an entire bottle of dog/cat shampoo. She said, "Son, you can read, why did you use something for animals?" He replied, "I was just doing an experiment."

Just to be on the safe side, she called the poison control hotline and read them a list of ingredients. The lady told her to ask Payne if his skin felt different in any way. So she asked him, "Does your skin feel funny?" After thinking it over, Payne replied, "No, but I am a little hungry."

How we are like this! We experiment with things we know are not meant for us. Sometimes it really is poison for us and we are blessed when it doesn't have lasting results. We rarely think ahead to how it might harm us. Smoking is a good example. Bill has emphysema caused from years of cigarettes, although he quit many years ago. Even after seeing him with his oxygen, we have several grandchildren who smoke. It is hard for them to realize that they will someday pay the consequences for this unhealthy habit. At least, Bill and I have the excuse of not knowing the dangers back then. But now after all the publicity and warnings, it is difficult for me to understand why anyone would walk into this same trap. It seems young people feel bulletproof.

Psalm 119:9 says, "How can a young man cleanse his way, by taking heed according to Your Word." Verse 11 says, "Your Word have I hidden in my heart that I might not sin against You."

Yes, we all need to think of the consequences when you begin to 'experiment' with things of the world that are harmful, whether physical or spiritual. Thankfully, there is a forgiving God, but He does let us 'face the music' sometimes, too.

March 7th ~ Rebuilding the Walls

In Nehemiah we read about the rebuilding of the walls in Jerusalem. The people did their work on the wall with one hand on their weapon - the Sword of the Spirit, the Word of God. (Verse 17, 18) Our enemy never sleeps either and so we have to continuously be on guard. He knows he cannot defeat us unless we let him, so he uses the weapons of discouragement, derision, deceit, despair, despondency, distrust and on and on. He has an arsenal filled with weapons to throw at us. So this is why we need each other.

Nehemiah 4:19-20 says that since the work was great and extensive and they were separated on the wall far from each other and had a trumpet to sound when they needed help. We also need a trumpet to sound when we need the others so they can rally to us wherever we are. Our rallying cry should be "Our God will fight for us." This is why we send prayer requests to others for support in our individual battles. Noticing the words "wherever we are," we are where we are and God will change us or others where they are. We are just to meet them where they are because He meets us where we are, too.

God Himself will revive us. Psalm 119 has several prayers for revival, as well as instances where He answers those prayers. (Verses 25, 37, 40, 50, 88, 98, 107, 149, 154, 159)

The woman at the well was restored when she came into contact with Jesus, showing that it is never too late. God promises our latter years will be even better than our former. (Job 42:10) Our future will be even better than our past. God is not interested in blaming us or others for our past. He is a 'now' God. We need to be confident and expectant of good things happening in our lives. Broken walls are being rebuilt.

March 8th ~ Welcome - You've Got Mail

We hear these words nearly every morning and so often that we don't think about them too much. Mostly a reminder about how many emails we need to delete. But this morning it occurred to me that the Lord is saying these same words to us each morning and we also take them for granted.

So, let's think about that for a moment. The God of the universe is welcoming us into His presence, daily! How fantastic is that? He is welcoming us with His open arms of unconditional love and forgiveness; how wonderful, how marvelous, how exciting. Jesus even says He is standing and knocking at the door of our hearts promising to come in and sup with us. (Revelation 3:20)

There are certain words, even simple ones that are hard for me to pronounce correctly. The word 'welcome' is one of them. I actually practice, with Bill helping me, to say it so it does not come out as 'walcome.' (Although, that is a little bit Texan anyway.) And since I am often the Master of Ceremonies for Love Overflowing, a Christian group that has been meeting monthly for over 37 years in Kilgore, Texas, that is certainly the first word I need to say – welcoming everyone attending. I haven't even improved through all that time. I have to make a conscious effort to say it the way I should.

"I've Got Mail" is also something God is speaking to us. He wants us to read our 'mail' from Him daily, too. The Bible is a wonderful love letter to His children. The most marvelous thing is that it is a living word that brings fresh revelation for us just when we need it: encouragement, wisdom, instruction, guidance and almost best of all, comfort. So, let's open His Word that never needs to be deleted.

March 9th ~ Waiting in Joyful Hope by Donna Payne, Daughter-in-law

One of the most amazing sights I have ever seen was during our winter in Hilo. I was so excited to learn we would be in Hawaii during the Humpback Whale migration! We learned that the whales migrate from Alaska to Hawaii every winter to give birth to their young. As we began to hear of sightings, we kept our eyes focused on the ocean at every opportunity. December and January passed without our seeing even one whale. As February approached, we were told that the whales weren't as active as in previous years, but that they were 'out there.' We were taught to watch for 'poofs' of water, signaling the existence of one of these magnificent creatures expelling water from its blowhole. The key, we were told, was to watch patiently. (I've always struggled with that one!)

Gradually we developed a habit of going to a local scenic outlook to whale watch after dropping the boys off at school. We watched with great expectation, anticipating a 'poof' sign. Finally I saw one! My husband Lee missed it and claimed I was imagining things. But, it encouraged me and I was determined to continue our vigil. I wanted to see a whale! Soon Lee saw a 'poof' then the splash of a fin! One whale even appeared to be greeting us, splashing his tail repeatedly! Full of awe and excitement, we returned to the overlook frequently, watching from rocks at the beaches, and searching the horizon during our drives, hoping to share this vision of God's glory with the boys. By mid-March, we had witnessed a whale breaching, her full body nearly out of the water! Then the *coup de grace,* a mother and baby whale breaching side by side!

The Bible tells us to wait on the Lord, to be patient and wait. (Psalm 37:7, James 1:4) The waiting isn't easy. We struggle with too much to do to be patient. But as we set our priorities, with our hearts focused on eternity, God rewards us with visions of His Glory more magnificent than we could ever imagine. Thank You, Father!

March 10th ~ X-Cancelled

After a meaningful time of worship at our weekly Bible Study in Palm Springs, our teacher, Rev. Gerie Martin, was prompted by the Holy Spirit to say that someone would then have a message from the Lord. She encouraged us to speak it forth even if it was only one word. Sure enough, one of the young ladies said the Lord was showing her an X and she felt that it meant 'cancelled.' So immediately we acted on that word and accepted God's cancellation of whatever was needed. All 14 of us made different requests of things for God to cancel.

The list began with cancellation of debt. We all received that one. Then disease or any sort of infirmity, doubt, fear, worry, addictions, and on and on. We knew God was promising to cancel just about anything we could think of if we would only receive His Word. God is so faithful to watch over His Word to perform it. (Jeremiah 1:12)

I well remember as a new Christian the first time the Holy Spirit gave me a 'word' for a friend. I was too timid to go to this very nervous and anxious business partner of ours, but finally I got up the nerve and told him the Lord wanted him to have peace. The Lord had told me to give him Isaiah 26:3, that says, "You would keep him in perfect peace, whose mind is stayed on You because He trusted in You." He really seemed touched and received it with joy. Glory be to God! This gave me the courage to continue giving 'words' and sometimes even pictures or visions that the Lord graciously showed me.

The Word says that in the last days old men/women would dream dreams (Acts 2:17) so I love it when that really happens to me. Most of the time my dreams do not make much sense, but I do try to be attentive to them. God speaks in many ways and I want to always have open ears to hear.

March 11th ~ Jesus is Coming – Look Busy

I saw a sign that said: "Jesus Is Coming - Look Busy." Jesus is coming and there is work to be done and He commissioned us to do it, but not at the expense of the opportunity to sit down with Him, face to face first, above all else. Being busy for God is not the same as being present with God. Matthew 6:33 says, "Seek ye first the Kingdom of God, and His righteousness; and all these things shall be added unto you." The Lord gave me that Scripture twice in one day. Do you think He might be trying to tell me something?

We can expend enormous effort with the best intentions but human effort will never produce heaven's results. John 3:6 says that "flesh gives birth to flesh but the Spirit gives birth to spirit." Wow! Do I know that since my eating had gotten out of control! I have really been giving birth to more flesh.

Psalm 46:10 says, "Be still, and know that I am God; I will be exalted among the nations, I will be exalted in the earth." Being still and worshiping reminds us who God is...and who we are not. My name is spelled S-I-S-T-E-R and not G-O-D. But sometimes I act like I'm in charge, as though it is all up to me. That's when I start to grow weary and also get whiny. It's comforting to know that some of the great men and women of the Bible had whiny moments.

(Examples of Elijah are in 1 Kings 18-19.)

Our job is to believe God can do His job. John 6:28, 29 says, "Therefore they said to Him, 'What shall we do, so that we may work the works of God?' Jesus answered and said to them, 'This is the work of God that you believe in Him whom He has sent.'"

Jesus is coming and there is work to be done, but your 'work' and my 'work' are not the same. Be still, sit at His feet, worship, seek His face, then obey and believe God can do His job. He is worthy of your praise and He will be faithful to show you everything you are to 'do.'

March 12th ~ Rhyming

Bill often reminds me that rhyming and poetry are not the same but I have always been impressed by those who could do either. This morning I caught myself saying a rhyme to the Lord: "Thank You, Lord, for wonderful days with lots to do, and countless blessings, too." Then I began to recount my many blessings. Of course, this is an endless list.

I remembered Psalm 16:5-6 that says, "O Lord, You are my portion and my cup; You maintain my lot. The lines have fallen to me in pleasant places, yes, I have a good inheritance." They sure have and I am forever grateful. Verse 11 says, "You will show me the path of life, in Your presence is fullness of joy; at Your right hand are pleasures forevermore." I am learning more every day how important it is to believe in the goodness of God and to be a good receiver of all His blessings. We must believe in His goodness and His desire to bless us with His goodness before we can expect them to come to us. They do not come automatically; they only come to those who believe they will. God honors faith.

All my life, even before I knew Jesus, I believed that good things would come my way. I was always the one who got the door prize, or won a contest. I think Mother worried a little about me getting my feelings hurt, as I wore them right "on my sleeve for all to see," as the saying goes. But my trust always paid off. I truly believed everyone loved me and wanted the best for me. So it has not been hard for me to believe in the unconditional love of God.

However, God was speaking to my heart this morning about not blocking His blessings by unbelief or negative and critical thoughts. Don't LET your heart be troubled. Quickly cast out the very first anxious or doubtful thought that comes into your mind. Keep saying, "Life is good, all is well." Then just let the blessings flow with pleasures forevermore.

March 13th ~ I Woke Up

Have you ever said, "I woke up" to some fact? I thought about what that really means: to awaken, to have it dawn on, to realize, to understand. One of the most "woke up to" times in my life was when certain scriptures becametruth to me. Psalm 119:160 says, "The entirety of YOUR WORD IS TRUTH, and every one of your righteous judgments endures forever." Wow! Then 1 Peter 2:25, "But the Word of the Lord endures forever." Peter is quoting from Isaiah 40:8, "The grass withers and the flower fades, but the Word of the Lord endures forever."

FOREVER means forever - eternally. His Word is truth so if what the doctor, or the banker or even the preacher says is not in line with the Word of God, it is not truth. What the Word says about our situation is truth. So when it says, "by Jesus' stripes we are healed," that is truth. (2 Peter 2:24) When the Word says that "He supplies all our need according to His riches in glory," He means it. (Philippians 4:19) When the Word says that "He will restore the hearts of the fathers to the sons and the sons to the fathers," we can believe He will do it. (Malachi 4:6)

These are just a few of the precious promises that we can 'awaken to' when we begin to really BELIEVE His Word is truth. Jesus says that He Himself is the way, the TRUTH and the life and no man comes to the Father except through Him. (John 14:6) In the first chapter of the gospel of John we are told that Jesus Himself is the Word of God and He was made flesh to dwell among us. Glory be to God. So, we can 'waken up' to the truth of the Word of God and take Him at His Word; forever and ever, amen.

March 14th ~ John Wesley Hardin

Supposedly one of the most notorious gunfighters in the Old West was a great uncle of my grandmother Clara Hardin Smith. There have been several movies and TV shows made about his life, one even played by Rock Hudson.

My first cousin, Helen "Biddy" Smith Cairns sent me a postcard with his picture showing him to be a very handsome young man. Still, I am certainly not proud of this ancestor.

I was always told by my mother, who tended to color everything beautiful, that he only killed people in self-defense or those who needed killing. (So much for the legend that said he once killed a man for snoring.)

He did live in Texas in the period after the Civil War and the carpetbaggers were really hated. However, I think that was hardly a reason to kill them.

John Wesley was the son of a Methodist minister who had 'a lovely family' as my mother would say. I recently read a book by Longview friend Peppy Blount who said he was also distant kin to 'Cousin Wes' and grew up hearing the same stories that I did; the family trying to make him a hero instead of a deadly killer.

Is this like what it means in the Bible about calling evil good and good evil? (Isaiah 5:20) The verse goes on to say, "Who put darkness for light and light for darkness." This makes me think of how today the world seems to be doing that same thing, calling evil good and good evil and certainly living in the darkness instead of the light. We see that especially in the entertainment world where Christians and their righteousness are made fun of and every evil is shown for all to see.

Maybe I have rose colored glasses like my mother, but I do sense a turning back to the light; that finally the devil has had his way for too long. Jesus the Light of the world is coming soon and every knee shall bow. Come, Lord Jesus, before it gets any worse.

March 15th ~ Are You Making the Right Choices?

We must choose life to enjoy God's blessings daily. Choose this day who we are going to serve – "as for me and my house we will serve the Lord." (Joshua 24:15) There is a lot of power in making the right choices. What kind of year we have is going to depend greatly on the decisions we make. Are you making wise choices?

Have you made some bad decisions in the past that have gotten you in trouble? Of course, we all have. Galatians 6:7 says "…for whatever a man sows, that he will also reap." Many people today are living in bad circumstances and they blame their situation on something or someone else. The truth is that most of the time it is due to wrong choices made in the past.

If I make wise choices, then I will reap the benefits of wisdom. If I do a lot of foolish things, I'm going to reap the consequences of foolishness. What if I have already made a lot of bad choices? Jesus can change things as we come to Him in true repentance.

He gives us opportunities to overcome the results of a series of bad choices, and shows us how to make a series of good choices. Little by little, day after day, as we continue in obedience to Him, continuing to do what we know to be right and what we know God's Word says to do, we will gradually see positive changes in our situations.

It isn't always convenient and it isn't always easy but

it is definitely worth it. Many times we make emotional choices and that is when we get in trouble. The Bible tells us to prize wisdom. "Wisdom is doing today what you will be happy with tomorrow."

Jesus wept over Jerusalem because they did not choose to know Him. (Luke 19:41-44) That is the first and most important choice we must make - to know Him.

March 16th ~ Lessons From Paul and the Shipwreck

Acts 27:4 says, "When we had put out to sea from there, we sailed under the shelter of Cyprus, because the winds were contrary."

Do you have any contrary winds? I suppose we all have had them at various times in our lives. We can learn many lessons about dealing with them from this passage:

1. Sailing at the wrong or dangerous time; timing is all important. (Acts 27:9)
2. Listening to people instead of God or a proven man of God. Even experts sometimes miss it although their way often sounds better. (Acts 27:11)
3. Realizing a mistake had been made, they just let themselves be driven. (Acts 27:14)
4. Lightening their load, now they are listening to Paul's advice. (Acts 27:18-19)
5. All hope was gone, NOW God could come in. (Acts 27:20)
6. Total commitment, cutting all their ropes and ties, leaning on God's Word alone. (Acts 27:32)

It is interesting to note that Paul's testimony to the centurion probably saved him. Our boat needs to hear our testimony. ALL were saved: 276 people. (Acts 27:37) The Lord told me way back when I was a baby Christian that I could have "all sailing with me" - all saved! All in our boat would be saved: all our children and grandchildren and extended family. (Acts 16:31) "Believe in the Lord Jesus Christ and you and your entire household will be saved."

March 17th ~ Guess Who Shifted?

A young Christian linguist working among the aborigines in Western Australia felt he was not as close to God as he should be. He had a friend though who encouraged him in his faith. One morning at breakfast he found a note under his plate. It read: "If you feel further from God than you used to be, guess who shifted?" The statement was rather pointed, but he accepted it as the answer to his problem.

Often we feel that God has forsaken us or that He is not really close to us. At such times we should ask ourselves the same question: "Who shifted?"

It is always good to remind ourselves of His wonderful promises that He will never, no, never ever leave us or forsake us. (Hebrews 13:13) He never moves away from us. He goes with us everywhere we go. Deuteronomy 31:6 says, "The Lord your God, He it is that does go with you; He will not fail you, nor forsake you."

There are many more scriptures that assure us of His faithfulness to always be with us. He is always close to strengthen and guide us in our daily lives, in our work, our fun, our disappointments, and our successes. I cannot count how often He has given me assurance that He would be with me. Especially when I need to hear that He will be going with me when we are traveling, moving or other big events in our lives. But never more than when I am going out to speak in His name. He always gives me the perfect scripture to cause me to know that I know that I know that I am in His will and He will speak through me.

It is never God who forsakes us; it is you and I who draw away from Him. James 4:8 says, "Draw near to Me and I will draw near to you, says the Lord."

March 18th ~ Grieve Not the Holy Spirit

Ephesians 4:30 says, "And do not grieve the Holy Spirit of God, by whom you are sealed for the day of redemption."

O dear, this sounds like we can grieve the Holy Spirit. I pray please show me right now what in my life causes You grief, Lord. Show me so I can deal with it. Forgive me for allowing my attitudes or actions to dishonor You. Starting today, I want to live every moment with the intent to please You and never cause You grief again. In Jesus' name, amen.

He quickly answered my prayer. "Yes, it grieves me when you judge My other servants, especially when you're critical of the way they minister. You must realize we are all different and we should not compare one another. Your lack of compassion can be fixed by leaning on Me and using My compassion. About judging, just stop each time a judgmental thought comes, giving it up to Me. Like I say, take every thought captive to Christ. (2 Corinthians 10:5) It takes practice but it can be done. With My help, that is what I'm here for, to give you strength and power to live each day in the spirit and not in the flesh. Just rest in Me knowing that as you choose not to judge and compare, I will be right there to remind you.

"Quit saying that you do not have patience, you do! It is a fruit of the Spirit and so is love and self control. Just receive it by faith and you will manifest those gifts. You talk about watching the words of your mouth and then turn around and claim that you have no patience or not enough love. Don't you think My love is enough for you? Also don't you think I would not have told you to do something you could not do? I told you to fear not and you can do that. I told you to judge not and you can keep from doing that, too. I told you to wait patiently and you can do that, too. In the flesh you don't have the strength, but supernaturally you do. Trust Me to help you. I love you and expect you to love one another."

March 19th ~ Good Passage from Job

The Book of Job has never been my favorite book of the Bible, but I was surprised when lately I found something 'new' to encourage me. What caught my attention in my New American Standard Bible was page 808, my secret code from the Lord. (The number 808 was our family's telephone number growing up. When I see these numbers, I know it is a special nod from God.)

Anyway, the entire page from Job 5:8-27 seemed to be important words for me. "But as for me, I would seek God, and I would place my cause before God; who does great and unsearchable things, wonders without number." I love that. He certainly does do wonders without number. The entire passage is full of encouraging words about not being afraid of famine or war or the scourge of the tongue or even violence.

I love Verse 24, "You will know that your tent is secure, for you will visit your abode and fear no loss." And what about Verse 25: "You will know also that your descendants will be many, (true for us with 23 grandchildren and 17 great grandchildren and probably many more) and your offspring as the grass of the earth."

Since Bill and I are 80 years old, Verse 26 is my favorite, "You will come to the grave in full vigor, like the stacking of grain in its season." How good is that? That goes with another of the ones I claim for us both, "According to our days so shall our strength be" (Deuteronomy 34:25). Or as the NAS says, "According to your days, so will your leisurely walk be." I really identify with the idea of a leisurely walk since I guess you might even say I have always been a tad lazy.

I believe these promises are for me, still I know He meant them for all His children, too. His promises endure forever. His word is truth. PTL!

March 20th ~ Mind of Christ

1 Corinthians 2:16b has always been hard for me to receive when it says that we as believers have the "mind of Christ."

Our pastor said this morning that another way to say having the "mind of Christ" was thinking the thoughts of Jesus. I liked that. What must I do to have the thoughts of Jesus?

1. Spend more time with Him.
2. Spend more time with Him.
3. Spend more time with Him.

I get it! So, at first I thought that meant fellowship time alone with Him. But it also means reading and meditating on His Word, praying to Him, talking about Him to and with others, and practicing His presence daily.

He yearns to give us His thoughts, to let us know who He really is. We cannot know anyone without spending time with that person. So, how could we expect to know Jesus if we don't spend the time getting to know Him?

And another good quote from our pastor, "When you don't know what to do…do what you know to do." So that means to me to go back to the basics that I learned as a new Christian. Pray and ask the Holy Spirit to help me do what I need to do in order to know Him better. "Apart from Him I can do nothing" (John 15:5). This is one of the best lessons I have ever learned. (Certainly it is the Holy Spirit who helps me get up early in the morning to spend that special time with Him.)

After almost 40 years of being saved, I do see more often the thoughts of Jesus coming to my mind – especially when I start to head in the wrong direction. I do claim the promise that I have the "mind of Christ" believing for it to become truth in my life.

March 21st ~ The Tool of Offense

This is our enemy's method of operation. As the seed of God's Word is planted in our hearts, he starts working to get rid of it before it has a chance to take root. The tool he uses to achieve this is the tool of offense. He may send a person along to say something mean to us that will hurt our feelings. He may get someone to irritate and provoke us until we step over into strife.

The very word 'devil' in the Greek carries the idea of a constant irritating, poking, pressing or pecking away at something in order to penetrate and get entrance into it. That's the way he functions and he cannot change his pattern. He goes after the seed of the Word in your heart by poking at you through someone's unkind words or actions. He tries to provoke you into reacting so you'll violate the commandment of love because, when you do that, he gains entrance into your life. This enables him to pierce your soul like a thorn would pierce your finger. Then he keeps working from that place to infect you more and more with his poison. If we truly understood what an evil thing offense is, most of us would steer clear of it like a rattlesnake.

No wonder Ephesians 4:26-27 says, "Give no place to the devil but to be angry and sin not." Giving place to the devil in our lives through offense and strife opens the door for him to steal the Word from us, and it's the Word that heals, prospers, delivers and leads us into a life of blessing.

Proverbs 26:21 says, "As charcoal is to burning coals, and wood is to fire so is a contentious man to kindle strife."

The more we practice obeying the commandment of love, the more rooted and grounded in love we become. Before long, walking in love won't even seem like a commandment anymore. It will become a privilege, an honor and a joy. "Hatred stirs up quarrels, but love covers all offenses" (Proverbs 10:12).

March 22nd ~ Take Root and Grow Fruit

When I was concerned that maybe some of God's words I had spoken in a friend's life might have fallen on deaf ears, the Lord assured me that many of the words would "take root and grow fruit." Wasn't that precious of Him to give me that assurance? I suddenly thought of how I certainly hope His words are taking root in my life and bearing good fruit, too. The fruit of the Spirit is love, joy, peace, patience, kindness, goodness, faithfulness, gentleness, self-control. (Galatians 5:22-23) Yes, I need them all to take root and grow more fruit.

Some will bear fruit in due season if we do not grow weary. Psalm 1:3 says, "...which yields fruit in its season." Yes, we will see the fruit growing in us and in the others in whom we have planted seeds in due season. I have really seen this come to pass in my family members. I have been planting God's Word into their lives for almost 40 years now and have seen them taking root and growing fruit. Some are in the blade stage, some in the ear and some in the full corn stage. (Mark 4:26-29) Oh, dear, I just realized I have changed from fruit to vegetables.

It's nice to know that others are probably sowing seeds in the same person's life. Jesus' words in John 4:36 say, "Already he who reaps is receiving wages and is gathering fruit for life eternal; so that he who sows and he who reaps may rejoice together." For in this case the saying is true "one sows and another reaps."

So my prayer for myself and others is in Colossians 1:10: "That we will walk in a manner worthy of the Lord, to please Him in all respects, bearing fruit in every good work and increasing in the knowledge of God." Amen.

March 23rd ~ Bulb Snatching

As I was taking a light bulb from one lamp to put in another, I thought about the old GE commercial about being a bulb snatcher. I have done this many times mainly when a reading light by our bed goes out. Bill and I both are avid readers and read in bed till midnight nearly every night.

This made me think of how important light is in our lives. I am so glad I did not live in the days before electricity and had to read by candlelight. Also, being a bulb snatcher made me think of the parable that Jesus told of the 10 virgins in Matthew 25:1-13. Five of them were wise and had their lamps filled with oil and five were foolish without oil for their lamps. When midnight came, the cry was heard that the bridegroom was coming. The foolish virgins tried to get some oil from the wise (modern day bulb snatching) but could not. So they went out to buy some oil for their lamps. While they were gone, the bridegroom came and those who were ready went in with Him. And the door was shut to the foolish ones.

Oil is symbolic of the Holy Spirit. It seems to me that all the 10 virgins were Christians but obviously the five foolish ones did not keep close to the Holy Spirit. Perhaps they were ones who did not read their Bibles or pray for themselves (expecting others to do it for them). Suddenly it was too late. Certainly we do not have to do "works" for the Lord, but He does expect us to stay in communion with Him. This passage of the virgins appears to be speaking of the rapture. Probably the foolish ones will eventually get to Heaven, but have to go through the tribulation here on earth first. Yuck. I want to fly with Jesus. I don't want to be foolish. I want to always be able to say, "Come, Lord Jesus." (I love reading about the rapture in 1 Thessalonians 4:16-17.)

March 24th ~ Practice What You Preach

The message the Lord was giving me this morning was: "Sis, practice what you preach." I understood this to remind me that I am constantly saying to look at the answer and not the problem but I needed to be reminded of this truth. For in my prayer time I was dwelling on how one of my family members was in an awful situation. I was busy thinking of all the horrible consequences, etc. So the Holy Spirit brought my own words to my mind. 'Believe the truth of the Word and trust Him to fix it in His way, not mine.'

After all, I have been standing on the promise of the Lord that the seed of the righteous is delivered. (Proverbs 11:21) That is the truth and I don't care how bad it looks in the natural. God is in control and will work it all for good, not with my own ideas, but His perfect ones. I believe the Holy Spirit is touching my loved one right now and all is well.

Sometimes in the natural it does look totally hopeless but I must remember that I serve a supernatural God. Nothing is too difficult for Him. I often forget to keep believing the truth of His Word. Instead, I sometimes fret about the problem. No matter how bad it looks, I can trust in the Lord to work it out; not 'some way' but 'His way'...not 'someday', but 'His day'…not my 'good' ideas, but His 'perfect' ones. Glory be to God. I believe the Holy Spirit is touching my grandson right this minute and all is well. He is the Author and Finisher of his faith so I can trust Him to work out all things for my loved one's good.

Believing the promises in God's word does not mean that I can be passive. Instead, I need to continually pray and speak the specific Word that applies to the need at the time. I quote Psalm 91 almost daily for my family so surely I can believe the Lord is watching over His word to perform it. I am practicing what I preach!

March 25th ~ Forgiveness is a Choice

The first person you probably have not forgiven is yourself. More people lack forgiveness toward themselves than anybody else. They are unwilling to forgive themselves and to recognize that God says, "As far as the east is from the west, so far has He removed our transgressions from us" (Psalm 103:12).

If you are a believer, He has already cleansed your conscience from dead works so that you might serve the living God. (Hebrews 9:14) God cleanses us for service in order not to leave us with the guilt of past sins that should be dead, buried and forgotten.

The second person we have to forgive if we have bitterness is God Himself. There are people who blame God because a child died, a husband ran away, they are sick, they do not have enough money. Consciously or unconsciously, they think all of these things are God's fault.

The third person you may have to forgive is a member of your family. You have to get rid of resentment, especially toward those closest to you. The husbands, wives, children, parents - all must be forgiven when slights and resentments have built up in family situations. Many people say, "Well, I didn't think that counted. I thought that was just a family matter." A lack of forgiveness has to be eliminated, especially toward a family member.

Finally, there has to be forgiveness for anybody and everybody else who has ever done anything against you. It may be that you feel your resentment is justified. But if you want to see Kingdom life and power flow in your life, it is absolutely imperative that you forgive, beginning right now.

Remember, forgiveness is a choice, a decision. If we set our wills to forgive, then the Lord will do the rest.

March 26th ~ Good Things

One of my special friends used to say to me to tell her only good things; she did not want to hear anything bad. I don't think she even knew that this was biblical or that Paul tells us in Philippians 4:8 to give good reports. Thinking about this made me wonder how often I give bad reports.

I looked up the verse in the Amplified Bible and instead of good reports it said, "Whatever is kind and winsome and gracious - that is the sort of reports we should give."

In measuring our words in that manner, we can stop and think of what we are saying. Is it kind? Is it gracious? And, most of all, is it necessary? Will it edify? Will it really be a good report or is it a bad report? Deep questions that convict us about our speech.

My daughter Grace is especially good about only bringing good reports and many times when I begin to tell her something bad she will question me with, "Do I need to hear this?" Then I tell her yes, I need her to pray about the matter. But I can tell sometimes she thinks I could have kept it to myself.

She is always careful not to pass anything on to anyone not involved, even to Dennis or her children. She really is an anointed pray-er and since I certainly believe in the prayer of agreement, I often do need her to agree with my prayers. She refuses to even listen to gossip or tell another prayer warrior unless led by God to do so, knowing that we can even gossip in prayer.

Back to Philippians 4:8, we are admonished to not only speak of good things, but to think on them, too – things that are true, noble, just, pure, lovely and of good report. If there is any virtue and if there is anything praiseworthy, meditate on these things. And if our thoughts are on these things then our words will fall into line. For out of the abundance of the heart the mouth speaks. (Matthew 12:34)

March 27th ~ Dr. Larry Lea - 3-27-11, Victory Christian Center

Imagine our surprise when Bill and I were walking into church and I saw Dr. Larry Lea waiting to speak to us at the entrance into the sanctuary. He immediately told us he was waiting for us! The Lord had told him someone was coming in from the parking lot that he needed to see. He was real excited when he learned we were from Longview since he was from Kilgore, Texas.

The big surprise was that the first thing he did when he

began his message was to say that the Lord had told him that he was going to meet someone coming in from the parking lot and he knew immediately it was us.

He said this 'sweet lady' from Texas reminded him of his mother who had died two years before. He had me stand up and say my name and then said, "Clara, this day is for you." How special did this make me feel! Bill and I both felt this was sort of a confirmation of the Word from the Lord that I had just sent the children. It was about a time of breakthrough in prayer for our family. Yea!

His message was on Anointed Prayer. He had blessed me and countless others in teaching us to pray the Lord's Prayer back in the 80's so I felt he was well able to teach on prayer. I also remember hearing him in Dallas and he said when he was a new Christian he would "read the red and pray for power."

His definition of Anointed Prayer was the ability to talk to God and have Him talk back to you. We already have the anointing dwelling inside us (1 John 2:27). We just need to have it released. He laid hands on all of us at the night meeting and released the anointing; sort of like activating, or re-charging, a battery. He reminded us that Jesus is interceding for us continually.

March 28th ~ Dr. Larry Lea #2

Bill thinks it is so funny that I have always loved 'front stage center' and he thought the recognition from a famous preacher was a special gift to me from a loving Father God.

Dr. Lea asked if any of us had a promise from God that had not yet been fulfilled. Of course, we all had one or more. So we were encouraged to not give up.

He taught from 1 Samuel 30, the story of David and his time at Ziklag when all was stolen from him. He told the three steps that David took to recover ALL:

1. No Shame

Verse 6 - David strengthened himself in the Lord and received no shame. Dr. Lea stressed that we should give up all our past and feel no shame at all. No matter what had happened to us to forget it and go on to newness of life.

2. Pray and Obey

   Verses 7-8 - David called for prayer support and got specific instructions from the Lord to pursue.

3. Give

   Verses 26-31 - David gave crazily. (I had never noticed all the people he gave to before.)

He also stressed to have no fear. We are told over 365 times in the Bible "DO NOT FEAR." It is a commandment, not a suggestion. God has not given us a spirit of fear so we don't have to fear. (2 Timothy 1:7) He is with us!

God recognizes that there will be times of natural fear. In Psalm 56:3-4 David says whenever he is afraid he will trust in God. Fear is stepping back when you should be going forth. We all do it, but with God's help we can pray and obey the commandment to "Fear Not."

March 29th ~ Bragging

I guess all mothers warn their children not to brag. I know I did mine. And my mother certainly admonished me as I would get so excited about a new dress or bracelet that I would want to show it off to my friends so they would be happy for me. Blessedly, I have learned that there are times when I can brag.

It is alright to brag about exciting prayer answers from the Lord. I was pleased to read Galatians 6:14 that says, "But God forbid that I should boast except in the cross of our Lord Jesus Christ…" I can now brag or boast without feeling guilty. Since I am bragging on Jesus and not on myself or as the Bible says "my flesh," I realize that I can do nothing in my own strength. Whatever talents or abilities I have, are all from Him.

Jesus' sacrifice on the cross bought me everything I could ever need. I just heard a Bible scholar give a graphic picture of how awful Jesus' suffering for us was. He said Mel Gibson's *The Passion of Christ* did not even begin to portray the horror. The Jews never gave over 40 stripes as they considered that any more would kill a person but Jesus received the awful 40 stripes five times! As I was listening I was stirred again to think that all those stripes He received should not be taken lightly as they really had bought my forgiveness from sin, healing, my peace, my prosperity and so much more. So if I don't receive what He did for me, then I am denying their power. He bore all this for me!

To finish Galatians 6:14 it says "by whom the world has been crucified to me, and I to the world." O my, I think this means that I should not be so seduced by the world's attractions and distractions. I am so willing to accept the blessings Jesus purchased for me, but seem to forget the power He gives me to resist temptation. Thank You, thank You, Lord.

March 30th ~ Letting Go of Control by Donna Payne, Daughter-in-law

Taking the ferry to Vinalhaven is an experience of its own. You race and stress about getting to the boat on time and then, once you are there, you are no longer in control. Anything you forgot to bring is left behind or you'll miss the boat. Once on the ferry you have no choice but to relax and enjoy the ride.

As we pull away from the dock, I often feel as if my worries and anxieties are drawn away and left behind. I love this feeling of letting go and often use it to visualize the relinquishing of my care to the Lord. So, often I ask God to take my burdens from me but then proceed to take them back, to try to control the situation myself, and keep stressing and worrying about it. Just like the ferry ride is out of our control and in the hands of a competent captain, we find that when we actually trust God to take control of our problems, He provides a safe journey. 2 Corinthians 13:12 says, "God Himself is our Captain."

One day as I was walking to the Post Office and grocery store, proceeding down our sidewalk towards town, I met a man who was photographing our house. "What an awesome house!" He remarked. I thanked him, agreeing that it was awesome in many ways – architecturally, historically, as well as financially. I mentioned that sometimes I become overwhelmed by the awesomeness of the responsibility of maintaining it.

Many times I recall that encounter and am reminded that God promises that He will never give us more to handle than the grace He gives us with which to handle it. If He has entrusted us with such an awesome responsibility, He must have an awesome amount of grace just waiting for us to accept! And I am awed by His confidence in us and encouraged to meet the challenge.

I still tend to get overwhelmed but my loving husband gently reminds me that faith in His promises will lead us through. Psalm 55:22 says, "Cast your burden on the Lord and He will sustain you. He will never permit the righteous to be moved."

Author's note: Lee and Donna Payne and their two sons, L.F. and Collin lived on Vinalhaven Island, off the coast of Rockport, Maine, that can only be reached by ferry. They own and operate Payne Homestead Bed and Breakfast, formerly known as the Moses Webster house.

March 31st ~ Confidence in God's Word

Nehemiah's wall builders were surrounded by enemies but they were able to celebrate because they understood all the promises God had given them. (Nehemiah 8:12) God's Word gives us confidence! Where does that sort of trust come from? We learn to trust God's promises when we daily feed on God's Word.

Satan does not fear our sin; he knows God can forgive it. He doesn't fear our depression. He knows God can drive it away. He doesn't fear our lack, he knows God can provide. He fears our discovery of God's Word, because our ignorance of it is the most effective weapon he can use against us. And our knowledge of it is the most effective weapon we have with which to fight him. "...the sword of the Spirit which is the Word of God" (Ephesians 6:17).

Mark Twain is quoted as saying, "Most people are bothered by those passages in the Bible which they cannot understand; but as for me, I always notice that the passages in the Scripture that trouble me the most are those which I do understand." How true is that? If we only would walk in the truth that we do know, instead of being concerned about what some of them mean for the future.

And if we will only ask the Holy Spirit to reveal to us the truth of the Word as we read it He is the Teacher and is more than willing to reveal the relevance it has in our life today. (James 1:5-6)

"All scripture is given by inspiration of God and is profitable for doctrine, for reproof, for correction, for instruction in righteousness that the man of God may be complete, thoroughly equipped for every good work" (2 Timothy 3

April 1st ~ Favor of the Lord

Evangelist Kenneth Copeland told fellow Evangelist Jerry Savelle that he had a problem with his big mouth and needed to learn the vocabulary of silence. That was not a revelation Jerry wanted to hear.

The Holy Spirit then told Kenneth that he had the same problem and pointed out all the things that had come out of his mouth, even played them back for him.

We would all be shocked at what we have said, if we really listened to ourselves.

God told Jerry there were lots of battles in his life that

would not have lasted so long if he had consistently declared the the favor of God.

Sometimes we don't even recognize that favor. God has no favorites; He is no respecter of persons. But some people receive more blessings than others because they search the Bible for words to believe and confess.

"Our fathers told us the stories their fathers told them, How single-handedly You weeded out the godless from the fields and planted us, How You sent those people packing but gave us a fresh start. We didn't fight for this land; we didn't work for it, it was a gift! You gave it, smiling as You gave it, delighting as You gave it" (Psalm 44:3, the Message Bible).

The blessing was not because of something they did but because of the favor of God. That favor will change things for us, also, and we need to declare it before we leave the house. But sometimes we forget and let this and other good habits slip away.

Circumstances change when we speak the Word of God into our situations. It's His free gift and He is waiting for us to realize we live in God's favor when we live in His Word.

God delights in His favor and so do we.

April 2nd ~ Question: Do You Really Believe in Miracles?

How many of us can say we have had a miracle in our life? How about lots of them?

What is your most pressing need right now?

We have no problem accepting the wonders that Jesus performed for the multitudes in the Bible, but we have trouble believing that Christ will do the same for us today and meet our most urgent needs. When it comes to believing Him to work miracles in our own crisis, something important is necessary: belief. It is possible to say, "I believe God can do the impossible" and still be so calloused the Lord can't get through to us.

How many of us have spoken words of faith and hope to others who were facing distressing, seemingly hopeless situations, then had a problem believing for our own miracle? The question Jesus asks is this: "Do you believe I can work a miracle for you? And not just one miracle, but a miracle for every crisis, and every single situation we face?"

Think of the one difficulty you're facing right now, your greatest need, your most troubling problem. You've prayed about it for so long. Do you believe the Lord can and will work it out in ways you can't conceive? That kind of faith commands the heart to quit fretting or asking questions. It tells you to rest in the Father's care, trusting Him to do it all in His way and in His time.

We can do this with his help.

Isaiah 65:24 says, "It shall come to pass that before they call, I will answer and while they are still speaking, I will hear."

April 3rd ~ Rivers

In Ezekiel 47:1-12, we are told about the waters that flow from the temple of God. These are called the healing waters. Sometimes we have rivers that cannot be crossed. (Verse 5) Sometimes we are ankle deep in problems, then the water comes up to our knees and other times the water is so deep we must swim a river that cannot be crossed. We may even feel as though we are drowning.

Got any rivers too deep to cross? Often we feel like it, don't we? And without God's help, we do have those kind of rivers. In Ezekiel 47 verse five, we are told that the water was too deep and the river could not be crossed. This really jumped out at me when the Lord was telling me to quit trying to help Him help me.

In the Amplified it says in verse five, "A river that I could not pass through, for the waters had risen, waters to swim in, a river that could not be passed over or through. "

So the passage goes on to tell me to return to the bank

of the river where the many trees will be for my healing and even my food (provision). Verse 12 says that their leaves will not wither, and their fruit will not fail. They will bear fruit every month, because their water flows from the sanctuary. Their fruit will be for food and their leaves for medicine. I love it. Maybe "returning to the bank" means to again trust in the promises of God.

The entire chapter in Ezekiel is good to meditate on and there is so much more to be gleaned than I ever touched on.

I also thought of how the Lord made a way for His people through the Jordan River as well as the Red Sea. So, even when we are in deep waters over our heads, He always has a way out for us.

April 4th ~ It Was Nothing by Julie Setzer, Daughter

It was Easter morning 2003 and I was tired and worn from a hard season of feeling "battered" by life and all its disappointments and inconveniences. I was constantly tense.

My husband Frank and I were celebrating Jesus' resurrection with my family at my parents' and sister's church, Longview Christian Fellowship. At the end of the sermon, Pastor Craft invited people to the front who needed to let go of things or who needed a touch from God. I immediately went forward along with several other people.

As I was standing there, I realized my sister-in-law Laura had come to stand beside me. I don't think she touched me and I'm certain she didn't speak directly to me but I knew she was there and I knew she was there for me. She just came and stood alongside me, shoulder to shoulder – a very simple gesture.

Instantly my whole body began to relax and I felt God's presence wash over me. I have no idea how long we stood there. It probably wasn't more than a minute or two but when it was over, I felt like I had been on a two-week vacation and received a deep massage every day! I honestly don't even remember the conversation that God and I had that day as I stood there but I do remember Laura being with me. I remember feeling her giving me her strength and feeling very much revived, refreshed and relaxed all at the same time. It was one of the most peaceful, serene moments of my entire life.

I imagine if you asked Laura if she thinks she did something great for me that day, she would say, "Oh it was nothing." But I know it was something I will always remember and treasure. Plus, it reminds me that even the smallest gesture can have a gigantic impact.

April 5th ~ Curse of Anxiety

Jesus told Martha, "You are worried and upset about many things" (Luke 10:41). In one short sentence, Jesus diagnosed the problem that has plagued humankind since the beginning of time: the curse and ongoing burden of anxiety, worry and fear.

The words used most often for worry and anxiety in the New Testament come from the same Greek word *meridzoe* which means "to be divided, to be pulled in opposite directions, to choke." The old English word for worry meant to "gnaw" and worry certainly gnaws on us.

The ongoing burden of worry and fear! I read about worry beads from the Greek Island Naxos called *komboloi* – "worry beads." It is an old Greek custom that actually started out as prayer beads but have turned into worry beads.

I was a born worrier. It seemed that if I was not worried, I was worried about not being worried. When I was born again, I was delivered from the curse of worry, but the habit had to be broken. Finally I realized when the Bible tells us not to worry, it is a command not a suggestion. And that it is a sin to worry. This knowledge makes it easier to stop worrying but only with the help of the Holy Spirit.

Proverbs 12:25 says, "An anxious heart weighs a man

down." The heavy burden of anxiety does not help us, as Jesus tells us in Matthew 6:27. Worry is not only futile; it is actually bad for us.

Dr. Charles Mayo of the Mayo Clinic pointed out that worry affects circulation, the glands, the whole nervous system, and profoundly affects the hearing. Oh my, all that comes from worry. No wonder Jesus warned Martha about her anxiety and tells us more than 350 times to "fear not." We are simply not made to worry. If we want to live healthy lives, we must have the Holy Spirit to help us leave our chronic anxiety behind.

April 6th ~ Father Tim

I dearly love Jan Karon's Mitford Series books. They are full of humor and wisdom. Father Tim, an adorable Episcopal priest, is the central character. I also enjoy the North Carolina mountain town of Mitford residents - they begin to feel like family after reading these books. I am on the eighth and newest: *Light From Heaven* and, as usual, it is wonderful. Some of the old-timers' sayings are especially funny such as when Old Granny exclaims, "I'll be et f'r a tater."

Father Tim quotes James Hudson Taylor, "There are three stages in the work of God: impossible, difficult, done." And Winston Churchill, "We're always getting ready to live, but never living."

I always learn a great deal spiritually as I read about Father Tim and his darling artist wife Cynthia. He prayed a prayer attributed to St. Francis, "Watch, O Lord with those who wake or watch or weep tonight and give Your angels and saints charge over those who sleep, Tend Your sick ones, O Lord Christ. Rest Your weary ones. Bless Your dying ones. Soothe Your suffering ones. Pity Your afflicted ones. Shield Your joyous ones. And all for Your love's sake. Amen."

Cynthia spoke about the phrase that jumped out at me:

"Shield Your joyous ones." Her words: "Joy is a terribly fragile thing and the enemy is bent on stealing it from us. Such a wise thing to ask for." Truly it is wise to ask to have our precious joy protected since it is given us by the Lord Himself. (John 17:13)

This reminds me of a book by Jerry Savelle that I re-read often entitled *If Satan Can't Steal Your Joy, He Can't Keep Your Goods*." Our joy is actually a way of worshipping God – having a thankful, grateful heart to Him for all He has done and is doing.

April 7th ~ What About Today?

"What about today, Sis?" The Lord asked me this question this morning as I was thinking to myself about all I was going to do during the week. I was saying to myself, "I can't wait" till my massage day after tomorrow, or "I can't wait" till the kids come over for game night, or till that book I ordered arrives, or till it is time for our vacation, and on and on.

God whispered to me, "Why not enjoy today?" Quit saying you can't wait, for, in the first place, it is not a true statement because you can and will wait.

Seems as if "I can wait" to call that certain person that is lonely and talks too long or to send that sympathy or get-well card or "can wait" to start exercising or "can wait" to say I'm sorry or ask forgiveness or lots of other things. In fact, I "can wait" for all those other more pleasant things, too, since I simply must. Many times I don't have a choice. So why not live in today? Each day is the day the Lord has made, why not rejoice and be glad in it? (Psalm 118:24)

Our church school gives out character awards each year and it is always great fun to see which one our grandchildren will receive. This year Scott, age nine, was given "Contentment." Well, I could hardly think of a better trait. He is a precious boy that lives in today.

I love Paul's writing to the Church at Philippi when he

said he had learned to be content in whatever circumstance. He goes on to say that he knows how to get along with humble means and also how to live in prosperity; in any way and every circumstance. (Philippians 4:11-12) Actually, I am for the most part a very contented person as I count my many blessings. Just need to live more in the present tense - counting each moment as a gift from God - which it really is.

April 8th ~ Confusion

In reading Acts 19, I actually laughed at verse 32 as it sounds like what is happening in our world today. "So then, some were shouting one thing and some another, for the assembly was in confusion and the majority did not know for what reason they had come together."

Oh, I hate to think about our Congress being in confusion but that is what may be happening. And the majority doesn't even know what they are there for; forgetting that they are there to represent the people, not their own political agenda.

We read in Acts 21:34, "Some in the crowd shouted one thing and some another, and since the commander could not get at the truth because of the uproar, he ordered that Paul be taken into the barracks." Yes, it is hard to find the facts or the truth when there is a crowd shouting first one thing and then another. This is what I suppose we can call mob rule.

My daddy told me to always be fearful of a mob because, when he was a teenager, he was innocently caught up in a mob of people bent on lynching a man. He said he had never been so afraid in his entire life, before or since. He could tell that an evil deed was going to be done no matter what he said or did although he knew it was horribly wrong. He explained that the mob was like an angry beast attacking a wounded animal. That awful scene resulted in the tar and feathering of the victim and then afterwards they ran him out of town. That made a tremendous impression on my daddy that he never forgot.

God is the author of peace not confusion. (1 Corinthians 14:33) So we can trust that when there is confusion, it is not of the Lord. Ephesians 2:14 says, "For He Himself is our peace."

April 9 ~ Chosen

When I was growing up, I was not very athletic and so was the last one chosen for any team sport. I always wished that someone would call my name for games. (Like Red Rover, Red Rover, let Sister come over—remember that one?) Sometimes it was embarrassing still standing when others were called. Thankfully, I had many friends and lots of confidence so this wasn't too bad for me. But I have known others whose lives were truly colored by this sort of thing.

Now I am chosen. Yea! "You did not choose me but I chose you and appointed you that you should go and bear much fruit..." (John 15:16) I am chosen for the Kingdom of God. It doesn't get any better than that. Chosen, elected, selected. I am among the elect! "God chose the weak to confound the wise" (1 Corinthians 1:27). No matter how weak I am in the flesh, I am still chosen and can boast in the Lord and not myself.

I used to wonder about the verse, "Many are called, but few are chosen" (Matthew 20:16). What could this possibly mean? Finally I heard a preacher explain that God calls everyone in the world to Him but not everyone accepts that call. That we have to choose to be chosen. I raise my hand and choose to be chosen right now, Lord.

1 Peter 2:9 says, "But you are a chosen race, a royal priesthood, a holy nation, a people for God's own possession, so that you may proclaim the excellencies of Him, who called you out of darkness into His marvelous light." We are all chosen for a purpose - to proclaim the excellencies of Him

who died to save us all. The gospel—the good news.

April 10th ~ Letters From Grace, Daughter

This morning while running through the elementary school yard near our house, I witnessed the clearest picture of Matthew 6:26 I've ever seen: "Look at the birds of the air, they never sow, nor reap nor gather into barns, and yet your heavenly Father feeds them. Are you not worth much more than they?"

The children were running toward me (very excited, I might add) with something hanging from what looked like string in their hands. As I got closer, I could see that they were holding pinecones covered in peanut butter and bird-seed and they were taking them to their teacher who was on a ladder hanging them from branches of a huge tree. (I know, because my own children have made these and I also ran past all the birdseed, peanut butter mess.)

The children are not scared of me as I talk to them on a regular basis so I said, "You sure are going to feed lots of birds today!" As I said it, I was reminded of Matthew 6:26 and the Lord encouraged me to share with all of you how much more He loves you than the birds of the air.

I got so excited thinking of the super abundance of food those birds were going to enjoy, not at all what they were expecting, over and ALL they could ever ask or think - that's how much He loves them and again how much more He loves you! Read the verse again - expect God to provide for you. He is your provider!

Written by Grace LaMaster, Daughter, to Her Dad and Brothers, April 10, 2009

April 11th ~ Draw Near to God

What a promise! "Draw near to God and He will draw near to you!" (James 4:8) I like to say it, "Draw near to Me and I will draw near to you" - the Lord speaking to me personally. I believe it with all my heart and stand on His promise. So even when I don't feel His presence, I know He is there because He said He would be.

A lady in our Wednesday Bible Study in California asked me why she did not always feel His presence during her quiet times and I told her just to trust that He was with her because He said He would be. We need to go by faith, not feelings. His promises are always true and we can trust Him to do what He says He will do. And in our Bible reading, we are also actually fellowshipping with Him as He is the Living Word.

Our two darling 18-month-old Shih Tzu puppies are very affectionate with me but run from Bill. (Possibly in the puppy mill, they were rescued from a man who was mean to them.) So the only time they come near Bill is when he gives them cheese or other treats. They take the gifts and quickly back away from him.

Aren't we sometimes like that with Father God? We take His gifts, but are just a little afraid to get too close to Him, especially when we are new Christians. We haven't quite learned to fully trust Him. We find it hard to believe that He really desires to fellowship with us and that He enjoys our company.

We can feel so unworthy at times but God is calling us to come just as we are. He loves us so much more than we could ever imagine. So let us continue to draw near to Him and know He is near to us.

2 Corinthians 13:14 says, "The grace of the Lord Jesus Christ, and the love of God, and the communion of the Holy Spirit be with you all. Amen."

April 12th ~ Judging

Jean Fossett, a darling new lady in our Tuesday morning Joy Group, gave a good example that emphasized our study this week. The lesson was about fasting our negative, judgmental, hateful words. She had just returned from a spring break skiing trip with her daughter and grand kids where they had been blessed to stay in a fabulous home.

Jean likes to read and had carefully looked at the titles of all the books in the bookshelves. She commented that she did not think the owners of the house were Christian because she did not find a Bible. Her daughter quickly convicted her by saying, "Mother, you should not judge people you do not know - maybe the lady is like you and takes her Bible everywhere she goes and thus has it with her."

How often do we all do this same type of thing? Way too often we judge a book by its cover, so to speak. We truly do not know what is going on in others' lives, behind closed doors or faces or whatever. However, the Bible does say that you will know a tree by its fruit; whether good or evil. (Matthew 7:15-20)

I laughed at hearing a man say that he did not want to die with certain books in his house. Occasionally Bill's Mystery Book Club or the Literary Guild sends him books that he did not order. If they are bad, we like to send them back as soon as possible.

But there are good judgments. Our postman said that he had been our mail carrier for several years and it seemed to him that we were Christians because of all the publications we received. This made me think that people really are looking at our fruit. It makes me want to be more careful with my witness in every way.

Heard a cute story about a boy watching a preacher build a fence and the preacher asked if he was interested in carpentry and the boy said, "No, I am waiting to hear what you say when you hit your thumb with the hammer."

Yes, people are watching.

April 13th ~ Author and Finisher of Our Faith

The Lord told me in my quiet time with Him this morning to picture a horse with blinders on so that he has to look straight ahead and for me to shut the world out and focus completely on Him. Focus on Him, the Author and Finisher of my faith. (Hebrews 12:2)

He began my faith walk and He will finish it! That takes a lot of pressure off of me. I know I'll finish the race because He is in it with me – right beside me. "He who began a good work in me will complete it till the day of Jesus Christ" (Philippians 1:6). Yea!

I was looking at a dead tree outside my sunroom window and wondering why it died when all others around it are living and thriving. What makes one dry up and become brittle and others be green and growing? Its leaves look all shriveled. Oh, I do see one reason – the big trees overshadow it and it doesn't get much sun. That's it! We all need to bask in the light of the Son. Sometimes all that's going on around us keeps us from the light, overshadowing us, keeping us from looking up, from looking unto Jesus, the Author and the Finisher of our faith. One version says, "Originator and perfector" of our faith.

The word "looking" in the Greek is *aphorao* from *apo* which means "away from" and *horao* means "to see." The word signifies undivided attention, looking away from all distractions in order to fix one's gaze on one object. "Looking" here in Hebrews 12:2 is having eyes for no one but Jesus.

The Lord told me not to concentrate on the dead tree but to look at all the green ones, to always look for the best, the way He does! I was singing, "I have decided to follow Jesus" – I'll go with Him all the way and best of all He will go with me all the way as I keep my eyes focused on Him.

April 14th ~ Boston Marathon, April 14, 2000, by Burke Patterson, Son

I had just finished zipping up my bag to head to the airport when my wife Lovey bounced into the bedroom and handed me a wrapped present. "I got you a little something," she said with a sheepish grin. It wasn't my birthday, so what could this be? I opened to find a brand new Bible. I had been hoping that someone would find the one I had lost at church a month earlier. Nobody had turned it in and I had gone without a Bible for too long. My new Bible was navy blue and had my name printed in white on the cover. "Look inside, I wrote something for you," she said. Tears poured down my face as I read her note.

I found myself smack dab in the middle of a miracle. In this exact same room, in almost this exact spot, just a few months ago, I had cried out to God in despair to save me and my marriage. In a moment of pure desperation, I cried out to God to rescue me and He answered. Right there in that room I had been born again. I was set free from the destructive grip of alcohol that had almost wrecked my life.

He saved me but our marriage seemed doomed. Too much damage had been done. We spent several months apart until one day, after a series of miracles, she asked me back into the house. Just a few weeks ago, she couldn't stand the sight of me and now she had just given me this gift with a love note written in it. We'd gone from barely speaking to now headed on a trip to Boston, just the two of us. Our marriage had gone from being in a death spiral to a restoration mode. We were a true miracle couple.

So we sat there reveling in this miracle and I opened the Bible to where the blue divider had been placed and my eyes went straight to this verse.

Psalm 18:33-36 says, "He makes my feet like the feet of a deer; He enables me to stand on the heights. He trains my hands for battle, my arms can bend a bow of bronze. You give me Your shield of victory and Your right hand sustains me; You stoop down to make me great. You broaden the paths beneath me so my ankles do not turn." As I read those words, we both looked at each other and said, "Wow."

Why was this verse so meaningful? Because the reason we were going to Boston was that I was going to be running in the Boston Marathon and, to finish a 26.2-mile race, I needed a miracle. I hadn't been able to finish any runs over 18 miles because of severe knee problems. After 15 or so miles, my left knee would feel like someone was twisting a knife right through it. Regardless of my knee problems, we had planned this trip and were excited to be going to Boston.

April 14 ~ Boston Marathon, Continued

The marathon was a big deal to me but the bigger deal was the fact that my wife was with me. If He could heal our marriage, He could heal my knee. That verse was just a "wink" that He had me covered.

At mile 22 of the Marathon, you come to a spot where downtown Boston is clearly visible and you know you're almost home. Heartbreak Hill is behind you now and it's just a matter of a few more minutes to the finish line. So as I paused for a drink at the mile 22-water station, I had tears of joy because everything felt great. I was tired, but free of any knee pain. Thank you, God. So I started running again. Within the first few strides, pain hit my knee like a knife and it was unbearable. Panic came over me as I slowed to a walk and, as runners went by me, I started to get angry.

I looked again at downtown Boston and in a state of desperation cried out to God, "Please God, PLEASE, I'm too close to the finish, please don't let this happen, make my feet like that of a deer. You promised, please Lord, help me!" And with that plea, He answered me in a voice that was as clear as if He was coming through iPod earphones — "GO FASTER."

So I just ran as fast as I could. The last few miles were my fastest miles of the entire race. I sprinted the last quarter mile, weaving through the traffic and crossing the finish line with no pain whatsoever. That was a miracle! But the fact that my beautiful wife was cheering me on at the finish line, louder than anyone else in that huge crowd, that was super-miraculous!

My Bible is now more than 10 years old and has many

verses marked and underlined and notes written all over it. All those verses are special. But if I ever need to be reminded of how incredibly faithful God is, how loving, and how He speaks through His Word, I can turn to page 918 and see Psalm 18:33-36, highlighted in yellow and written next to it "4/14/2000 The Day WE Left For Boston." If you need a miracle in your life, expect it. God has you covered.

Author's notes: I cannot read this wonderful testimony about a healed marriage without tears of joy. I stood on the words from the hymn, "My Hope is Built on Nothing Less Than Jesus' Blood and Righteousness" during their separation. I would sing it at the top of my lungs. Not only were we heartbroken for Burke, but we loved our precious Laura (Lovey) so dearly, too, and we did not want to lose her. God was faithful to answer ours and others' prayers.

April 15th ~ High Horse

My mother used to tell me "not to get on my high horse" or "not to be too big for my britches." I always understood what she meant, but only recently thought that, like a lot of old sayings, these might have had their roots in the Bible.

While I was reading Acts 9 about Saul/Paul's conversion, I realized that he was knocked completely off his horse. Since he was very self-righteous in his zeal for God, he was probably on his "high horse." Although he believed that he was justified in persecuting Christians, he was definitely too big for his britches and doing it in his own strength. So the Lord had to knock him off his horse to get his attention.

O dear, I don't want to have to be knocked off of my "high horse." I want to get down from it by myself when He corrects me. There are ever so many verses in the Bible about how God hates pride and judging. I guess judging is similar to persecuting Christians. That is what He has really been convicting me of lately. Pointing a finger at other Christians can even be done in your thoughts.

Matthew 7:1-2 says, "Judge not, that you not be judged.

For with what judgment you judge, you will be judged, and with the measure you use, it will be measured back to you."

April 16th ~ *Applause from Heaven*

This is the title of a book by author Max Lucado. As usual, he has great lessons for the reader to learn. It really touched my heart because God had asked me not long ago, "Sister, do you want compliments from people or Me?" I answered truthfully, "Both." He went on to remind me that I was to do everything as unto the Lord and not to expect the thanks of people or even for them to realize how hard I had worked or whatever.

It has been very gratifying to hear many praises about my first *Morning By Morning* book. I must constantly remind myself that I did not write it alone. Without Him I can do nothing, and I need to give all the glory and praise to Him.

Pastor Russell Craft conducted a funeral that I attended for a man named David who was a dedicated prayer warrior. This young man (young to me, he was only 53) had been an invalid for the last 10 or12 years but, while in the nursing home, he had constantly prayed for the other patients. (I almost dreaded to get this young man's emails on the prayer line as he always had a long list of people to pray about whom I did not know or even their slightest problem. How ashamed I now feel!)

Pastor Russell said that when he visited David, he was known and loved by all. He will truly be missed by all the other patients. I was so impressed when he asked us to stand up and give David a standing ovation for his caring prayer ministry – stating that although he had not been recognized here on earth, there was awaiting applause for him in heaven. There was not a dry eye in the place.

The Lord is always looking for prayer warriors to stand in the gap and this precious man will have stars in his crown. I learned a big lesson. He did not have a showy ministry but I truly believe with Pastor Russell that he had the heavenly applause. What do I really want most?

April 17th ~ Advertising

In a college psychology course at the University of Texas in 1950, the professor said that Ford Motor Company's advertising campaign was the best ever, at that time. It consisted of a huge billboard presentation of just a baby and followed each week with another teaser. Finally they unveiled their new model.

My daddy had been working for the Ford dealership in our home town all my life and was now the owner, so the advertising campaign meant a lot to me. He was born in 1901 and grew up with the century. He began sweeping out the Ford place when he was 15.

My all-time favorite slogan was "Ford has a better idea" which makes me think of how God really does have a better idea and has an individual plan for each of our lives. All we need to do is ask Him to show us what His plan for us is all about, praying each day "give us this day our daily bread," asking for daily provision – physical and spiritual.

Asking is so much better than trying to think up our own agendas which often are in direct opposition to the "better idea" He has in mind for us. God has prepared beforehand good works for us to do. (Ephesians 2:10) He has planned them, not us.

Ephesians 4:7 says, "But to each one of us grace was given according to the measure of Christ's gift." He not only gives us gifts (or talents), He also gives us the grace to use them in whatever measure we need. God really does have "better ideas." And we need to advertise His willingness to give them to us.

Praise His name.

April 18th ~ Growing Weary in Worship

When we do not rest, we do not worship. When we do

not worship, we do not trust. Therefore, we should not grow weary in worshiping Him.

Psalm 131:1-3 says, "My heart is not proud, LORD, my eyes are not haughty; I do not concern myself with great matters or things too wonderful for me. But I have calmed and quieted myself, I am like a weaned child with its mother; like a weaned child I am content. Israel put your hope in the LORD both now and forevermore."

Here is what I am learning: EVERYTHING is too great for me. I don't need to try to run away from it. We all are weary trying to accomplish His work our way. It's exhausting trying to be God. That's because He is and we are not.

The Jews observed and still practice the custom of the Sabbath, a day of rest and worship following their six days of labor. (Exodus 31:12-17) God's intent for Sabbath was "so you may know that I am the Lord, who makes you holy." (Verse 13) When God's people fail to observe Sabbath rest, it is a sign we have forgotten who He is.

By keeping Sabbath (resting in Him), we acknowledge that we know who the Lord of every part of our lives really is. What happens when we neglect God's Sabbath rest? Our spiritual, emotional, and material resources become overworked, worn out, dried up. There is no rest in that!

According to Isaiah 28:12, God told His people, "Here is a place of rest; let the weary rest here. This is a place of quiet rest." But they would not listen.

I'm listening, Lord!

The Greek word "to be weary" signifies to shrink back like a coward in a war. Let it not be this way with us. Let us not shrink back from worshipping our Prince of Peace. God is never weary of doing us good.

April 19th ~ Tomorrow

Lovey, my precious daughter-in-law Laura, called to tell me about a speaker at the "Chick Night" at Healing Place, her church in Baton Rouge, Louisiana. The lady was with Hillsong Church from Australia. She pointed out something I had never noticed before from Exodus 8:1-15. It really excites me to get a new revelation.

This passage is about the plague of frogs and the speaker told them to imagine how awful it would be to have frogs all over you: stinky, noisy, croaking frogs crawling all over you. Imagine them in your bed, where you walk, where you sit, where you eat, in your food bowls, everywhere, even on your head when you lie down. Can you imagine anything as awful?

OK, here is the big revelation: Moses asked Pharaoh when he wanted God to remove the frogs, and amazingly, Pharaoh answered, "Tomorrow." Why not today, Pharaoh? Why wait? It is hard to believe that he would not want immediate relief.

Do we do that, too? Sure we do, not willing to give up our stinking thinking of depression, self pity, anger, worry, resentment, unforgiveness or whatever "frogs" we have all over us.

This convicted me of times I knew the Lord's healing was readily available but I would make a decision to take a day off "enjoying" ill health, using that as an excuse to rest and stay in bed all day just like I used to do before I was a Christian. It made me feel better to be "sick" rather than just lazy. It is shocking how many ways we can fool ourselves!

Moses answered Pharaoh, "Let it be done according to your word, that you may know that there is no one like the Lord our God." Our relief often comes according to our words, too.

Lord, help us to never put off receiving our deliverance until tomorrow. Amen.

April 20th ~ The King Of the Flood

Psalm 29:10-11 says, "The Lord sat enthroned at the Flood and the Lord sits as King forever. The Lord will give strength to His people, He will bless his people with peace."

Isaiah 59:19 says, "When the enemy comes in like a flood the Lord raise up a standard or banner against him."

Sometimes floods come into our lives like *Tsunami* waves, catching us completely off guard. They can be so big and scary that they carry us or our loved ones away. Our job is to look to the King of the flood for His help. He's King of all our floods. He is in control, so all is well!

Psalm 29:10 in the Message Bible says, "Above the flood waters is God's throne from which His power flows, from which He rules the world. God makes His people strong. God gives His people peace." Even in the floods, He gives us peace and makes us stand strong, IF we will only trust Him. He will be enthroned above the waters so they won't overflow us.

Isaiah 43:2 says, "When you pass through the waters I will be with you, they shall not overflow you." PTL!

Psalm 66:12 says, "We went through fire and water, but You brought us out to a place of rich fulfillment" (Amplified: abundance). Super abundance - so it's sometimes good when the rivers overflow their boundaries instead of a flood always being thought of as bad. Many times it overflows with blessings. He's the King of the Flood - a mighty flood of blessings.

Water speaks of life, sustenance, fertility, blessing and refreshing. We can rest in the fact that God has everything under control. The God who controls the storms is also the God who gives us strength and peace.

April 21st ~ Seasons of Life

Every one of my decades has been different and blessed. I never want to forget what being young felt like. I want to be able to identify with young people as well as my contemporaries. Of course, I think it is easier for me to remember being young than it is for young people to understand elderly people like me.

I used to hear older folks talking about eating cereal for supper and I was horrified. They did not eat a real meal? How drab. Now that I eat cereal nearly every night and Bill eats popcorn and a banana, I rethink my judgment of them. In fact, we have learned that if we eat a big meal at night, especially a late one, we end up with indigestion and do not sleep well.

Despite all the negatives, there are a great many pluses. For one, we don't sweat the small stuff anymore, worrying so much about what others will think, and we adjust to changes and problems with more ease. Yes, we have more wisdom to cope with life in general. Experience really is a great teacher.

Here are some Scriptures that refer to elders: 1 Peter 5:5 says, "Likewise, you younger people, submit yourselves to your elders." 1 Timothy 5:1 says, "Do not rebuke an older man, but exhort him as a father." And then we elderly are told in Titus 2:2,3: "That the older men be sober, reverent, temperate, sound in faith, in love, in patience; the older women likewise, that they be reverent in behavior, not slanderers, not given to much wine, teachers of good things."

Solomon, in looking back on his life (Ecclesiastes 12:1) gives this good advice, "Remember now your Creator in the days of your youth, before the difficult days come and the years draw near when you say, 'I have no pleasure in them.'" Hopefully, we will never have to say those words because in His presence is fullness of joy and pleasures for evermore. (Psalm 16:11)

April 22nd ~ 3 Don'ts

While in Palm Springs, we enjoy attending Victory Christian Center in nearby Rancho Mirage and are always blessed to hear the wonderful pastor Dr. Jeff Walker. He is super anointed as a great teacher/preacher/encourager. We always come from the services inspired in our spiritual walk. We are also excited to know that three to six people are saved at nearly every service. Only once do I remember a service when no one was saved. It is such a joy to be a part of this miracle of rebirth.

Since Pastor Jeff is always upbeat and never at all negative, we were surprised to hear him announce that for a change he was going to tell us some "Don'ts." He said that this was a message for times of devastation and destruction, not his usual message at all.

The Three Don'ts:

1. Don't throw away your confidence. Hebrews 10:35 – "Therefore do not throw away your confidence which has great reward."
2. Don't be weary in well doing. Galatians 6:9 – "And let us not grow weary while doing good, for in due season we will reap if we do not lose heart."
3. Don't forget His benefits. Psalm103:1-5 – "Bless the Lord O my soul and all that is within me and forget not all His benefits."

Of course, Pastor Jeff enlarged on these "Don'ts" and reminded us from Hebrews 6:12 that we are not to become sluggish, but imitate those who through faith and patience inherit the promises. This is good advice since His promises are always true, yes and amen. (2 Corinthians 1:20)

April 23rd ~ 3 Do's

Last week Pastor Jeff taught on "Three Don'ts for Troubled Times" and this week on "Three Do's." Both were very anointed sermons.

Now the Three Do's:

1. Encourage yourself in the Lord ~ We read in 1 Samuel 30:6 that King David encouraged/strengthened himself in the Lord when all appeared to be lost and even his own men were ready to stone him.
2. Go to the house of the Lord ~ Ps. 122:1. A Psalm of David, "I was glad when they said unto me, let us go into the house of the Lord." He knew he needed to be

with other believers to strengthen his faith. Hebrews 10:25 says, "Not forsaking the assembling of ourselves together."

3. Take every thought captive into the obedience of Christ ~ 2 Corinthians 10:5 says, "Casting down arguments and every high thing that exalts itself against the knowledge of God, bringing every thought into captivity to the obedience of Christ. Instead, think on and mediate on how good God is." Philippians 4:8 says, "Think of and mediate on whatsoever things are noble, just, pure, lovely and of good report, if there is any virtue and if there is ANYTHING praiseworthy."

I don't know which I find harder to do: the Do's or the Don'ts. At least I know there is no way I could possibly do either without the help of the Holy Spirit.

April 24th ~ Supernatural Breakthrough

Keys to a supernatural visit from the God of the Breakthrough can be found in 1 Kings 17:8-16. It's the story of Elijah and the widow of Zarephath.

1. Hearing a prophetic word from God
2. Having a willingness to obey
3. Sowing a significant seed

The most important thing we can do to receive our breakthrough is to give the Lord praise and worship. I found this quote, "The depth of our praise will determine the magnitude of our breakthrough."

Say over and over till it sinks into your spirit: "God loves me and nothing can separate me from the love of God." (Romans 8:38-39) The compassion of God is constantly being revealed. Psalm 145:8 tells us, "The Lord is gracious and full of compassion, slow to anger and great in mercy." He not only is all powerful, He is all giving.

Has He ever done a miracle for you? Then He can and will do it again. No matter how big it is. WE think a really big money matter is too hard. A marriage problem, work problem, children in rebellion, or whatever seems too big for God is NOT too difficult when there is a supernatural breakthrough.

Remember, nothing is too difficult for our God. We need to understand how much God loves us and that he hears our prayers and loves us just as much as His Son Jesus. No matter how impossible your situation may look, the God of the breakthrough is working behind the scenes in your life right now!

April 25th ~ Looking Good

Once at a big party I said to a friend that she just looked wonderful. She replied, "Thank you because this is the very best I can look - I just had my hair done and these are the best clothes I own so I could never look any better than I do right now, this is it." Was that funny or what? I laugh every time I think of her remark.

I personally have wasted a lot of time in my life concerned about how I looked to others; wanting to buy the prettiest clothes, makeup, and so on. Certainly this is a pride issue. It's wonderful to get older and not care so much. But I'm ashamed to say when I was young, it mattered a great deal to me. I was not concerned about how I looked to God, just to people.

He is helping me to change but what is hard for me to believe is that He loved me just as much when I was living in the world as He loves me now that I spend much more of my time seeking to please Him. His love is constant and never ever changes. Praise His name.

The book of 1 John could be called the love book as 1 Corinthians 13 is the love chapter. In 1 John four, we read several verses about God's love toward us. Verse 19 says, "We love Him because He first loved us." And to paraphrase verses 17-18 we learn that love has been perfected in us that we may have boldness in the day of judgment, because as Jesus is, so are we in the world. There is no fear in love, as perfect love casts out fear. God's love is perfect and we are perfect in His sight.

We look good to Him all the time. He will never love us any more or any less, no matter what we do. He loves us with an everlasting love. It can't get any better than that.

April 26th ~ "He Leadeth Me"

"He leadeth me, He leadeth me, by Hs own hand He leadeth me" - the first line of that wonderful old hymn. I got very excited singing that song this morning thinking about how marvelous it is that God really does lead each of us.

Just think about how God has put an internal guidance system in birds that direct them to fly south when winter is coming. And we are more important than sparrows. (Matthew 6:26)

How could we ever doubt that He will lead us, too? He truly leads us by the hand if we only trust Him. Of course, we must ask for His direction. He is such a gentleman that He will not push His way into our lives. He waits for us to ask.

The Book of James tells us that if we lack wisdom, we are to ask and the Lord will give it to us without reproach. (James 1:5-6) In fact, He is delighted when we ask for His special directions rather than relying on our own ideas.

Now that our children are all grown, they seem to seek our counsel more often than when they were younger. It really blesses me when I see our kids take the advice we give them, especially Bill's. Not that we always know best, but our experience has given us some knowledge. Our God has all knowledge so don't you think He is pleased when we avail ourselves of His wisdom?

It seems that our problem is that we actually forget to ask Him before we jump in and try to solve something in our own limited abilities. If we only obeyed Proverbs 3:5-6, our lives would go so much smoother. "Trust in the Lord with all your heart, and lean not on your own understanding; in all your ways acknowledge Him and He shall direct your paths."

April 27th ~ Heart Surgery

Being told by his cardiologist that he was a walking time bomb was a huge shock to dear friend Jim Asbury. However, he is an extremely strong Christian who immediately put his faith in God and asked the saints to pray. His precious wife Bonnie, after hearing he needed heart surgery, began to pray the scripture: Philippians 4:6-7 in this manner, "Be anxious for nothing but in everything by prayer and supplication, with thanksgiving, let your requests be known to God, and the peace which passes all understanding will guard 'Jim's heart' and mind through Christ Jesus."

Jim knows that before, during and after his heart surgery, many people all over the country and even in Europe were praying for him. His 11-year-old granddaughter was at a church camp in Oklahoma and was excited that the theme for the week was Proverbs 4:23, "Above all else guard your 'heart' for it is the wellspring of life." This she prayed for Grandpa Jim. Because of all these prayers, Jim was calm and without fear during the heart cauterization and the actual surgery. He says, "When your heart is filled with faith, there is no room left for fear."

The surgery on Thursday morning went fine but on Saturday evening his heart began beating in a very erratic manner and he was near death. But once again prayer prevailed. At that very moment, special friends came to the hospital to see him and immediately began praying outside his room when they realized there was an emergency.

The family later learned that on that same Saturday evening a friend from Houston heard from the Lord, "Pray for Jim, Pray for Jim," which she did. She had no idea that at that very moment he was near death.

Bonnie, who was at Jim's bedside, could hear him saying, "Come Holy Spirit, Come Holy Spirit, Come Holy Spirit." A short time later he improved, gaining strength daily. The doctors are amazed at his rapid recovery and the fact that he was without pain after the first few days. Jim says when people say to him, "It's good to see you," he replies, "It's good to be seen."

John Wesley said, "God does nothing without prayer and nothing happens without it." James 5:16b says, "The effective fervent prayer of a righteous man avails much."

April 28th ~ Gone With the Wind

My all-time favorite movie and book is *Gone with the Wind*. I have read the book at least three times and seen the movie even more. I even had *Gone With the Wind* paper dolls. I wish I had saved them as they would be worth lots today. A little trivia: My mother's first cousin John Arledge was the actor in the movie playing the soldier having his leg amputated at the Atlanta train station.

I loved Scarlett O'Hara's indomitable spirit and her most famous line "tomorrow is another day" at the close of the film after Rhett Butler had left her and all seemed lost.

This, of course, reminds me of Lamentations 3:21-23 that says, "This I recall to mind, therefore I have hope. The Lord's loving-kindnesses indeed never cease, for His compassions fail not, they are new every morning, great is Your faithfulness."

We can start anew every morning with hope knowing that God is faithful to have compassion and loving-kindness for us. Hope springs eternal! And my favorite verse from the hymn "Great Is Thy Faithfulness" is "strength for today and bright hope for tomorrow," a good prayer that I pray often.

Jesus in the Sermon on the Mount told us not to worry about tomorrow. (Matthew 6:34) He said that tomorrow will take care of itself. In verse 33, He gave the instructions as to how to keep from worry: "Seek first His kingdom and

His righteousness, and all these things will be added unto you." Before I knew Jesus as personal Savior, I was a world class worrier. How I praise Him that He changed me completely and I've exchanged a worrying attitude for a trusting one.

I don't know what tomorrow holds, but I know Who holds our tomorrows. Wonderful! I can and will trust Him with all my tomorrows.

April 29th ~ EXTRA

Looking for something to give the group at Love Overflowing to remind them of how much God loves them, I thought of the gum called Extra. I gave them each a piece and told them what I thought the Lord was saying to His children. First, that we are each EXTRA special to Him and He always gives us EXTRA blessings. I began to look up EX words in the concordance. I knew the word EXTRA was not in the Bible but there were lots of EX ones that spoke to me.

EXAMPLE ~ Jesus is our example.

EXAMINE ~ He requires us to examine ourselves to see how close we are becoming to our Example.

EXACT ~ He is exacting in being faithful to change us into His image.

EXCEED ~ He always does exceedingly abundantly more than we can desire or pray for.

EXCEL ~ He expects us to excel and helps us to do it in His strength.

EXCESS ~ He wants us to get rid of all our excess baggage.

EXCUSE ~ He excuses all our sins and overlooks our faults.

EXERCISE ~ He teaches us to exercise our faith.

EXHORT ~ He exhorts us to do our very best and calls on us to exhort others.

EXPECT ~ We are to expect Him to act on our behalf, to wait for Him expectantly.

EXPERIENCE ~ We can experience His grace, mercy and favor and especially His presence.

EXPRESS ~ He expressed His love to us on the cross, now we can express our love to Him with praise and worship.

EXTEND ~ He extends His outstretched arm to us to lift us up. His mercy and grace are always extended to us.

EXTREME ~ He is an extremely good and great God; an EXTRA special God, so we EXALT Him daily.

April 30th ~ Cutting Yourself Down

Mark 5:5 says of the man with the unclean spirit, "He was…in the tombs…cutting himself." Stop cutting yourself down!

Discussing his low self esteem, cartoon character Charlie Brown says, "It goes back to when I first set foot on the stage of life. They looked at me and said, 'He's just not right for the part.'"

You may smile but when you've spent your life engaged in self-flagellation, you know exactly what he means. The man in the tombs spent his days, "cutting himself" because he thought he was worthless. Many of us wear a game face in public but spend our days doing the same thing.

Your self-image is second only to your faith in God. It doesn't matter what others think of you, what matters is what you think of yourself based on what God thinks! Self-esteem has to come from self. That's why it's hard to believe the good things people say about you when you can't see them in yourself.

How you treat others flows directly from your reservoir of personal dignity and self-respect. It's impossible to "love your neighbor as yourself" (Matthew 19:19) when you don't even like yourself. Paul says a man should love his wife like he loves himself. (Ephesians 5:28) But when you detest yourself, how can you love your mate?

The only time any of us even comes close to perfection

is on a job application! Stop cutting yourself down! God made you the way you are in order to use you the way He planned. Start complimenting Him on the great job He did. And remember, He loves you unconditionally and that's the only reason you need for loving yourself.

*Copied from, "The Word for You Today."

May 1st ~ God's Unlimited Blessing

We must get it deep down in our spirits that there are no limits to God's goodness and He is absolutely unlimited in His ability to pour out His resources upon us. Nothing delights Him more. He has abundant good stored up for those who honor Him.

The Jewish people have an easier time grasping these truths. The very word "glory" in Hebrew means "to be heavy with everything good." The Jewish people understood that it was God's goodness that would deliver them, bless them and bring them to victory. They depended on the glory of the Lord to go before them and would proclaim His goodness as they went out to battle. (2 Chronicles 20:21)

Jewish scholar David Baron, born in 1855 in Russia, had an understanding of the goodness of God. When he accepted Jesus as his Savior, he already had a wonderful insight into God. He wrote some commentaries on the Old Testament still used today. "God's goodness is without limit," he wrote. "This good His goodness bestows on all and each, according to the capacity of each to receive it; nor is there any limit to His giving, save His creatures capacity of receiving, which also is a good gift from Him."

How did this man get such a revelation back in the early 1900s before anyone was preaching the goodness of God? Well, he was brought up in a Jewish home and not exposed to the poverty teaching in the Christian churches at that time. He read and believed the Old Testament scriptures about the goodness of God.

Just think, today we have a new and better covenant and

better promises because of Jesus. Hebrews 8:6. PTL

May 2nd ~ Great Grandchildren

I really believe children are getting smarter. I had thought ours were all brilliant, the grandchildren even smarter, but I think our great-grandchildren may be geniuses.

Recently daughter Kathy was reading to her grandchild, seven-year-old Allie, and asked her if she knew what "foe" meant. Allie thought for a moment and replied, "Nemesis." Wow, imagine Kathy's surprise. She would have been pleased with a simpler 'enemy' for an answer. Kathy is a special education teacher and familiar with testing children's IQ's. She is constantly amazed with Allie's brilliance.

My mother thought J.G., my brother, and I were brilliant and so did Bill's mother about him. I guess all mothers think that about their children, but I really am convinced that the children of today are more knowledgeable than our generation; probably in a great measure due to TV that gives them a lot of information, whether we like it or not. I am quite sure that at age seven, I did not know what the word "nemesis" meant or even the word "foe". (Allie is also the child who could win at the game of Free Cell on the computer at age four.)

Daniel, speaking of the last days, said, "At the time of the end, many will run to and fro and knowledge will increase" (Daniel 12:4). Does that sound like today or what? Just think of all the changes I have seen in my lifetime and how many more my parents saw. Knowledge really is increasing.

1 Corinthians 8:1 reminds us that "knowledge puffs up (or makes arrogant), while love edifies or builds up." So, no matter how much we know, if we don't know God who is love, all our learning is nothing.

Proverbs 1:7 says, "The fear of the Lord is the beginning of knowledge, but fools despise wisdom and instruction." (Thankfully Allie is being taught about knowing the Lord as well as her other studies.)

May 3rd ~ "Ponder Anew What the Almighty Can Do"

This phrase from the old hymn "Praise Ye the Lord, the Almighty" jumped out at me as I was singing it this morning. I began to consider the words and this thought came to me: What can't He do? After all, nothing is too difficult for Him. Why then is it so hard for us to ask? He is always willing to answer us. Another line in the hymn is, "Surely His goodness and mercy here daily attend thee." (Reminds us of Psalm 23, doesn't it) Interestingly, the author, Joachim Neander, was in bed with tuberculosis when he wrote it.

As I was taking communion, I began to ponder anew how afraid Jesus must have been during the last supper, knowing what horrors were waiting for Him the next day. It dawned on me that is why I need never be scared or afraid again, because He bore ALL my fears. (Isaiah 53:5)

I was such a "scaredy cat" until I was born again. I would even look under my bed, afraid someone or something would come out and get me. I honestly don't know why or what I was afraid of, but always wanted Mother or Daddy to come into my bedroom and assure me all was well. Usually they would lie down beside me till I fell asleep. Daddy used to tease me that if someone "got" me they would quickly bring me back. I did not think that was funny.

After I married at 19 and Billy went to work at 5 a.m., I would sit with a butcher knife and watch the doors until it was light. How silly can you be? But Billy died and I sought the Lord, I was completely delivered of all fear. (Psalm 34:4, is my personal verse, "I sought the Lord and He delivered me from all my fears.)

We have the wonderful promise that "...the chastisement needful to obtain peace and well-being for us was upon Him..." (Isaiah 53:5, Amplified Bible).

May 4th ~ Anxious Thoughts

Do you ever feel guilty about having anxious thoughts? When you really know God loves you and you ask him to be in control? I was reading one of my favorite prayer scriptures and it comforted me that He knows that at times I have anxious thoughts. Psalm 139:23, 24 says, "Search me, O God, and know my heart; try me and know my anxious thoughts; and see if there is any hurtful way in me and lead me in the everlasting way." The New King James Version says "anxieties" instead of "anxious thoughts" and "wicked" instead of "hurtful."

So, it sounds like God considers "anxious thoughts" as being "wicked" and they are hurtful to Him. Certainly He forgives us for them, but it grieves Him for us not to completely trust Him in everything. He showed me this morning that it hurts Him for me not to believe He cares about everything that concerns me; even the little bitty, tiny things. He reminded me that He loves me with an everlasting love and is Jehovah Shamah, the God who is always there, and Jehovah Rohi, our Shepherd God who will always lead us. It is an offense to Him when we doubt that He is interested in every single thing that interests us. (How wonderful is that?)

Writing rhymes is not my thing but I wrote: "Oh, Lord, help me not to fret, to remember and not forget. To know You will always be there for me, so help me to just let it be. To acknowledge You in all I do, and know You will ever see me through. I praise You and thank You and worship You and most of all just love You."

May 5th ~ Older Son

In the parable of the Prodigal Son in Luke 15:11-32, the emphasis is on the younger son who repented from his wild ways and was forgiven by the father. But there is also an important message for us concerning the older son. He was angry at his father for welcoming the younger son with a huge party. All he could think of was how his brother had wasted his inheritance off wandering in the world while he himself had been faithful to his father and worked hard at home.

Interestingly enough, while he was pouting and not entering into the joyous celebration for his brother's homecoming, the father went out and pleaded with him. (Instead of pleading with him, I would have been furious with one of mine for acting that way.) But this father is a type of Father God who is always loving and forgiving.

When a friend and I were brand new Christians, another Christian who had been active in the Charismatic movement in the 1970s along with us admitted that she felt like the older brother. We were receiving the gifts of the Spirit just like she was, although we had wandered out in the world for almost 40 years while she had been faithful to Jesus all her life. She was saved early and had never strayed from the straight and narrow way. Certainly we could see how she would feel. Of course, she quickly repented of her attitude and rejoiced with us that we had finally seen the Light.

I guess this is also like the Parable of the Vineyard where the workers complained that the ones who arrived late got the same pay as the ones who had worked all day. (Matthew 20:1-16) This means to me that it is never too late to come to Jesus. Praise His Name for His forgiveness and love that never fails.

May 6th ~ "Safe in the Arms of Jesus"

Rev. Gerie Martin shared with us at our Bible Study a vision she had of the conquering Christ on His white horse. (Revelation 19:11-16) I was excited as this is one of my favorite pictures of Jesus as He goes forth to battle with the sword of the Spirit and His robe dipped in blood and the titles KING OF KINGS AND LORD OF LORDS written on his robe and thighs.

Anyway, as Rev. Gerie had this vision of Him, she begged to go with Him and He immediately swooped her up on the horse behind Him. As I thought about this vision this morning, I told Jesus that I, too, wanted to ride with Him and He reached down and cradled me in His lap with His arms encircling me and we rode off. Isn't that sweet?

The words of the old hymn — "Safe in the Arms of Jesus" — by Fanny Crosby rose up in my spirit. I had felt safe when He picked me up and held me tightly in His strong arms. It didn't matter if we were going forth to battle. I knew where I was just as the old hymn says: "Safe in His loving arms, safe on His gentle breast, there by His love o'er shadowed, sweetly my soul shall rest.

"Safe from corroding care, safe from the world's temptations, sin cannot harm me there; free from the blight of sorrow, free from my doubts and fears."

No matter what our battles, we can lean on His gentle breast and rest with His strong arms of love tightly around us. Whenever doubts or fears try to come in, we can piggyback on Rev. Gerie's vision and remember whose horse we are riding on when the enemy acts like he's going to attack. We can never lose when riding with the conquering Christ, whose name is called FAITHFUL and TRUE, THE WORD OF GOD.

May 7th ~ Little Frets

One of the many devotionals I read daily touched me with a message from the Lord: "Little Frets - your lack of control is not due to big burdens, but to your permitting the little frets and cares and burdens to accumulate. If anything vexes you, deal with that and get that right with Me before you allow yourself to speak to or meet anybody or to undertake any new duty. First cast all your cares on Me."

After reading this, I immediately made a list of cares that I needed to cast on the Lord. Then I tore up the list and threw it away, giving it all up to Jesus. This symbolic act helps me remember that they are now His problems and not mine.

Jesus tells us in the Sermon on the Mount (Matthew 6:25-33) to not worry. In fact, He commands it. We are not to take the pressure of forethought upon ourselves. It is not only wrong to worry, but it is infidelity because worrying means that we do not think God can look after the practical details of our lives and it is rarely anything else that worries us.

Have you ever noticed what Jesus said would choke the Word that He puts in us? The devil? No, the cares of the world, the little worries. (Matthew 13:22) Infidelity begins when we will not trust God for the answers we cannot see. The only cure for infidelity is obedience to the Spirit. One of the great words to His disciples is "abandon" — all cares, thoughts for tomorrow, anything that is troubling us.

In Philippians 4:6, we are commanded again, "Do not fret or have any anxiety about anything, but in every circumstance and in everything by prayer and petition (definite requests) with thanksgiving continue to make your wants known to God." (Amplified Bible) This was the very first verse I ever memorized and it comes back to my spirit often when I begin to fret or worry. God wants us to have the peace that passes all understanding. (Verse 7)

May 8th ~ Forgiving Aunt Alma by Rachel Rice, Friend

Over and over in my mind, I heard my pastor's words as I drove home: "If you mean business with the Lord, but don't know if you need to ask forgiveness, just ask the Lord to have that person call and she will. You just watch what I say and let His forgiveness reign in you!"

Aunt Alma kept popping into my thoughts. Let me tell you, she was something else!

I pulled into my garage at 2 a.m. from a conference several hours away and "bone weary" quickly dropped into bed. The next thing I realized was the phone ringing at 6 a.m. "Hello? Hello? Aunt Alma?"

"Rachel, will you..?" My mind flashed back to the promise I'd made Jesus only hours ago. Before I reneged and turned yellow, I blurted out, "Aunt Alma, just a minute; before you say anything else, I need to ask your forgiveness. It's been so long since I've called you to babysit. I could have taken you shopping and to the drug store, or to church. I've been wrong to treat you this way. Will you please forgive me?" There, I said it and gulped air with a sigh of release.

She began to cry. "Oh, Rachel, I don't fit. My life's useless here. I can't drive, so days are long. I miss all my old friends since moving here. It's awful to say, but I've been thinking suicide just could end it all!" With her sudden admission, we both sobbed and resolved to stay in touch and plan some projects together.

A whole new relationship sprang up with this elderly, little pediatric nurse living her last days in a bedroom. I'd thought of her as tough, overbearing and hard to please. I'd meant business with the Lord when I prayed that prayer and I'm ever so glad because our Aunt Alma met Jesus, peacefully in her sleep, several months after my "big amends." We'd had some mighty good times, too, all because forgiveness reigns! Sometimes I find myself smiling when I remember her and those precious words, "If you mean business with the Lord and don't know if you need to ask forgiveness…" I can recommend them to you also but don't be surprised if you're called too early, even before the very first sunbeam glints. (Matthew 5:23-24; James 5:16)

May 9th ~ Hide and Watch

Once when I was praying about a situation in a child's life, the Lord whispered to me, "Hide and watch to see what I am going to do." I was thrilled to have Him remind me that He was in control and I only needed to hide myself in the shadow of His wings (Psalm 91) and see how He was going to work it out.

Since then I have thought of this calming thought with every prayer need. For instance, I had been almost panicky about the upcoming election with candidates that did not have the experience or even the love of America necessary to serve as Commander in Chief of our great nation. But the Lord again reassured me that He was working even when I did not know it and all I had to do was keep hiding and watching as He showed His power. I can hardly wait to see what He does.

It's always safe to trust the Lord. He desires above all things for us to have the abundant life He died for us to have. (John 10:10) He yearns to lavish His blessings on us. If we truly believed these truths, we would never worry at all. We would really let go and let God.

Since then I have shared this word from God – Hide and Watch – with many people and it has blessed them, also. He says to hide yourself in Him and watch Him "go to town." I love surprises and sometimes I pray for others to have glad surprises. God's surprises are always glad ones!

May 10th ~ Praise Hymns

Rick Godwin, pastor of Eagles Nest Church in San Antonio, taught on the subject that many of our hymns are not really praise to God but only about ourselves. This caused me to look closely at each one that I sing in my morning quiet time. I use four different hymnals and it has shocked me to see that he is right. In fact, I have to search for the ones that are pure worship and praise to our wonderful Lord, like most of the Psalms.

I Also noticed there are a great many older hymns refer to when we get to heaven. I love them and am sorry that we don't sing them much today. Even when I first came into Charismatic movement, we were singing songs about Jesus' return such as "I'll Fly Away" and "Jesus Is Coming Again."

He IS coming soon and I want to celebrate it.

I do so want to sing songs of adoration and thankfulness to Him! I was thinking about one such hymn that praises Him and also relates to our needs. I often sing this one first as a prayer to Him: "Come Thou Almighty King, help us Thy name to sing, help us to praise, Father all glorious, o'er all victorious, come and reign over us, Ancient of Days." How good is that! Then the second verse, "Come Thou Incarnate Word gird on Thy mighty sword, our prayer attend. Come and Thy people bless and give Thy Word success." Then, "Come Holy Comforter, Thy sacred witness bear, in this glad hour: Thou who Almighty art, now rule in every heart and never from us depart, Spirit of Power."

The last verse says, "To Thee, great One in Three, eternal praises be, hence evermore, Thy sovereign majesty may we in glory see and to eternity love and adore."

What a great hymn of praise and a blessed prayer. Psalm 150:6 says, "Let everything that has breath praise the Lord."

May 11th ~ Parades

When I read my giant print New American Standard, it is like reading the Bible for the first time. I had worn out a NAS many years ago and had since been reading the New King James. There are, of course, many similarities, but occasionally something just jumps out at me that is different, for instance Psalm 73:9. The heading on this Psalm is "The End of the Wicked Contrasted with That of The Righteous." Anyway, verse nine says, "They have set their mouth against the heavens, and their tongue *parades* through the earth." Is that funny or what? Picture a parade of tongues.

I looked up the verse in the Amplified and it says, "Their tongue swaggers through the earth (invading even heaven with blasphemy and smearing earth with slanders)." O my, I don't want to smear the earth with slanders. Do our tongues ever *swagger* or *parade* through the earth? I hope not. The New King James reads, "Their tongues *walk* through the earth." Who would have ever thought that our tongues could walk, swagger and parade?

I had thought that I knew almost all the many verses reminding us to watch the words of our mouths, or about our tongues being hard to tame, and even that there is life and death in the power of the tongue. I had even taught Bible study lessons about the tongue, but this was a new one to me.

It will take some meditating on this as I sure don't want to be counted as one of the wicked. Just yesterday, I spoke something with my tongue that I regret having said. Of course, the Lord forgives me and I have forgiven myself, but still I know those words are out there and can't be taken back. God calls non-faith-filled words wicked so I want the Lord to help me remember to not *walk, swagger* or *parade* with my tongue.

May 12th ~ God Wants Us Blessed

God wants us blessed! Do you believe it? This takes faith. Staying in the Word and learning what it says about everything will build that faith in you. It's so important to spend quality time with the Lord. You cannot have it while watching TV, even though it might be a good program, or being about busy work. Time must be set aside only for the Lord.

God cannot drop blessings on us just because He wants to, and believe me, He wants to more than we realize. He offers us a covenant of blessing just like He did Abraham. But He can only bring forth those blessings to the extent that we believe His Word.

Once you decide to take God at His Word, there will always be someone who will warn you against it. They will say things like "be realistic, don't get your hopes up too high, that could never happen, there are natural limitations, you know." Yes, but we serve a supernatural God who has no limitations. He can create, recreate, produce, reproduce, or whatever we need if we believe and claim His promises.

I thank the Lord that Abraham did not listen to the peddlers of doubt and unbelief. Instead, we read about him in Romans 4:18-20 that says, "Against all hope, Abraham in hope believed and so became the father of many nations, just as it had been said to him, 'so shall your offspring be.' Without weakening in his faith he faced the fact that his body was as good as dead…" Abraham never could have dreamed all he eventually received from the hand of God. Unless God Himself had offered them to him, it never would have occurred to him that he could have them. But he took them by faith and refused to let go. God wants you and me to be blessed and I'm not letting go of that promise! How about you?

May 13th ~ Not About Trying

Without God, we can do nothing. Jesus said, "I am the vine, you are the branches. He who abides in Me and I in him, bears much fruit; for without Me you can do nothing" (John 15:5). In other words, it is not about trying, it's about dying.

Genuine sanctification is not about trying, it's about dying, nothing less than a daily dying to self and conformity to the will of God. He wants us to die to all our "self" energy and trust Him to do the work. Understanding this truth is a major step to receiving the greatest life of all, the life in Christ.

God does the work and it is an inside job. On TV or in the movies, an inside job tells about somebody who worked inside the bank, got the 'goods' and brought them outside. That's exactly what the Holy Spirit does on the inside of us. He works from inside our spirit, taking all the 'goods' that God put in us at salvation and works them out through our soul until they're eventually seen on the outside, in our words, attitude and actions.

When Jesus died on the cross, my flesh died with Him. I

have ceased trying, I'm dead. When God raised Him from the dead, my spirit was raised to new life. Every characteristic of Christ is in me and eventually it is going to show up. Yea! Sometimes when my flesh is acting up, I find this very hard to believe.

Our daughter Kathy, after hearing a bad report from the doctor concerning her husband Johnny, said one of the funniest things. When her prayer group rallied around her, she declared, "I intend to handle this in the flesh." Of course, everyone laughed and prayed anyway. (Thanks be to God, Johnny was healed.)

Christ is our all in all. Abiding in Him, and His Word dwelling in us, we can bring forth fruit to the glory of the Father. Jesus helps us remember that nothing is impossible with Him. (Luke 1:37) Without Him we have no life that can bring forth fruit.

May 14th ~ Blessings Stored Up for You

One thing is obvious, the more we understand and receive the goodness of God, the more wonderful our lives are going to be. The Lord takes pleasure in our prosperity in every area of our lives. He even gets a benefit from bestowing His goodness on us, as well. He turns us into witnesses to the world! We become walking demonstrations of the goodness and care of God.

The Lord has always wanted that for His people. All the way through the Scriptures, we see God wanting to give His people such abundance and victory that it would get the attention of the heathen. He told the Israelites He wanted to bless them so extremely that "all people of the earth shall see that thou art called by the name of the Lord" (Deuteronomy 28:10).

Jeremiah 33:9 says that He would restore Israel with such goodness that "it shall be to Me a name of joy, a praise and an honor before all the nations of the earth, which shall hear all the good that I do unto them; and they shall fear and tremble for all the goodness and for all the prosperity that I procure unto it."

Why does God want people to see and hear about His goodness in our lives? Because He loves them and wants them to recognize Him as good and turn to Him! He wants people to know the truth about Him instead of the lies.

He wants us blessed going out and coming in. He wants our lives overflowing with good. He wants people to look at us and see we are different. We are not worried or depressed. We are prosperous whether the economy is up or down. Nothing seems to take us off our path. We just keep going on our way, blessed and full of the joy of the Lord. People are hungry for goodness and joy. I believe it's time we showed it to them. Don't you?

May 15th ~ Power Outage

A note on our doorknob said "Planned Power Outage" and named the specific time and date. This made me think that we never plan to have a power outage with the Lord, but sometimes our disobedience causes it to happen.

Why would there be a planned power outage? The note said it was for upgrading aging infrastructure or completing other repairs to make needed improvements. Of course, there is never a power shortage with God. He is the source of all power. But are we always tuned into our Source?

Maybe we should pause and check our aging infrastructure or complete other repairs to make needed improvements. Is our simple trusting faith in Jesus still standing strong? Or are there cracks? We all need to make improvements all the time.

The note told us how to prepare for a power outage:

1. Safeguard your computer to prevent loss of data (remembering the Word of God, Hebrews 2:1).
2. Unplug sensitive electronic equipment (such as forgiveness and anger Ephesians 4:31-32).
3. Minimize opening refrigerator doors to maintain

temperature (keeping our tempers and lusts in check. Ephesians 4:26).

What a good lesson this is for us all as we check up on ourselves and our walk with the Lord. For outage status, please call and reference outage numbers: 1 Corinthians 13:4-8.

May 16th ~ No Walls by Gloria Thomas, Missionary

In Belfast, Northern Ireland, there is a 40-foot wall dividing the Catholic and Protestant communities. It is known as the "Peace Wall." However, it was built in order to keep the two groups of people separate, and to lessen the violence between them.

My husband Marvin and I first moved to Northern Ireland as missionaries in 2005 and lived in Belfast. God placed us there, right beside this so-called "Peace Wall." Marvin refers to it as the "Hate Wall" since it was built because of man's hatred for one another.

We being Americans were accepted on both sides of this wall, so we were able to move freely from one side to the other. As we ministered to both communities, we realized that many of the Catholics had never been to the Protestant side of Belfast and vice versa!

For over a year, we led a Bible study home group in a born again Catholic woman's home. On July 4, 2006, there was a large gathering at her house. During the meeting, one of the Protestant ladies raised her hand, asking to speak. She gave her testimony about her former affiliation with the Protestant para-military group that had terrorized the Catholics for years! She broke down and wept when she said that this was the first time she had ever been on the 'other side' of the wall.

The Catholic woman hosting the meeting got up and carefully made her way through the people sitting on the floor to this woman. She put her arms around her and also wept. Others in the group that night spoke of their similar experiences. There was such a breakthrough in the Spirit and everyone was touched by God! Tears flowed and healing flowed as well!

God is no respecter of persons. Jesus died on the cross for us all! There are no walls and no division in His Kingdom. Ephesians 2:14 says, "For He Himself is our peace, who has made us both one and has broken down in His flesh the dividing wall of hostility."

May 17th ~ Laborers for the Lord by Gloria Thomas, Missionary

2 Corinthians 1:11 says, "You also must help us by prayer, so that many will give thanks on our behalf for the blessing granted us through the prayers of many."

In September of 2005, my husband Marvin and I left our families, our jobs, our country and answered the call of the Lord on our lives to move to Belfast, Northern Ireland. Our decision was made after five years of traveling back and forth to Ireland, much prayer and confirmation. It was very difficult at first, especially for me. I had given up everything comfortable and familiar and found myself in a place that was cold, rainy and dark (especially spiritually).

The time difference from California to Ireland is eight hours, so the first few weeks I found myself wide awake at 3 a.m. In our tiny sitting room, I would pray, cry out to God for guidance, direction for our ministry and for our protection. Back home, our family and many dear friends were praying for our safety. Even though things had settled down in Belfast, there were still incidents of violence. We knew we were being covered daily by the prayers of the Saints and those prayers provided a hedge of protection for us. 1 Timothy 2:1 says, "First of all, then, I urge that supplications, prayers, intercessions, and thanksgivings be made for all people."

Once, Marvin was called upon to pray and minister to

a family in the Catholic community being terrorized by the IRA (Irish Republican Army). Other members of their family had been forced to leave when their houses were burned. Just as he was driving away from the home, a white van passed by and pulled up to the house. A number of IRA men forced their way into the house at gunpoint, threatening the family and harassing them. Without a doubt, I know it was prayer and the prompting of the Holy Spirit which led my husband safely out of that place just moments before the IRA arrived!

Please remember to pray for those who are laborers for the Lord, especially those servants of God on the mission field. You may never know the difference your prayers can make!

May 18th ~ An On-Time God by Marvin Thomas, Missionary

Philippians 4:19 says, "And my God shall supply all your need according to His riches in glory by Christ Jesus." Have you ever heard this saying, "God may not come when you want Him to, but He is never late"? We often have to wait, but the waiting stretches and strengthens our faith.

As Independent missionaries, my wife and I live by faith. We have family members who give to our ministry, but we are not sponsored by any church or organization. The donations we receive from family and friends are enough to keep us warm, dry and fed with not much left over.

While on the mission field in Northern Ireland, which is part of the United Kingdom/England, we are not allowed to work in a secular job. That is a stipulation of our missionary visa status. When our first-year visa was about to expire, we needed to leave the UK and return to the U.S. to apply for a visa extension. But we could not afford the airfare and there was no one we knew who could help us. Most of our local friends had little left over after their basic needs were filled. All we had was 40 British pounds, just enough to buy food.

Suddenly, and very unexpectedly, Christian friends from the Catholic community began to drop by at different times to give us money! We did not tell them of our financial need, only that it was necessary for us to leave Belfast for awhile. As the finances began to add up, we knew that God was at work in our situation. People from the Protestant community, where we lived, also began to donate! Soon we had enough money to purchase our airline tickets, with some left over!

God met our needs through unexpected sources. To add to this blessing, the people had taken the time to exchange their currency to bring us American money. God is so good! Time and time again, He has met our needs and He is always on time! Praise His name.

May 19th ~ His Mercy Endureth Forever

Psalm 25:6 says, "Remember, O Lord, Your tender mercies and Your loving kindness." Although many people doubt it, He does have tender mercies and loving kindness toward us. They know He can heal, but doubt that He would show mercy and heal them because they have no knowledge of His Word. Jesus calls healing "the children's bread." (Matthew 15:26)

It would really tick me off and be insulting if my children were hungry and did not think I would give them food. And it hurts God's feelings also when we do not believe he will show mercy toward us and heal us.

Theology teaches man about God's power but, for the most part, it denies His willingness to use that power on man's behalf. Theology lacks the vital experience of the father/son relationship that we can enjoy in Jesus as children of God. Man's idea of God always comes up short and lifeless.

Time after time, we see Jesus moved by compassion in His earthly ministry. He yearns to meet our needs. One who does not know the Scriptures might wonder why God does not heal all those who are sick, regardless of their faith. God's mercy is given in accordance with His covenant, the Word. Because He has bound Himself by His Word, He can only move freely toward those who are willing to believe and receive His mercy.

Mercy is God's attitude toward you in freely bestowing whatever is necessary to meet your needs. According to *Vine's Word Studies*, mercy "manifests itself in action and assumes the adequate resources to effect the proper result." Mercy is the result of compassion and God delights in mercy. (Micah 7:18)

May 20th ~ Homeless

There seem to be a great many homeless people here in Palm Springs. Bill says that because of the good weather, they can live outside and are more visible. I have a hard time passing them by although Bill reminds me to be sure I am led by the Spirit in what to give as some might want to spend it on alcohol. There is always one or more in the shopping center where I buy groceries and I almost always give them something. I ask them if they know Jesus and the answer is usually 'yes' and sometimes they even quote a Bible verse.

Some of them carry cardboard signs saying something like, "God will bless you for helping me" or "Need of funds, any amount will help." Yesterday, I saw a man with a sign reading, "Need a beer." I was shocked, but Bill said at least he was honest. I couldn't help but wonder how much he received.

I truly believe that except for the grace of God, any of us could be on the street looking for a handout. In the current economy, I don't know many people who haven't felt a pinch in their finances. Bill says our income has been cut in half which is pretty frightening. (Hairdresser and friend Carlo said to tell Bill that was his half – pretty cute.)

But I know in whom I believe and I know He desires the prosperity of His servants; in fact, He delights in it. (Psalm 35:27) We've lived Psalm 37:25 that says, "I've been young and I am now old and I have never seen the seed of the righteous forsaken nor their seed begging bread." So why are these homeless people, who profess to know Jesus, begging? Is it a lack of belief or trust? I don't know, but I just thank the Lord and count my blessings and pray I am blessing them. It really is more blessed to give than to receive.

May 21st ~ Orders

"Lord, PLEASE tell me Your will for my life!" Every Christian has prayed these words. Most of us have prayed them hundreds of times. Without a doubt, that is a prayer God wants to answer. Yet, all too often, believers remain frustrated, seemingly unable to hear specific instructions from the Lord. Hence, they end up wandering around in a spiritual twilight zone, incapable of clearly seeing the unique path God has planned for them.

This might be the reason: If we are ever going to receive God's specific orders and plans for our lives, we must first obey the general instructions He has given us in His Word. (Matthew 22:36-40)

We must learn to receive God's Love, then love God and others. Those are the general orders of the Kingdom of God, and direct orders to each member of the Body of Christ. They are easy to remember and simple to understand. Yet have you ever failed to live by them? As a result, you may have been unable to find God's specific will for your life and a breakthrough to your destiny? If so, you're not alone.

It does not have to be that way. There are definite things you can do to step up and step into obedience to those two all important orders and commands:

1. Receive God's love for you.
2. Believe God's love is in you.
3. Practice, practice, practice His love on others.

4. Don't just sit there, do something! Look for ways to bless other people.
5. Become God-inside minded, cultivating the Word.

Proverbs 4:18 says, "But the path of the just is like the shining sun, shining brighter and brighter unto the perfect day." God's love is a light that shines brightly on the pathway to His will for your life!

May 22nd ~ Anchor in the Lord by Anne Crabtree, Granddaughter

Working in sales for a corporate company can be very stressful; hitting monthly budgets, margins, ticket averages, and so forth. You can imagine how I felt when I went to work on the last day of the month and found my store had not yet hit its budget. That day was my last chance to do it! I needed one big sale. I knew it was possible, but 5 p.m. I had no customers! Since my store closes at 9 p.m., I lost hope.

I was angry, anxious, annoyed and just mad! A few minutes after five, a man using a cane came walking slowly up to the door. It was really windy outside and our doors are hard to open, so I ran to the door and opened it for him. I thought he was a customer, but I was disappointed when I learned he had only come in to get directions. I gave him directions to his doctor's office which was across the street.

As we were walking to the door, he handed me his business card. He had been in the Air Force in 1944 and had fought in World War II and other wars. On the back of his card it read: "IN THE MIDST OF YOUR CHALLENGE, KNOW GOD CARES. Be anxious for nothing, but in everything by prayer and supplication, with thanksgiving, let your requests be made known to God; and the peace of God, which surpasses all understanding, will guard your hearts and minds through Christ Jesus" (Philippians 4:6-7).

After I read the verse, I felt an instant peace and about 20 minutes later a customer came in and purchased a very nice bed and that put me over budget.

But it wasn't the customer who bought the bed that made my day. It was Harold Payne (no kin to our family) – the nice man asking for directions. His business card sits on my desk at work and I read it every day and it still helps me EVERY day!

All I can do during the "storms" of life is to have a sure foundation, an unshakable faith, in an unchanging, trustworthy God!

May 23rd ~ Feather Beds

In reading Oswald Chamber's book on prayer entitled *If You Will Ask,* a statement in the book triggered old memories. It said, "Circumstances are like feather beds, very comfortable to be on top of, but immensely smothering if they get on top of us." He went on to add, "Jesus Christ, by the Spirit of God, always keeps us on top of our circumstances." That's very comforting.

This made me remember Granny Sypert's fantastic feather bed that she would occasionally let her granddaughter Boopy, my friend, and me sleep in. It was so soft and comforting and we would just sink down in it, feeling warm and secure. I always felt that Granny was my grandmother, too, because Boopy was like my sister. My Smith grandparents had died before I was born and my Grandmother Hurst was very prim and proper and not loving like Granny. So I always enjoyed going with Boopy to her grandparent's farm right out of Hallsville.

I still remember the celebration each year at the cemetery near their home that I think was called, "All day cleaning and dinner on the grounds." The tables were laden with delicious homemade goodies. Bill says he went with his grandparents to similar cemetery cleanings in Pickton, a small town near Sulphur Springs. It might even have been titled, "All day singing and dinner on the grounds." But the primary purpose was to clean the tombstones and grounds. While the adults worked, we children just played.

Back to Jesus being on top of our circumstances – our part is to turn them over to Him and then to trust Him for the victory. Romans 8:37 says, "Yet in all these things we are more than conquerors through Him who loved us." 1 Corinthians 15:58 says, "But thanks be to God who gives us the victory though our Lord Jesus Christ."

May 24th ~ You Have Not

"You have not because you ask not" (James 4:2b). I have quoted this verse quite often, but sometimes still forget to ask. God is such a giving God who yearns to act on behalf of His children, but He wants us to humble ourselves and admit our need. There are many, many promises in the Bible that are ours for the asking. But they are not automatic, they don't simply happen. God is waiting for us to ask.

We got a promotional notice from our Citi Bank Visa Card showing how we could earn 20 percent more American Airlines Advantage miles for every dollar spent on eligible purchases. To activate this offer, we had to call an 800 number. This was not hard to do, but I usually put off this type of thing. Bill made a good point – why did they just not give us this deal? Instead, we had to ask. Calling them did not take long at all and it will be a blessing to get more miles. But it would not have happened if I had not called.

This made me think again of how important it is to speak forth the promises of God for ourselves and our loved ones, making declarations and proving to the Lord that we believe His Word and that it is for us personally. How exciting to think of that! I love to claim His Word as there is always a perfect answer for every situation.

God cannot lie – He will fulfill His promises. Jeremiah 1:12 says, "He watches over His Word to perform it." But we must speak it out. Voice it. Psalm 103:20 says, "Bless the Lord, all you His angels, mighty in strength, who perform His word, obeying the voice of His word!" Sounds too good to be true, but I have seen it proved over and over. Isaiah

55:11 says, "So will my word be which goes forth from My mouth, it will not return to Me void but it shall accomplish what I please and it shall prosper in the thing for which I sent it."

May 25th ~ Crucified With Christ

Born again believers have been crucified with Christ, hence they are free from sin. We all believe that Christ died for our sins, but have a hard time believing that He also destroyed the power of sin in our lives. Galatians 5:24 says, "And those who belong to Christ Jesus (the Messiah) have crucified the flesh (the godless human nature) with its passions and appetites and desires." (Amplified)

It is a done deal. In other words, when Christ died on the cross, we were buried with Him and just as He was raised to a new life, our spirit was also raised to new life. (Romans 6:4-6)

Why is it so important to believe that our flesh has already been crucified? Because God's Word says it has, and because what we believe about ourselves is what we're going to manifest in our lives. We can never get beyond what we believe. (Proverbs 23:7)

If we keep recalling our past mistakes, we will never overcome them. In order to break free from wrong thinking and behavior, we must first believe that we are free. We need to stop seeing ourselves as wretched sinners saved by grace, and start seeing ourselves as the righteousness of God in Christ Jesus. No one can do this for us; it is our own personal choice. (Romans 6:11) We can tell ourselves daily, "I am dead to sin and alive to Christ and will not be afraid of sinning nor am I expecting to sin. I am expecting God's power to strengthen me to submit to Him and overcome every temptation that comes my way."

We activate our faith by confessing with our mouths, "I'm dead to sin. When Jesus died on the cross, my flesh died with Him. When God raised Him from the dead, my spirit was raised to new life. Every characteristic of Christ is in me and eventually it is going to show up. It may take some time but it's on its way. I can't make it happen in my own strength, but I can cooperate with the Holy Spirit and He will bring it to pass. Amen."

May 26th ~ A Fly in the Ointment

An annoying fly kept buzzing around me in my quiet time this morning, and I found it difficult to concentrate on the Lord; I kept concentrating on the fly. So I had to make a determination to focus on Jesus and sing praises to Him, instead of trying to find ways to kill the fly. I think there is a lesson here. I spend too much time trying to fix a problem when I really should just be praising the Lord.

This made me think of the old saying about there being a "fly in the ointment" meaning a small, but irritating flaw, that ruins the entire thing. As with many of our old sayings, this phrase has its origin in the Bible. Ecclesiastes 10:1 says, "Dead flies make a perfumer's oil stink, so a little foolishness is weightier than wisdom and honor."

One thing I learned early in life was not to touch anything on my daddy's, or my husband's desks. All of the children and grandchildren also understood the desks were "sacred ground." I remember that my daddy's desk looked like a disaster with piles and piles of papers, although he actually knew exactly where everything was.

His secretary of many years told the story that when she first went to work for him, she tried to straighten up the desk. She never did it again as this usually mild-mannered man became highly enraged. It became a large "fly in his ointment" and all her good intentions came to naught.

Since ointment is supposed to be a healing balm, I realized that even a small irritant will keep it from soothing. Often when the Lord is healing our bodies or our spirits, we still may have some pain. But if I can focus on the Healer and give Him the praises He deserves, it will definitely make it easier to bear. Lord, help me to remember this truth.

May 27th ~ Choose This Day

Joshua 24:15 says, "As for me and my house, we will serve the Lord." I must have read Joshua's statement hundreds of times but had never caught the meaning of the rest of the verse: "Choose for yourselves this day who you will serve." I thought I had done that and it was a done deal, but I read a devotional that pointed out that we need to choose EACH DAY who we would serve. That put it all in a new perspective. If we consciously choose to serve Him first thing in the morning, it will surely make us more aware of the importance of our actions during the day and will bring glory to him and not ourselves.

This is not a one-shot deal. We must bow to His authority every day and make a choice to obey His commands. But as for me and my house we WILL serve the Lord. (This is a good verse to pray for our families.) It is always good to be reminded that the Christian life consists of choices made each day.

We can actually choose to have a good day by setting our course to praise Him for who He is and thank Him for all our blessings. We could never praise or thank Him enough for what a mighty, glorious God He is and how thankful we are that He loves us unconditionally. Psalm 68:19 says, "Blessed be the Lord, who daily loads us with benefits, the God of our salvation!" Selah – Pause and think on that. We can choose to serve Him each day and He daily loads us with benefits. We can't beat a deal like that.

But note, no one can do it for us. We have to choose to do it for ourselves. We can pray for our unsaved loved ones that their hearts will be softened toward the gospel message and that the Holy Spirit draw them, but they have to make the choice for themselves. God does not have any grandchildren – just children. We are all brothers and sisters in Christ.

May 28th ~ Grow in Grace

Peter tells us in the last verse of his second letter to grow in grace. 2 Peter 3:18 says, "Grow in the undeserved favor and spiritual strength of God." How good is that? This was one of Peter's favorite themes as he tells us at the beginning of both his letters that grace and peace will be multiplied to us in the knowledge of Christ.

Reading in the Amplified, 2 Peter 1:2 says, "May grace (God's favor) and peace, (which is perfect well-being, all necessary good, all spiritual prosperity and freedom from fears and agitating passions and moral conflicts) be multiplied to you in (the full, personal, precise and correct) knowledge of God and of Christ Jesus our Lord."

It seems that grace and peace are multiplied to us as we grow in the knowledge of God. 1 Peter 1:2 calls grace a "spiritual blessing." And we are certainly blessed as we study His Word and grow in our knowledge of Him. That is the only way we can grow in grace, by knowing Him, the living Word.

After I was born again in January of 1971, our daughter Julianne gave me a Living Bible for Mother's Day. This translation made it easier for me to understand the Scriptures and I read it avidly. I now like to look up verses in several translations and then meditate on the meaning. In college, I had read the Bible through, but since I did not have the Holy Spirit to help me understand, it did not mean as much to me.

I had also read a children's Bible almost every night to my children so I had some familiarity with the stories, but did not understand the true meanings. I had even missed the fact that David was depending completely on God when he fought Goliath. It was just a story to me as were so many of the others. I have certainly grown in the knowledge of God, but I yearn to have a full, personal, precise and correct knowledge of Him and thereby grow in grace.

May 29th ~ "His Way With Thee"

The old hymn "His Way With Thee" was written in 1889 and was not one that I was familiar with. But when I read the words, it touched my heart with its truth. I looked up the author, Cyrus S. Nusbaum, and learned he was a Methodist pastor.

We can think about these words in the hymn when we want God's grace to help us change our hearts so that He can have His way with us:

Chorus: "His power can make you what you ought to be; His blood can cleanse your heart and make you free; His love can fill your soul, and you will see; T'was best for Him to have His way with thee." AMEN

Verse 1 asks the questions, "Would you live for Jesus and be always pure and good? Would you walk with Him within the narrow road? Would you have Him bear your burden, carry your load?" If you answer yes, he then tells us to, "Let Him have His way with thee."

Verse 2 asks, "Would you have Him make you free, and follow at His call? Would you know the peace that comes by giving all? Would you have Him save you, so that you need never fall? Let Him have His way with thee."

My favorite question in the hymn is: "Would you in His Kingdom find a place of constant rest?" Sure, I would. So what do I have to do? Let Him have His way with me. In other words, submit to Him and let His power make me what I ought to be. Not my power, but His. His blood can cleanse my heart and make me free. His love can fill my soul so it is best to let Him have His way with me. (Romans 12:1)

May 30th ~ Good Works

Ephesians 2:10 says, "For we are His workmanship, created in Christ Jesus for good works, that God prepared beforehand that we should walk in them." It says in the

Amplified "...that we may do those good works which God predestined (planned beforehand) for us, taking paths which He prepared (ahead of time) that we should walk in them—living the good life which He prearranged and made ready for us to live."

Obviously, if God planned and prearranged them then we can do good works. They will only be "good" though if they are His idea. Many times we get off in the flesh and do what we think is right in our own eyes and those "works" don't turn out so good.

Lately in meditating on this verse, I have been much more aware of where I am during the day, being alert to ask the Father if a certain person I see is one I should be ministering to or praying silently for.

Yesterday morning at Walmart, the greeter, in response to my question, said she was tired because of a sleepless baby. She was delighted when I asked her if I could pray for her. Then as I was leaving, she told me she was feeling the supernatural strength I had prayed for her to receive. God knew I would be going there at the right time to pray for and bless that lady.

Now I think back on the many opportunities I have missed when in a hurry. I just rush past people without stopping to see if they are the ones I am to bless. It dawned on me that I can refuse to do the "good works." He did give us a free will. Sorry, Lord, HELP, change me. After all, sometimes it is just a kind or encouraging word that is the "good work" I am to do. My prayer is to ask the Holy Spirit to make me more aware of His prearranged plans. I want to be a person who lives to do HIS "good works."

May 31st ~ Benefits

Almost daily I quote Psalm 103:1-5. In meditating on Verse 2: "Bless the Lord, O my soul and forget not all His benefits," I kept thinking about what His benefits actually are. It seems to me that we hear a lot about jobs with benefits. In fact, those jobs are sought after. More than even salary, benefits are of great importance.

All this is very well and good as long as we remember where and from whom all benefits come. "Every good and perfect gift comes from above" (James 1:17). This we must never forget.

Psalm 68:19 says, "Blessed be the Lord our God who daily loads us with benefits. He is the God of our salvation." Do you love that? He DAILY loads us with benefits. Wow! Every day in every way - His mercies are new every morning. (Lamentations 3:23)

He gives us superabundantly more than we could desire or pray for. To load means, among many other things, to supply in large quantities; give much of something to (to load a person with honors); to add to or to add extra. I think this should excite us that the Lord DAILY LOADS us with benefits. And our only job is to believe in Him. John 6:29 says, "Jesus answered and said to them, 'This is the work of God, that you believe in Him whom He sent.'"

The work of God has the best benefits anyone could imagine. We receive as we believe. God truly yearns to bless us even more than we know. 1 Corinthians 2:9 says, "But as it is written: Eye has not seen, nor ear heard nor have enter into the heart of man the things which God has prepared for those who love Him."

June 1st ~ "The Sun in the Morning and the Moon at Night"

I love the Irving Berlin song from the musical *Annie Get Your Gun.* "I've got the sun in the morning and the moon at night, who could ask for anything more? Got no checkbooks, got no banks, still I'd like to express my thanks, and with the sun in the morning and the moon at night I'm alright." There are many more upbeat lyrics.

So I thought of this old song when I read a testimony about Jeremy Taylor, a 17th century clergyman and author, to whom everything seemed to go wrong. His house was plundered, his family driven outdoors, and his worldly possessions confiscated. He pointed out, however, that he still had the sun and the moon, a loving wife, many friends, a merry countenance, a cheerful spirit and a good conscience. Taylor also had the providence of God, the promise of the gospel, and his hope of heaven. Despite his losses, Taylor had real possessions, most of the great intangibles, and was THANKFUL.

In days of disaster and deep discouragement, when the storms of life beat down upon us, do we still appreciate the unnumbered blessings that are still ours? We can get bitter or better. James 1:2 says, "Count it all joy when you fall into various trials." Count your blessings and name them one by one; not forgetting all His benefits. (Psalm 103:2)

More lyrics say, "Got no silver, got no gold, what I got can't be bought or sold. I got the sun in the morning and moon at night. Sunshine gives me a lovely day; moonlight gives me the Milky Way. I'm alright."

I dearly love the fact that I can count on the sun shining in Palm Springs. It is such a blessing. But even on rainy days in Texas, I always have the 'Sonshine' and so every day I'm alright with Him.

June 2nd ~ The Finished Work of the Cross

Jesus did not say, "To be continued." He said, "It is finished." Praise His name. It's not about what He will DO for us; it is what He has already DONE. We just need to receive it by faith.

I never liked the TV shows that just when I am really interested, flash a "to be continued" up on the screen. I want them to finish what they had begun. I don't want to wait until next week to know the outcome. With Jesus, it is already done. We don't have to wait to see what He will do, He has already finished it. We've read the back of the book. We know the outcome. All His promises are fulfilled. Glory be to God!

There is no way we could ever express our gratitude for all that Jesus bought for us on the cross; of course, primarily the forgiveness for our sins, past, present AND future, resulting in our reconciliation with our Father God. The cross allows us to come boldly to His throne; it's almost too wonderful to be true. So we need to read Isaiah 53 often just to realize all the things His suffering delivered us from.

In the Amplified Bible, Isaiah 53:4 says, "Surely He bore our grief's, sickness, weakness and distress, and carried our sorrows and pain (of punishment)."

Isaiah 53:5 says, "But He was wounded for our transgressions. He was bruised for our guilt and iniquities; the chastisement (needful to obtain peace and well-being for us) was upon Him, and with the stripes, that wounded Him. we are healed and made whole."

Thanks be to God who sent His only Son so that we could be saved, healed and delivered – past, present and future – every day. Amen!

June 3rd ~ Sidewalk Sunday School

There are many things to make us proud of our daughter Kathy Payne Harville, but one of the most impressive is that she directs a Sidewalk Sunday School on Saturdays in the poorer "project housing" areas in her hometown of Paris, Texas. This includes a Vacation Bible School in the very hottest part of the summer. What a dedication she and the other workers show! We are also proud that our other Paris daughter, Julie Setzer is one of the volunteers. (Actually, she says Kathy "volunteered" her.)

In the summer of 2005, they ministered to over 120 children (and adults) in four days. One of the children gave his life to the Lord. According to Kathy, "That is worth it all; blood, sweat and tears. The kids had a wonderful time and many relationships were formed and solidified through face painting, crafts, snow cones, Bible stories, puppet skit, praise and worship, hugs and kisses."

Here's a letter from Kathy to the volunteers:

"During my lowest point, when the temperature was at its highest and all I could see was people snatching, grabbing, stuffing decorative letters into their pockets, and smuggling snow cones onto the bus, I felt really discouraged. However, the next day when God mercifully brought cool, overcast weather, I once again saw more clearly. I saw beautiful smiles on faces, heard the infamous "Big Boys" singing praise songs as they did their crafts, and heard sincere thanks from parents and grandparents who were truly grateful for our presence. It made me see once again with His eyes and feel the urgency to help them meet the only One that can ever really make them whole. My humble thanks go out to each and every one of you for your sacrifices to leave your air conditioners and families to wash the feet of a group of people that the rest of the world doesn't consider important."

She has already started planning for next year. "Whoever receives one of these little children in My name, receives Me." (Mark 9:37)

June 4th ~ Planting Your Faith

The seed is the Word of God and when we plant it (by speaking and believing it by faith), we will be planting that faith in good soil. Matthew 17:20)

If you treat your faith like a seed, by planting it, nothing will be impossible for you. If the Word of God is going to produce results, it has to get off the pages of the Bible and into the ground called the heart.

When you need healing, for example, plant the Word concerning healing in your heart. Whatever your need is, go to a Bible concordance and get all the scriptures pertaining to that need and confess them daily out loud, several times a day if your need is desperate. Words are seeds and the law of receiving says that whatever goes through your eyes, your ears and your mouth in abundance, when acted upon, will come out, overwhelm and overtake you. (Proverbs 4:23)

In the Amplified, Matthew 6:33 says, "Seek for (aim at and strive after) first of all His Kingdom, and His righteousness (His way of doing and being right), and then all these things taken together will be given you besides." God's way of doing things. This is talking about us living in the Kingdom of God here on this earth.

Here's the story of a man and a glass of water: The man believed that if he drank the water he would live, but he did not drink it and so he died. We have to not only believe the Word of God, but act on it. Plant it in our lives and those of our loved ones. We can give mental assent to the Word, but still not act on it. Really believe that it is truth, but often do not take a step further and claim it for ourselves.

So plant the Word of God and see it grow.

June 5th ~ Let My People Go

In Exodus chapters 5-12, we read about Moses and Aaron pleading before Pharaoh, then the plagues, and finally the deliverance of the Israelites from Egypt. Recently while studying these chapters, I had some new insights into this old story.

We know that Pharaoh kept going back on his word to allow the Israelites to leave Egypt. Think of Pharaoh as Satan and it takes on new meaning for us. Begin with him asking, who are the ones that are going? And Moses answer was: we will go with our young and our old; with our sons and our daughters, with our flocks and our herds, for we must hold a feast to the Lord. (Exodus 10:8-9) So Moses is saying that they must take their families and goods with them, too.

That's what we say, too. I love Acts 16:31, "Believe on the Lord Jesus Christ and you and your entire household will be saved." I claim this often.

We also notice that Pharaoh still argued with them, first wanting them to stay in Egypt to serve the Lord; then saying they could go, but not very far; next saying that just the men could go; then the children could go, too, but not their flocks and their herds. This is so much like Satan wanting to keep us in the world, then even letting our families stay with us, but still wanting to keep our finances (flocks and herds) in his control.

We can stand strong as Moses did and not allow Satan to keep us or our families from worshipping the Lord. We do not have to let the enemy have the victory in stealing our goods, either - we know that he comes to steal, kill and destroy, but we have authority over him. We can even plunder his house, too, as the Israelites did the Egyptians. How do we do this? By daily using the sword of the Spirit - the Word of God — against him. Then praising the Lord for the blessings.

June 6th ~ Nothing to Fear

President Franklin Roosevelt brought us through World War11 with the wonderful slogan: "We have nothing to fear, but fear itself." This is a great Biblical truth and I can't help but wonder if FDR knew he was speaking Biblically. I do know that as President he prayed often and his prayer on D-Day was one of the best prayers ever. (What would critics say today about a Christian prayer from the White House?)

The only antidote to fear is the Word of God. We are told over 365 times in the Bible not to fear. One for every day of the year! We are commanded "fear not." Also, 2 Timothy 1:7 says, "God has not given us the spirit of fear, but of power, love and a sound mind." So wonder who gives it to us? We certainly don't have to receive it and we have authority over it - we can cast it out. 1 John 4:18 says, "There is no fear in love and perfect love casts out fear because fear involves torment. But he who fears has not been made perfect in love." And we know God is love itself and love never fails.

And in the Old Testament, the New Century Version, Psalm 49:5 says, "Why should I be afraid of bad days? Why should I fear when evil people surround me?"

In these days with the economy and the government in such a bad state, it is very hard not to fear. Satan pulls out every stop to get us to believe everything is hopeless. But we just need to remember that God is in control and no matter how horrible it looks, He is still on the throne. I keep reminding myself of this truth and remember Psalm 56:3, 4 that says, "Whenever I am afraid, I will trust in You…in God I have put my trust, I will not fear, what man can do to me. And Romans 8:31, "If God be for me, who can be against me?"

June 7th ~ The Rich Young Ruler

In Luke 18:18-30, it is easy to see the mistake the rich young ruler makes with his first question to Jesus, "What can I DO to inherit eternal life?" Like us, he wanted to DO something to insure his salvation, instead of just accepting it as the gracious gift that it is.

Some commentaries suggest that this young man was the leader of the local synagogue so he was very familiar with all the Law. That was his problem; he was into legalism. He also seems very self righteous when he says that he has kept all those laws from his youth. (Luke 18:21)

Jesus names several of the commandments in verse 20, but He does not mention, "Do not covet." I heard a preacher say the rich young ruler was probably guilty of that one. The preacher went on to say that we could even be guilty of coveting our own stuff. Wow! I certainly never thought of that.

If we are afraid of losing the stuff we have, that is coveting. We must remember that EVERYTHING we have belongs to God and nothing belongs to us. That includes our families, talents, time, possessions, money – EVERYTHING! When we look at it like that, it is easier to give it back to God; it's not ours anyway. We have just been given it all on loan from Him. Whenever we think it is ours, then we have broken the commandment, "Do not covet."

The preacher also used the example of trying to open a tightly closed fist. He then ASKED the congregation to open their fists. This made me think of James 4:2, "We have not because we ask not." We can open up and let God pour His riches into us or hold on too tight to what we already have and even lose that. When "We let go and let God" then we realize who we are in Him; His beloved children that He yearns to bless.

Had you rather hold on or be held?

June 8th ~ One Plus One is Two, by Julie Setzer, Daughter

It just so happens that twice in the span of two days, I have heard two very dear friends say their daddy's either never said they loved them or rarely said it. It blows my mind as there is no way I can even imagine what that must be like. You see, for no reason that I can think of, God gave me not one, but two very loving fathers.

My biological father was a pleasant, outgoing, good-natured man who loved me and I knew it. He died when I was 12 years old and in a couple of years my mom remarried my Poppy, who has absolutely no reason in the world to love me yet does love me unconditionally. First impressions are important and I'm sure I made a horrible one when introduced to Poppy. I was young, mad, unpleasant and hateful when I met him and I treated him disrespectfully for years. He has reciprocated with kindness, love, mercy, grace, generosity and a great amount of humor. Poppy genuinely likes me and he never misses an opportunity to express his affection for me. He knows me; he understands me, he enjoys me – through good times and bad.

I've been pondering the effect of not having a loving father has on a child. How would that effect a person's view of a heavenly Father? What effect would it have on the shape of their personality? I guess it could make a person insecure, fragile, suspicious, and closed off emotionally.

However, both of my friends who had emotionally distant dads have turned out to be very loving, responsible, happy individuals. They both have had no trouble showing affection to their children or keeping their commitments to their spouses. I think it's because they forgave their dads through the power of the Holy Spirit and were able to love their fathers without conditions and reservations. Neither of them is walking around keeping score of how other people are treating them, but rather making sure they are treating others appropriately and with love.

The more I think about my two friends, the more I am impressed with God's greatness. Obviously, my friends sought God's help and assistance in dealing with their emotions and feelings about their upbringing, about the lack of encouragement and approval received from their male parents. I applaud them for their willingness to let God's love flood their wounded hearts.

Just hearing my friends say that their dads didn't express love verbally, reminded me of how truly spoiled I am. I have not spent one single minute of my life wondering if my father loves me. My Poppy has shown me a true father's love in thought, word and deed, just like my heavenly Father does. That is the mark of a real daddy's heart.

June 9th ~ Dreams

Of course, all dreams are not of God, but many are truly God speaking to us. Dreams are Biblical and we see them used often in the Word to warn, encourage or instruct. It is important to write them down and then ask the Holy Spirit to help us understand what God is speaking to us. Interpretation belongs to God. (Genesis 40:8)

Believers have been afraid to teach on dreams as the secular world and new agers have made us afraid of them. Too long we have let the enemy have the supernatural and forgotten that our God is a supernatural God and as long as we center on Jesus, we too can have dreams teach and bless us.

It is normal for us to receive correction or direction from God in dreams. Job 33:14-17 says, "For God may speak in one way, or in another, yet man does not perceive it. In a dream, in a vision of the night, when deep sleep falls upon men and seals their instruction. In order to turn man from his deed, and conceal pride from man."

Pretty clear, right?

Now that we are in the end times, dreams will become more and more commonplace. Guidelines for dreams: pray, pray, pray and write them down, label everything, and ask God to reveal to you if they are important for many times they are.

We don't have to be dream chasers, but sometimes it is a good idea to write them down and review them to see if the Lord is trying to tell us something. We will not necessarily remember all that we dreamed. So we are told in Habakkuk 2:2 to, "Write the vision and make it plain on tablets that he may run who reads it."

June 10th ~ Perish the Thought

One of our favorite sayings in our teen years, when someone would say something we did not want to hear, was, "Perish the thought." We had no idea we were speaking a Biblical principle. 2 Corinthians 10:5 says, "Casting down arguments and every high thing that exalts itself against the knowledge of God, bringing every thought into captivity to the obedience of Christ." Perish all negative thoughts that are against the way Jesus would have us to be.

For some reason, we choose another Bible verse to be our special car horn tune. We would tap out on the horn,

"Money is the root of all evil." Where we got that, I will never know. We certainly did not know that we were quoting it wrong, and could never have found it in the Bible. The true Scripture is: "The love of money is a root of (all kinds) of evil" (1Timothy 6:10). Certainly changes the meaning, doesn't it? Money in and of itself is not evil; it is the inordinate love of it that is.

I am always telling Bill that it is not money for money's sake that I love; just the things money can buy. Somehow he does not see the difference. I mean, I don't just want to have lots of money in the bank, I want to spend it. He still does not buy my theory and thinks that means I love money. O well, I am sure he may be right.

I want to "Perish the thought" that I love money. At least let the Lord change me. I am willing, Lord. Also willing to let the Lord help me to perish any negative thoughts and truly bring all my thoughts into captivity to the obedience of Christ. I have learned how important my thoughts are because "out of the abundance of the heart the mouth speaks" (Matthew 12:34). Our words have lasting results. Verse 37 in that same chapter says, "For by your words you will be justified, and by your words you will be condemned."

June 11th ~ Shalom

We all know that the word Shalom in Hebrew means peace. Shalom is a greeting that the Jews still give to one another - a custom that would be good for us to adopt. One of the Lord's special titles is Jehovah Shalom - God, our Peace. If that isn't wonderful enough, the Hebrew word also means nothing missing, nothing broken. I like to meditate on that as it seems that I may have some missing or broken spots in my life.

How precious is it that God does not desire that we have anything missing or broken that we need for an abundant life? We are told in John 10:10 that Jesus came that we might have life and have it more abundantly. It's the devil that comes to kill, steal and destroy. Satan is constantly trying to steal our joy and our peace. But Jehovah Shalom is always there to see that it does not happen.

Gladness and joy are mentioned over 382 times in the Bible. This certainly seems to mean that the Lord wants us to have them. I receive that joy and gladness right now.

As I was meditating on this thought, the Lord showed me that one of the ways to keep our peace, joy and gladness is to live one day at a time – in other words, not to borrow trouble. I certainly have a tendency to live in tomorrow's problems rather than enjoying the present. To keep thinking of what is coming and what might happen and forgetting that His mercies are new every morning. (Lamentations 3:23)

And Jesus reminds us in the Sermon on the Mount to not worry about tomorrow because tomorrow will worry about its own things. (Matthew 7:34)

Shalom!

June 12th ~ A Friend in Jesus, by Ray Woodruff, Nephew, Dallas, TX

I build houses and do remodeling for a living. I have often found myself in a situation where I could not sleep and dreaded the outcome of the next day. It often seemed that a problem was nearly unsolvable and that the customer was going to be very disturbed. In those instances, I prayed for patience, strength and insight. Since I have become accustomed to taking my problems to the Lord in prayer, my life has really changed.

It has been my experience that what seemed impossible only hours earlier, had a very simple solution and was no problem at all. I sometimes feel like I do not deserve all the help He gives me and I feel somewhat guilty for asking, but I am always gratified to see how wonderful things can be if the Lord and I are working together. I feel I do have a friend in Jesus.

Psalm 127:1 says, "Unless the Lord builds the house they labor in vain who build it; unless the Lord guards the city, the watchman stays awake in vain." Verse 2 says, "It is vain for you to rise up early, to sit up late, to eat the bread of sorrows; for so He gives His beloved sleep."

Author's note: Ray is my niece's husband and a true Christian gentleman, a West Point graduate and Vietnam veteran.

June 13th ~ An Emerging Bulb, by Grace Anne Woodruff, Niece

We just returned from West Point to help with the orientation of the new Plebes and their parents. Our job was to visit with the parents after their son or daughter had to report to duty. We talked with them about what an honor it was to be at West Point; how proud they must be of their sons; and in the end, the cadets will have had a wonderful experience and education.

As we sat in the Chapel listening to an organ concert, it dawned on me that these new cadets were like new Christians, emerging bulbs. They start out fresh, eager, naïve, and ready to conquer the world. We as new Christians feel the same way; we are out to convert everyone and anyone that will listen to us.

But as the cadets and new Christians move along their journey, they begin to see that baby steps must be taken before we can run, that each step is an important one, none are to be skipped. We learn that having faith in everything we do, we will one day conquer and convert the world, but the process is the major event for both of us. But until that day arrives, we must be patient, faithful, and loyal to our cause.

We pray for the safety of these new cadets and their families, and that they will feel God's presence in their lives as each begins to emerge into a new person. 2 Corinthians 5:17 says, "Now if anyone is in Christ, he is a new creation in Christ Jesus; old things have passed away, behold all things have become new."

June 14th ~ Forgiving Our Enemies

The Word of God tells us, "Bless them that curse you, and pray for them which despitefully use you" (Luke 6:28). We cannot easily stay mad at a person for whom we are praying. Sometimes we may have to pray for them through gritted teeth, but God will honor our efforts and our choices to pray and forgive.

We are to forgive them to the point where you actually feel yourself cleaned of resentment and bitterness. If we do not, the lack of forgiveness will make it impossible for God's power to be released to and in us. The miracle life depends 100 percent on our relationship to God the Father. That relationship is built strictly on the strength of His forgiveness of our sins.

Then we are to continue to let the Holy Spirit show us anyone else we may not have forgiven. Many times we might need to go to others and ask them to forgive us. (Matthew 5:23-24) If we know someone has something against us, we may need to go to them in a humble attitude and repentance. They may not always accept our apology, but we will have done our part and the Lord will reward us and release us.

There might even be people that are already dead that we need to forgive and the Lord will help us do this, too. For instance, we could picture the person sitting in front of us with Jesus in between. The Holy Spirit will help us if we just purpose in our heart to act in obedience to the Word.

We will never be called on to give more grace than God has given us. So let's go ahead, step into the river of God's mercy and let it flow over us setting us free as we forgive and pray for our enemies.

June 15th ~ Unforgiveness

Several years ago I heard a good teaching about forgiveness and I thought to myself, "Well, I don't have that problem as I do not harbor any unforgiveness in my heart." How shocked I was when the Holy Spirit pointed out an event that happened when Billy and I were at Fort Hood back in the early 50's. It seems I had not forgiven the person involved. This really showed me how serious the Lord was about forgiveness. (And how picky.)

I had not thought of this person, a sergeant, in years. He and his family lived on the other side of the duplex when we were at Fort Hood in Killeen, Texas. We did not have children yet and my two dogs were my babies. Tar-baby was a cute little mixed breed and Trouble was a boxer puppy about two months old.

One morning, as I washed dishes in the kitchen sink, I watched the dogs playing in the backyard. Trouble strayed into the neighbor's side of the yard and this big burly sergeant kicked him with all his might. I ran out the door exclaiming, "How dare you kick my puppy!" He replied that he would kick my "blankety blank" dog anytime he came in his yard.

Imagine my horror! Not only had he kicked my baby puppy, but he had cursed at me! Understand I had lived a very sheltered life and no one had ever spoken to me in such a way. Talk about a spoiled baby girl! I called Billy at Fort Hood and wanted him to come home immediately and for us to move. He appeased me and said to stay in the house with the dogs and we would see about it.

Thankfully my brother J.G. and his family were coming for the weekend, so after dinner we started driving around looking for a place to move. Sure enough, we found the perfect duplex, even nearer the base, and spent all the next day moving in. The neighbors there loved our dogs.

I never saw the sergeant again, but the Holy Spirit wanted me to forgive him. I quickly did. He has continued to bring others to my mind that I had not forgiven. It seems He thinks this is a very important matter. And since I certainly want my prayers answered, I have made a quality decision to forgive instantly whenever He brings anyone to my remembrance.

I have learned that every day we have opportunities to forgive, especially our loved ones. It really is as simple as making a choice and simply obeying God's command to forgive as we are forgiven. (Matthew 6:14-15)

Choose to forgive and God will take it from there.

June 16th ~ Confessing the Word

There are many who may not understand what it means to confess God's Word. They have always associated confession with confessing their sins or weaknesses. I am talking about confessing God's Word because what God said is truth, whether you have experienced it or not. By your confession, you make a demand on the provisions God has made through His exceeding great and precious promises. (2 Peter 1:3-5)

You have a free will to choose and then confess the words you speak. Each word has power to move you in the direction of God's plan for your life or in the opposite direction. Why not confess words that line up with God's plan?

As you confess God's Word, you establish God's goals by His Word. It gives you direction. You can hear your own voice speaking what God said and faith comes by hearing. God's Word can change you. That is really what confession is all about. It is calling things that are not as though they were before they are. (Romans 4:17, 1 Corinthians 1:27-28)

God told Joshua in 1:8 to keep speaking the Word. You must speak God's Word even when you feel like the very opposite is true. God wants you to stop all that the wicked one brings against you with the shield of faith. That shield is fashioned by the Word of God coming out of your mouth. "And the sword of the Spirit which is the Word of God..."

(Ephesians 6:18).

I encourage you to make your own list of scriptural confessions that will plant God's Word in your heart. This won't happen overnight, but when you continue to speak and confess the Word on a daily basis, it will eventually change present situations and bring in the reality of God's promises.

June 17th ~ Census

Often when I would read the account of King David insisting on taking a census, I wondered why God got so mad when He Himself told Moses to number the Israelites. (Numbers 1:2-3) But as I was reading 1 Chronicles 21:1-30 last night, I nearly fell out of bed when the revelation came to me. It was so simple that I can't believe it took me so many years to realize it. *He was putting his faith in man and not God; in numbers and not God's might. Also, not faith in God's promises – God had told him that he would multiply Israel as the stars in the heaven.* (1 Chronicles 27:23)

David desired to count how many armed men he had to fight for him when he should have trusted the Lord to fight his battles. It showed a definite lack of faith on David's part – he was worried about how many able-bodied men he had on his side. Even Joab, his general, knew it would be a sin against God.

1 Chronicles 21 begins by saying that Satan moved David to number Israel. (I guess what's where we get "the devil made me do it".) Satan counterfeits everything God does. This made me think of an old adage gamblers use, "Don't count your money – it will change your luck." It is probably derived from the mistake David made in counting his men.

I love David as he so quickly repents. (Verse 8) He begs God's forgiveness and then goes on to say that he would rather receive his punishment from the hand of God, since His mercies are very great, than to fall into the hand of man.

(Verse 13) This story is also told in 2 Samuel 24:1-25.

God's mercies are so very great, they are new every morning or we would all be under His wrath for our many sins. Especially displeasing to God is a lack of faith in believing that He will fight our battles for us, a belief that He is always on our side.

Always and ever. Amen.

June 18th ~ Identity Theft

Since identity theft is really becoming a huge problem, Bill has been staying on me to be careful about my numbers: Social Security, driver's license and credit cards. Imagine his horror when he found that I was using my bank deposit slips like calling cards. It seemed to me to be a simple way to give someone my address and phone number. Needless to say, I do not do that anymore after he had such a fit. He also had me take my driver's license number off our checks.

Trusting others to a fault was obviously my problem. But it does seem sad to me that we have to be suspicious of others nowadays. Growing up we did not even lock our doors, in fact, did not even have a key to our house. Now we have an alarm system and Tippy's loud barking. She gives us early warning when anyone comes near our house or even anywhere in the neighborhood. This is good except she also leaves the door open nearly all the time and anyone could walk in. The door just pushes open and she can go in and out at will. If it is not locked, she only has to jump on it hard to make it open from inside or out.

Bill and I both admit we should be more concerned about people just walking into our home. Although Tippy barks a warning, she really loves company and would welcome anyone in with great glee. She thinks everyone loves her. I guess I am a lot like that, too, and cannot imagine a person wanting to steal from me. I am still not fearful because of my complete trust in God.

I think of Psalm 127:1b that says, "Unless the Lord

guards the city, the watchman stays awake in vain." So we can rest in His watchful eye on us and our possessions IF we ask Him to be in charge. This does not mean that we can be foolhardy as I was, because the Bible does remind us that thieves do come in to steal. (Luke 12:33)

June 19th ~ Authority Over the Enemy

Luke 10:19 says, "Behold! I have given you authority and power to trample upon serpents and scorpions, and (physical and mental strength and ability) over all the power that the enemy (possesses), and nothing shall in any way harm you." (Amplified) God has already given us the power AND the authority over ALL the power of the enemy. We don't have to try to be good enough to get it. He has given it to us. How is this power released; through believing the Word and then speaking the Word.

Behold - look and see. "I HAVE GIVEN." It is a done deal.

Power (*dunamis*) here means ability and strength. Authority is taken from the Greek word '*exousia*' which means the right to act. We not only have the might, but we have the right. (Example – If I stood in the middle of the road and held up my hand to stop traffic, I might get run over. But if a policeman with the authority of his uniform does the same thing, then the traffic will stop.)

Believing is the key that opens the door to victory. We must believe it first and then we will see it. The truth is that God has already done everything for us. We just need to receive it. All our victories are through faith.

But we must SPEAK the Word to bring it to pass. Speaking the Word turns the key to unlock your breakthrough. Power and authority are not released through thinking, but through speaking. We have the power and authority, but we must open our mouths and speak, being careful not to speak the problem, but the answer. "God's Word will not return unto Him void without accomplishing what He purposes" (Isaiah 55:11). His word will break into pieces even the most stubborn problems we face. (Jeremiah 23:29) "God is alert and active, watching over His Word to perform it" (Jeremiah 1:12).

June 20th ~ Just As You Are

While having a quiet time with the Lord, I was bemoaning all my many faults and He spoke quietly in my spirit, "I love you just as you are." I said, "Yes, Lord, but I know You want me to change." He then told me that He would do the changing and for me not to try to do it on my own, just to trust Him to do it in His timing. That really takes the pressure off of me. Of course, I must be willing to let Him.

This immediately made me think of the well-known hymn "Just As I Am" that we associate with the Billy Graham Crusades. It goes on to say, "Without one plea, but that Thy blood was shed for me." Praise God for the blood of Jesus – our only plea which offers us forgiveness from all our sins, past, present and future.

And how about the secular song "It Had To Be You" with the line, "With all your faults I love you still." And God does – with all our faults, He loves us still. Are we thankful for that, or what? That is His unconditional love. It will never change no matter how awful we think we are. He sees us through the blood of Jesus. He thinks we are wonderful because He sees us perfect just like Jesus.

When our girls went to Camp Waldemar in the Hill country of Texas each summer, the most coveted and exalted honor a camper could receive was entitled "Ideal Girl." And the winner's names would be engraved on a permanent Hall of Fame plaque at the camp headquarters.

In God's eyes, we are all "Ideal Girls" (or boys) and our names are engraved in the Lamb's Book of Life, even on the palms of His hands. Glory be to God. (Philippians 4:3, Revelation 21:27, Isaiah 49:16)

June 21st ~ A Good Plan

Part of God's goodness is that He is a planner. And what a planner! He mapped out the plan of redemption before the foundation of the world so that when man sinned, that plan was already in place. And everything He has planned for the earth will happen right on time. Yes, God has a plan for us – a good plan. (Jeremiah 29:11)

He has prepared paths for us beforehand. (Ephesians 2:10) How will He lead us? By His Holy Spirit, according to the plan He has laid out for each individual life. He did not leave us on our own to try and figure out what to do with our lives. He had a plan for each of us before we were even born; a great, victorious, abundantly prosperous plan. He has a calling and purpose for every one of His children to fulfill. We don't have to all be preachers or teachers, but there is still a call for our lives.

Think about it – living the good life that He ordained for us. We are His handiwork, divinely designed to fulfill the good destiny God has planned for us. He prepared beforehand our paths! Wow!

When we were born, God placed certain abilities, dreams, and desires within us that would equip us for what He wanted us to do. Even when we were still sinners, they were there. So before we knowingly began to seek God, He already had a plan working for us. But without His Word and His Spirit to enlighten us, we can never grasp the plan God has for us. It has to be walked out by following the leading of the Lord, obeying His written Word, and walking in His plan BY FAITH, one step at a time.

Those two words BY FAITH are very important. We have to believe God has a plan for us, a good one or we will never be able to walk in it. Isn't it sad that there are millions of people who do not know what God planned for them; especially all the blessings He has stored up for them.

June 22nd ~ "Near to the Heart of God"

This is another favorite hymn I was singing as a prayer to the Lord this morning and I really thought about what it means to be near to the heart of God - total trust! Not always feeling His presence, but simply trusting Him no matter what. "Near to the heart of God - a place of quiet rest, a place of comfort sweet, a place full of blessings, a place where all is joy and peace."

Isaiah 40:11 says, "He will feed His flock like a shepherd He will gather His lambs with His arm, and carry them in His bosom, and gently lead those who are young."

One of my devotionals this morning said, "Allow God to show His love for you today." Song of Solomon 2:16 says, "I am my beloved and He is mine. He feeds His flock among the lilies." How wonderful is that? He really does want us just to rest in Him and let Him love us.

Many of our beloved hymns were written at times of grief in the author's life. "Near to the Heart of God" is no exception. Cleland B. McAfee was deeply grieved over the death of his brother's two small daughters who died of diphtheria within 24 hours of each other. He wrote, "Hold us who wait before Thee, near to the heart of God." It is a wonderful prayer in times of sorrow.

"It is Well" was another hymn that was penned during a time of deep grief. The author Horatio Spafford had just learned that his four daughters had drowned in a tragic shipwreck. He hurried to join his wife in Europe and, on the voyage, the ship's captain showed him the place where the luxury liner, with his daughter, went down. He later wrote the immortal words that have comforted millions, "Whatever my lot, Thou hast taught me to say, It is well, It is well with my soul."

These words continue to comfort us in our times of need.

June 23rd ~ God's Glasses

Have you ever thought about putting on God's glasses, seeing things sharp and clear the way He sees them? Oh, that would certainly change our perspectives – to see ourselves as God sees us, others as God sees them and our situations as God sees them.

This can only be done with the help of the Holy Spirit. On our own, we would either look through dark or rose-colored glasses or the kind the world thinks look good on us (fashion ones that are pretty to look at, but not too helpful, and ones we're trying to match our outfits), or maybe even broken glasses that resemble mixed-up attitudes.

Think about how God sees us if we have accepted Christ as our Savior. He sees us through the blood of Jesus and with such love and approval. He is the only one who can see us that way? Remember the expression "only a mother can love a certain type person?" Well, God really does love us in spite of all our faults and failures. He sees us as victorious winners, through glasses that filter out all our sins - past, present and future. He sees us just like He sees Jesus. Wow! He's not mad at us, He's proud of us. We are His special children and He sees us as a doting parent. He yearns to bless us and only wants us to be sinless so life will go easier for us. He thinks we are wonderful! How good is that?

And He also sees other people through glasses of love. He wants us to see them that way, too. The Amplified in 1 Corinthians 13:4-8 is a description of the lens through which he sees us and others. He looks on the inside like He did with David. (1 Samuel 16) We are told in Matthew 7:1-5 not to judge others or their intentions. We don't know the whole story! Thank God, He has given us His Holy Spirit to help us love ourselves and others. His love has been shed abroad in our hearts. (Romans 5:5) And 1 Peter 4:8 says, "Love covers a multitude of sins."

June 24th ~ God's Glasses #2

What are God's glasses? They give you the ability to see things through God's eyes, from His perspective. Seeing a situation through his eyes is determined by how much peace you have in the midst of a storm in your life. If you are anxious and fretting about it, then you are looking at the problem and not the solution. Agree with God and what He says about you, others and the storm you are going through.

Don't let others steal your God glasses. Keep them cleansed and polished with the scratches rubbed out. This can only be accomplished by the washing of the water of the Word. I was thinking about how hard I am on my bifocals; always getting them scratched up. My daddy was even rougher on his glasses and, when he died, I found an entire drawer filled with broken glasses and the stems twisted off. He hated to wear them, so would take them off and twirl the sides. We take our God glasses off a lot, too, and they become lost or broken.

We don't want to look through cracked glasses, but through God's glasses which will give us a much better prospective from His Word on our situations. He says He is in control and all is well. Just wait and see how He's going to handle the problem for you. "I know the end from the beginning and I promise you a good outcome" (Romans 8:28).

So let's shine up our God glasses and see everything as He does. He has the big picture. He sees even better than 3-D! Sometimes we magnify our problems or the faults of others but, with His help, we can use our magnifying glasses to magnify God and not our problems.

Let's put on His glasses and see victory!

June 25th ~ "Me and My Shadow"

Most who read this will be too young to remember a nightclub singer named Ted Lewis. He was one of my Mother's favorite performers and Daddy would take her to see him whenever he was in Shreveport, Dallas or Houston. I went with them several times to see him at the roof garden of the old Washington-Youree Hotel in Shreveport. His theme song was, "Me and My Shadow" and he would wear a top hat and carry a cane and would have behind him, doing the same motions, a small black boy. With effective lighting, this was very clever. He would begin his show with his famous catchphrase, "Is everybody happy?"

I heard a teacher say that the word "shadow" was mentioned around a 100 times in the Bible. Well, I immediately thought of Psalm 91 about being hidden under the shadow of the Almighty. There are several other mentions of being covered by His mighty shadow. This blesses me to think that "Me and my Shadow" are together all the time, just as the Holy Spirit is always with me. We can never be separated.

The teacher reminded us that we, too, cast a shadow as we go about our daily living, often touching many other lives and those whom our shadow falls upon. This makes me think of what a grave responsibility it is to be a Christian witness all the time. Especially to those we are around most often. Certainly our children are copying our every move. Scary, eh? Not only is God watching over us, others are watching us, too. My prayer is that I will be ever more aware of His Spirit in me giving me the power every day to become more like Him.

I just read on the Internet that Al Jolson and Billy Rose wrote the lyrics of the song, "Me and My Shadow."

June 26th ~ Time Marches On

Time out, time marches on, time goes by, time after time, time flies, time is fleeting, time waits for no man, and on and on. Time sometimes seems to be our enemy, but we also hear that time heals.

What Solomon says in Ecclesiastes 3:18 is still the most definitive definition of the word "time." He says, "To everything there is a season, a time for every purpose under heaven: A time to be born, and a time to die; a time to plant, and a time to pluck what is planted; a time to kill and a time to heal; a time to break down, and a time to build up; a time to weep, and a time to laugh; a time to mourn, and a time to dance; a time to cast away stones, and a time to gather stones; a time to embrace, and a time to refrain from embracing; a time to gain, and a time to lose; a time to keep, and a time to throw away; a time to tear, and a time to sew; a time to keep silence, and a time to speak; a time to love, and a time to hate; a time to war, and a time of peace."

Once when we were getting frustrated waiting for one of our daughters to give birth, I remember a nurse friend of mine saying "ripe apples fall." This blessed me and reminded me that God is in control and we want His timing and not ours. It's comforting to know that God has a season and purpose for everything, and His timing is always perfect.

In Psalm 69, David speaks of an "acceptable" or favorable time and in Isaiah 49:8, "Thus says the Lord: In an acceptable time I have heard you, and in the day of salvation I have helped you; I will preserve you and keep you." So we can pray for His acceptable or favorable time.

Yea! That's what I want — His perfect timing.

June 27th ~ Hear and Understand

Matthew 15:10 says, "Jesus called the crowd to Him. He said to them, 'Hear and understand.'" O, Lord, what good advice. I do so want to hear and understand what You are saying to me. Because, of course, anything You say is vitally essential for me to know.

Jesus goes on to tell us in Verses 11 and 18 that it is what proceeds out of the mouth that defiles the man because it is what he thinks or what is in his heart. Verse 19 tells us that out of the heart come evil thoughts. I noticed, not for the first time, that slander is right up there with murder, fornication, and stealing.

Of course, we do not need to dwell on evil thoughts, but even more importantly, we don't need to speak them out. Evil thoughts may come, but we don't have to entertain them. And if we don't speak them forth, they don't bear fruit. So I think Jesus is stressing to us again the importance of the words of our mouth.

Jesus often tells us that whosoever has ears, let him hear what the Spirit is saying. So when He tells us to "hear and understand," it is a matter of tremendous importance to Him because He knows it is to our benefit to watch our words. Proverbs is full of verses about watching what we speak. In fact, we are told that death and life are in the power of the tongue. (Proverbs 18:21)

One of my favorite verses to pray is Psalm 19:14, "Let the words of my mouth and the meditation of my heart be acceptable in Your sight, O Lord, my Rock and my Redeemer." Amen.

June 28th ~ Pails and Shovels

Reading about the pails and shovels used in the temple that Solomon was building to the glory of God, it occurred to me again how very much God is interested even in the small things in our lives. Just reading about the furnishings of the temple is mind boggling. Seemingly unimportant things were listed. I also noticed that the pails and shovels were made of bronze, which usually means judgment so I wondered about them. Also, there was a sea of cast metal for the priests to wash in. (2 Chronicles 4:2)

Anyway, reading about the sea, the pails and shovels made me think of our wonderful family trips to Galveston. Oh, how excited I would be when Mother would buy me my new bucket and spade for digging in the sand. I knew our trip to the gulf could not be far off. We would have a family contest to see who would spot the ocean first. Of course, Bubba always won. This has nothing to do with the Bible passage I am talking about, but it just proves that there is always something new to think about in the Living Word.

I truly believe that the Holy Spirit had the writers of the Bible list all these otherwise seemingly unimportant things to show us how much God cares about all of our little everyday problems; or better still, our joys. He is pleased when we are happy and give Him the glory for every blessing. They certainly all come from Him, anyway.

Sometimes I skip over all the temple adornments. However, they would not be there if each one was not important. For all scripture is inspired by God and profitable for us. (2 Timothy 3:16-17)

June 29th ~ Nothing's Too Good for Us If We Can Get It, by Rachel Rice, Friend

I remember it like it was yesterday! We all sat around our dining room table laughing at Gabe Palmer's words. He was our across-the-street neighbor. And he was Irish – a big burly roustabout who played third base on our oil company's baseball team!

"Why, nothing's too good for us if we can get it!" This was his exuberant declaration as he urged our team manager to send headquarters a purchase requisition for brand new uniforms.

"We can't miss! After all, we've got the best players, and we've got the 'winning streak' again this year!" Gabe was absolutely right on that count. Our team had come out on top last year, but everyone thought new uniforms for this year weren't even a possibility.

But not Gabe Palmer! "We'll get 'em," he argued, and get them we did!

How often I've thought back to Gabe Palmer with his catching, aggressive excitement. He was so assured all would happen just as he proclaimed, new uniforms, winning players, and a two-year winning team in our own oil field league. It was in the baseball bag for sure!

This vivid memory has helped me in my own faith walk.

Gabe believed; he spoke forth what he believed and what he wanted to happen. He urged and motivated others and a requisition was sent and rewarded with those actual and coveted uniforms! What a morale boost to "that winning streak" for the players as every game was played with even more gusto and assurance to win the championship two times in a row.

"Nothing's too good for us if we can get it!" That's it! Jesus won all things back for us believers; we have once again been restored to Adam's dominion in the garden of this world. After all, it is written in 1 Corinthians 3:21-23 that we truly have all things! Let's go get them with His blessings!

June 30th ~ Palm Trees

Psalm 92:12, Amplified, says, "The uncompromisingly righteous shall flourish like the palm tree and grow like the Cedars of Lebanon." Palm trees grow in warm, sunny climates and are long lived, stately, upright, useful and fruitful. Cedars of Lebanon are majestic, stable, durable and incorruptible. The seeds are dispersed by dropping on water in an oasis in the desert. Verse 13 says, "Planted in the house of the Lord they shall flourish in the courts of our God."

Verse 14 says, "Growing in grace they shall bring forth fruit in their old age, they shall be full of sap and (does this mean sappy?) of spiritual vitality and rich in the verdure of trust, love and contentment." The Lord always wants us to be fat and happy - fat and sappy, too. Since I have always been a little sappy and fat, this makes me glad.

I enjoy looking at the wonderful palm trees here in Palm Springs. Even though some of them are old, I think about how upright they are, how straight, stately and fruitful. Yea, we will still bear fruit in our old age!

Psalm 104:16 says, "The trees of the Lord are full of sap; the cedars of Lebanon which He plants." Unless the Lord plants us, we labor in vain but in Him we have plenty of sap, the anointing oil, to do whatever He asks us to do.

In thinking about the palm and cedar trees, it makes me think of the importance of having deep roots to stay upright in the deserts of life. Deep roots must be in Jesus and growing with the water of the Word of God. I'm reminded of the parable of the seed which is the Word of God; still bearing fruit in our old age. (Matthew 13; Mark 4; Luke 8)

July 1st ~ Concern or Worry

I once heard a pastor say, "Worry is allowing problems and distress to come between us and the heart of God. It is the view that God has somehow lost control of the situation and we cannot trust him. A legitimate concern presses us closer to the heart of God and causes us to lean and trust on Him all the more."

Concern addresses the problem; worry obsesses about the problem.

Concern solves the problems; worry creates more problems.

Concern draws us to God; worry pulls us from Him.

Oswald Chambers says, "Fretting is wicked if you are a child of God. All of our fret and worry is caused by calculating without God."

We need to start reminding ourselves of who God is. Jesus warned us about trouble in John 16:33, but reminds us that He has overcome the world. That's the reason we can leave our worries behind. Not because there's nothing to be concerned about, but because we have Someone who can handle them a lot better than we can.

Corrie ten Boom said, "Any concern too small to be turned into a prayer is too small to be made into a burden." When we choose to pray instead of worry and to have a grateful heart in not-so-great circumstances, then the peace of God comes and takes us into "protective custody." It stands guard over our hearts and minds. (Philippians 4:6-8)

July 2nd ~ Perfume

As I was reading Psalm 110, I noticed something about 'youth dew' and it made me think of the Estee Lauder Youth Dew Perfume that came out in the late 50's or early 60's and was all the rage. I realized that they got the name from the Bible.

It was much more expensive than the drug store brand Cody L'Origan that I had always used. But, of course, I had to go with Youth Dew regardless of the cost. After about a year, my dermatologist told me not to use any of the Estee Lauder products as they worked with the sun to cause brown spots. O my, I guess the most expensive isn't always the best?

There are many references to perfume in the Bible and how important it is to get the right ingredients. God is downright picky about certain things and the incense for a sweet smelling aroma to Him is one of them. Since incense is symbolic of the prayers of the saints, it behooves us to learn what type of prayer will bless Him. He doesn't expect us overnight to begin to pray like Paul and he does meet us where we are. But He also desires that we continually grow in our understanding. (We can pray like Paul because we can pray his prayers straight from the Word.)

It is so wonderful that when we pray the Word of God, we know we are praying in His perfect will. His word is His will. (We have a precious grandson named Will and I often pray Lord, Your will for our Will.) Another perfectly safe way to pray knowing that He hears us is in tongues - our own personal prayer language. He yearns to give us all the Baptism in the Holy Spirit with a special communication just between God and us. God's way is not for us to beg Him - just to ask Him in faith knowing how more than willing He is to answer.

July 3rd ~ The Hand of God, Testimony by Susan Taylor, Friend, Houston, TX

I remember back in the early 70's, an elderly lady passed me on the crosswalk of an intersection in downtown Houston. She said, "Baby, the Lord really has His hand on you. I could see such a bright light on your forehead as you crossed the street." Well, being unlearned concerning the Word, I went off thinking to myself, "That nut, I don't see no hand on me!"

Here I am approaching 60 years old on my birthday in October and can truly reflect back on situations and circumstances, and even assess my life today and say, "Surely the Lord is and has been with me."

One incidence that comes to mind immediately is how I chose drugs as a Band-Aid for the abuse that I suffered as a child including molestation between the ages of nine to 13. The mental anguish, the loss of self esteem, the feelings of rejection and all the false guilt and shame that Satan threw my way had me bent over in the mud of hell. It was so deep, I reached the place where more drugs, men, alcohol and any other ungodly habits were not enough. Eventually I overdosed and was flat line dead. Thank God for an old seasoned drug addict who was present and knew to shoot my veins full of salt water. His action truly was the hand of God upon my life.

I went on for another season and met another mother in Zion and once again I heard, "Daughter, the Lord really has His hand upon you." I thought the Lord didn't want me and believed the woman had to be crazy because I didn't see any hands on me. I wished that I had some of what she had been smoking.

It was at that time that I met Him, one on one with extended hands. John 10:28 says, "...and none shall pluck them out of My hands." He wants to extend His hands to all of us, suddenly.

July 4th ~ Lilies

We are told in Matthew 6:28-29 to "consider the lilies" and in Luke 12:27 to "think about them." So I began to do just that.

Song of Solomon mentions them often. In the Amplified, Chapter 2:1 speaks of a humble lily of the valley that grows in deep and difficult places. I certainly had never noticed that verse and I wondered about it. I read in verse 16 that "He positions His flock among the lilies." Does this mean that we are positioned around beauty in deep and difficult places? Sounds like it to me. And He Himself positions us so we are where He desires us to be.

Song of Solomon 6:3 says, "He feeds His flock among the lilies." He not only positions us but feeds us wherever He has placed us. In verse two, the beloved has gone to feed in His garden and to gather lilies. Then we are told we are our beloved's garden - wow, I like to think about being a garden.

Hosea 14:5 says that Israel shall grow and blossom as the lily.

I love the hymn, "The Lily of the Valley." It says, "He's the Lily of the valley, the Bright and Morning Star, He's the fairest of the ten thousand to my soul." Certainly our Jesus is all of that and so much more.

Verse one says, "I have found a friend in Jesus, He's everything to me, He's the fairest of ten thousand to my soul; The lily of the valley in Him alone I see all I need to cleanse and make me fully whole. In sorrow He's my comfort, in trouble He's my stay; He tells me every care on Him to roll."

And the last stanza begins with, "He will never, never leave me, nor yet forsake me here, while I live by faith and do His blessed will."

July 5th ~ The Foundation of Faith - Understanding God's Goodness and Love

Do we really know God loves us? And that He is a good God? Do we really believe in His goodness and mercy — not just as a concept but do we personally know it? I believe that unless a person believes in the goodness of God, they will not be able to trust Him. If there is even a lingering doubt that God is mad at us, then we won't trust His goodness. Or if we have the mistaken idea that we are not worthy of His blessings, we have a problem trusting Him.

1 John 4:16-17 in the Amplified, says, "And we know (understand, recognize, are conscious of, by observation and by experience) and believe (adhere to and put faith in and rely on) the love God cherishes for us. God is love, and he who dwells *and* continues in love dwells *and* continues in God, and God dwells *and* continues in him. In this [union and communion with Him] love is brought to completion *and* attains perfection with us, that we may have confidence for the day of judgment [with assurance and boldness to face Him], because as He is, so are we in this world."

God is not mad at you. He is a good God; He loves you. Understanding this will change your life. The more we know God's goodness, the more we trust Him. The more we trust Him, the easier it is for us to put our lives into His hands. He is endeavoring to help us so we can relax and receive and be overtaken by His blessings. (Deuteronomy 28) The revelation of God's goodness will help us have confidence and receive from Him whatever we need. Until we settle the fact that God is good and we can trust Him with our lives, our faith is never going to be great because we will always draw back in fear.

"I am still confident of this: I will see the goodness of the Lord in the land of the living" (Psalm 27:13). The more deeply you understand the truth of these words, the more you will be able to trust God in every circumstance of life.

Your confidence in His goodness and love will make you bold when others are timid.

July 6th ~ The Red Sea

Exodus 14:13 says, "Do not fear! Stand still and see the salvation of the Lord which He will accomplish for you today." That's good advice for us, too, when we have our backs to the Red Sea and the enemy is coming fast. But how hard is that? Real hard. We can think of a lot of things to do, but standing still is not one of them. Or how about Verse 14, "The Lord will fight for you while you keep silent." Silent?

These Verses are so rich that I don't know where to start. I love every point they are making. I even love the "today" part. He will accomplish it today. Yea.

But I am a tad confused about Verse 15 when the Lord spoke to Moses and said, "Why are you crying to me? Tell the children of Israel to go forward." Wait just a minute. Were they not just told to stand still? I think it must mean to stand still in their hearts by trusting in Him, not being afraid, and then to go forward.

Just read the Amplified and Verse 13 says, "Fear not, stand still (firm, confident, undismayed)." Verse 14 says, "The Lord will fight for you, and you shall hold your peace and remain at rest." Still hard, but a little easier to understand when we realize what standing still really means: being firm, confident, undismayed and to hold our peace and remain at rest. I love it, but it's still hard to do.

I love the fact that in every translation of the Bible there is the promise that God will fight for us. He will never let us down when we believe Him and quit trying in our own strength.

Sounds like 'Let go and Let God,' doesn't it?

July 7th ~ The Red Sea #2

Psalm 106:7-8 says, "....they did not remember the multitude of Your mercies, but rebelled by the sea – the Red Sea. Nevertheless He saved them for His name's sake..."

Cross references:

A. Psalm 106:7 : [ver. 13, 21]
B. Psalm 106:7 : Ex. 14:11, 12
C. Psalm 106:8 : Ezek. 20:9, 14
D. Psalm 106:8 : Ex. 9:16

It seems to me that the Lord delivered them from the hand of the enemy even when they rebelled against Him. They forgot all the miracles He performed for them in Egypt when they were spared from the disastrous plagues – none touched their land, or them.

Sounds like us – we so often forget all the times He kept us safe or pulled us out of some serious messes. But He will still save and deliver us when we call. He will also rebuke our 'Red Seas' and cause them to dry up and our enemies will be washed away.

In Verse 12, "Then they believed His words and sang His praise." Well, finally. O, Lord, help me to believe Your word and sing Your praise even before You deliver me.

Have you ever looked around and it felt like there were 600 chariots coming toward you? And you saw no way to get away from them? Well, maybe not that many but several. And what about the times when your back was to a sea with huge waves coming at you?

In Exodus 14:9 the Israelites saw all the chariots of Egypt coming towards them and they were literally between the devil and the deep blue sea. This was, of course, when they cried out to the Lord and He saved them. The pillars of clouds and of fire worked both ways. The clouds led them, but also acted as a shield of protection that hid them from the enemy. The fire gave them light and coverage.

Jesus, the light of the world, does that for us, too!

July 8th ~ "Let the Rest of the World Go By"

There seemed to be more distractions than usual trying

to come against me this morning during my quiet time with the Lord and I was having a hard time concentrating on Him. Then He whispered this song title into my spirit, "Let the Rest of the World Go By." He has such a great sense of humor and I had to laugh out loud.

Later I looked up the lyrics online and they were good and really fit into my thinking about being alone with God. The Chorus says, "With someone like you, a pal good and true, I'd like to leave it all behind and go and find some place that's known to God alone, just a spot to call our own. We'll find perfect peace, where joys never cease out there beneath a kindly sky, we'll build a little nest, somewhere in the west and let the rest of the world go by."

And since at present I'm in the west - Palm Springs, California — the words of the song — "A place that's known to God alone" — seemed to be speaking to me personally as God so loves to do. Doesn't that sound like a special time communing with God, leaving behind all the worldly distractions? And was there ever a "Pal so good and true" as our own Jesus who sticks closer than a brother? We are told in the Psalms that we find fullness of joy in His presence, joys that never cease. (Psalm 16:11) And perfect peace comes from knowing Jesus, the Prince of Peace. So the words all fit into what He was trying to tell me this morning.

I had a glorious "love time" with the King of Kings and Lord of Lords as I "Let the Rest of the World Go By." This took a little discipline on my part, but it was SO worth it. It felt heavenly to obey Him and just sit still for several minutes. Then I felt His presence in such a powerful way that I nearly jumped out of my skin. God is so good.

July 9th ~ Valuing the Person Christ Has Made You

Valuing the unique person you continue to become in Christ enables you to develop and use the gifts He gives for His glory, honor and praise. We've all been given personal, special, just-for-us talents and abilities, but we must allow God to help us develop them so they can be used to touch others.

Your talents weren't just given for your benefit, but for the benefit of others, just as their talents were given to benefit you. "A spiritual gift is given to each as a means of helping the entire Church" (1 Corinthians 12:7). God planned it that way. If others don't use their gifts, you get cheated. If you don't use your gifts, they get cheated. An unopened gift is worthless. That's why we're each commanded to discover and develop our spiritual gifts and natural talents.

Before God created you, He decided the role He wanted you to play; then He prepared you for it. He also planned each day of your life accordingly. "All the days planned for me were written in Your book before I was one day old" (Psalm 139:16). God wouldn't give you talents and life experiences unless He intended you to use them. You have certain abilities given to you by God. You don't earn or choose them – they're free. Paul writes, "He alone decided which gift each person should have" (1 Corinthians 12:11).

We can take the unique experiences and abilities that God provided us and allow Him to redeem them for external investment. It is important to talk with God privately about all these things. Ask Him to show you what He is presently accomplishing in your life. Ask God to reveal your strengths developed in the past which He desires to use in the future.

Until God showed me that I really did have value and that He could use even me, I had always said that I had been so babied that I could not do anything. I thought I was talentless, had no abilities at all and was completely helpless. Then I learned from His Word that I did have worth and talents that He could use for His glory. God also explained to me that He could use even my experiences. There is no event, situation, person, circumstance, or moment that occurs in our lives that God does no transform into a holy moment when we belong to Him: tragedies, joys, talents, abilities, family, or whatever.

How grateful I am for this truth.

July 10th ~ Hands, by Grace Anne Woodruff, Niece

One of my favorite things to do in life is to hold hands. As a child growing up, my Daddy always held my hand. I knew if Daddy was holding my hand, I was safe and no harm would come to me. I remember driving down the road with him and we would be holding hands. There were even times when I was in the back seat he would reach back and hold my hand.

He and my Mother held hands all the time, showing their love for each other. One of my favorite pictures is Daddy and me walking to a football game at T.C.U. my senior year holding hands and laughing.

I have also taught my children to hold hands. As they grew, we were holding hands with them through each stage of their childhood. When I would drive Medley to school, we held hands the whole way. It was just a natural thing for us and she was never embarrassed. When she is scared at night or just the two of us sharing a bed, we hold hands until we fall asleep. Hands — they give us strength.

After my Daddy's death, my dreams were about his hands. I would know they were his and would awake with new strength to get through another day without him.

Just like my earthly Daddy, my Lord has strong hands to give me the strength to face each new day. As Tennessee Ernie Ford sang, "He has the whole world in His hands." We can continue with our lives knowing He is holding us in His hands.

Isaiah 41:10 says, "Fear not, for I am with you, be not dismayed, for I am your God. I will strengthen you, yes, I will help you. I will uphold you with My righteous right hand."

July 11th ~ The Blessing Chapter

Until you settle the fact that God is good and you can trust Him with your life, your faith is never going to be great because you will always draw back in fear. You will always be thinking: What if He doesn't come through for me? What if He is not listening to me? What if He asks me to do something that is hard to do?

However, once your heart grasps the goodness of God, you won't be plagued by those questions. You'll be confident in the fact that He will never hurt you. He will never abandon you or let you down. As long as you follow Him, He will always be there loving you, helping and blessing you.

Deuteronomy 28:1-11 is the blessing chapter and tells us we have been freed from the curse. He knows what is good for His children. He wants us to be physically and mentally healthy and whole. On the other hand, He knows it is evil for us to be sick, poor, frightened or oppressed.

Religious traditions taught by long-faced, angry preachers have represented God as mad at the whole human race and furiously looking for someone to punish. There is even a song with the chorus, "God's gonna get you for that." How awful to make people think that. Certainly we have already given God many reasons to get us if He was going to.

Actually the Hebrew word *shalom* that the Lord uses so frequently to bless His people means to have wholeness in your life - spirit, soul and body. It means there is nothing missing, nothing broken. God knows that is the way things ought to be and that is the way He wants them to be; not for just a few of His people, but for every one of them.

Psalm 145:9 says, "The Lord is good to all."

July 12th ~ Believers Believe

Mark 5:36 says, "Do not be afraid, only believe." These were Jesus' words to the father who had just been told his

Dec. 3, 1972 Wedding of Clara Hurst Patterson and Bill Payne with her 3 children Grace, Julianne and Burke Patterson and his five, Kathy, Brant, Lee, Jim and Tim

1973 1st anniversary in front of home in Paris, TX   Now not his and her children but ours

1980 Christmas card in Longview, TX with 1st grandchild, Emily Harville. Sons in laws-Johnny Harville and Pat Crabtree.

1994 Christmas card with grandchildren

1992 Christmas card at the wedding of Laura Harvey and Burke Patterson

2005 wedding of granddaughter Laura LaMaster and Jeff Whitworth

Thanksgiving 2011 the original 10 back together. Back row: Brant, Kathy, Grace, Julie, Lee, Jim; front row Tim, Bill, Clara, Burke

Thanksgiving 2011 with the whole family – 60 in all. Also celebrating my 80th birthday coming up on Jan. 5, 2012.

daughter had died. Wow. How hard would that be? And Jesus tells Thomas (forever dubbed 'doubting'), "Do not be unbelieving, but believing" (John 20:29).

We are told over and over in the Word how important it is to believe. In John 6:29, Jesus says, "This is the work of God, that you believe in Him whom He sent." That is why we are called BELIEVERS, we are to BELIEVE.

The Greek word for BELIEVE is *aman*. It is also the root word for faith and amen and means so be it, to be firm, stable, established, firmly persuaded, to believe solidly, to consider trustworthy.

2 Corinthians 4:13 says, "And since we have the same spirit of faith, according to what is written, 'I BELIEVED therefore I spoke'." Psalm 116:10 reinforces this teaching. This is very important for it shows us three things we are doing: acknowledging God's ability, speaking so Satan will hear us and strengthening our own faith.

We are to speak forth our faith as David spoke his faith before he won the battle with Goliath. (1 Samuel 17:45-47) I love it when in Verse 48 it says that David hurried and ran toward the army to meet the Philistine. Sometimes we may want to run away, but David ran toward the enemy.

2 Chronicles 20:20 says, "Believe in the Lord your God and you shall be established." Believing is developing 20-20 spiritual vision. Choose to believe the Bible as the absolute Word of God. Rely upon its witness to God's nature, character and promises.

Jesus said, "All things are possible to him who believes." My prayer is, "Lord, I believe! Help my unbelief" (Mark 9:23-24).

July 13th ~ Proclaim God's Mercy

The Lord Himself tells us that "...He is a merciful God, gracious and long suffering, abounding in goodness and truth" (Exodus 34:6). Many doubt that He has mercy for them because they have no knowledge of His Word. Actually, God delights in mercy. (Micah 7:18) Acting on the Word, puts you in position to receive the mercy of God.

Mercy is God's attitude toward you in freely bestowing whatever is necessary to meet your needs. According to *Vine's Word Studies* we read, "Mercy manifests itself in action and assumes the adequate resources to affect the proper result. The inward moving of compassion results in the outward manifestation necessary to meet the need."

Time after time we see Jesus moved by compassion in His earthly ministry. He yearns to meet our needs. One who does not know the Scriptures might wonder why God does not heal all those who are sick, regardless of their position of faith. God's mercy goes forth in accordance with His covenant, the Word. Because He has bound Himself by His Word, He can move freely only toward those who put themselves in a position to receive.

Psalm 136:1, Deuteronomy 7:9, Psalm 86:5 say, "His mercy endureth forever." His willingness to act on man's behalf is still operating in the earth. His mercy never runs out. He is faithful to keep His covenant and offer His mercy to those who call on Him.

Proclaim His mercy! Mighty and powerful things happened when Israel proclaimed these words. They are words of praise and adoration to God. Proclaim God's mercy and compassion to those around you. King Jehoshaphat appointed singers to proclaim, "His mercy endureth forever" and their enemies destroyed themselves. (2 Chronicles 20:21-23)

With your spirit, dare to stretch your faith to take in the boundless mercy of God. Psalm 25:6 says, "Remember, O Lord, Your tender mercies and Your loving-kindness."

July 14th ~ Father's Good Pleasure

When we see in God's Word that it is the Father's good pleasure to give us the Kingdom (Luke 12:32), that no good thing will He withhold from them that walk uprightly

(Psalm 84:11), then we will realize that God is for us and not against us. Then we will be confident that His will is always better than our will and that He will never hurt us, abandon us or let us down. As long as we follow Him, He will always be there with us: loving us, helping us and blessing us.

David truly understood the Father's pleasure because he was a man after God's own heart. He would fall on Him for mercy. As a young shepherd, he worshipped and fellowshipped with God and got to know His nature.

A lesson for us is that only when we get alone with Him to get to know Him will we really learn to trust and know the Father's heart. David knew Him to be a loving God. David also knew that it was the Father's good pleasure to bless him, take care of him, and deliver him from danger.

The 23rd Psalm came from that revelation: "The Lord is my Shepherd (to feed, guide, and shield me), I shall not lack. He makes me lie down in (fresh, tender) green pastures; He leads me beside the still and restful waters. He refreshes and restores my life (myself); He leads me in the paths of righteousness (uprightness and right standing with Him—not for my earning it, but) for His name's sake. Yes, though I walk through the (deep, sunless) valley of the shadow of death, I will fear or dread no evil, for You are with me; Your rod (to protect) and Your staff (to guide), they comfort me. You prepare a table before me in the presence of my enemies. You anoint my head with oil; my (brimming) cup runs over. Surely or only goodness, mercy, and unfailing love shall follow me all the days of my life, and through the length of the days the house of the Lord (and His presence) shall be my dwelling place." (Amplified Bible)

July 15th ~ Why Jesus Chose Us

Pastor Jeff pointed out something in Mark 3:13-15 that I had never noticed before. There are three reasons why Jesus chose His disciples: (1) That they could be with Him, (2) That He could send them out to preach, and (3) To give them authority and power to heal the sick and drive out demons. Since we are His disciples, we need to heed this.

1) That we could be with Him. This shows us the most important thing we can do as His disciples is to spend time with Him by setting apart time getting to know Him and His heart's desire for us and for others. Matthew 6:33 says, "Seek you first the kingdom of God and His righteousness and all these things will be added unto you." We should seek him the first thing each day for there is no way to become close to someone unless we spend time with them.

2) That He could send us out to preach. This doesn't mean all of us have to be ordained ministers, but it does mean that we can all carry the message of the good news of the gospel. In other words, be witnesses for Jesus everywhere we go. Telling others the glorious things He has done for us. Being encouragers. Letting His love be shed abroad in our hearts and overflow to people we meet every day. We are His ambassadors to the world. (2 Corinthians 5:20)

3) That we would have the power to heal the sick and cast out demons in His name. Wow! Do we really believe we have that power residing in us by His Holy Spirit? If we did, we would be out praying for everyone we meet. Jesus gave us His very own authority and power so we need to start practicing it.

Jesus Himself commands us to go and preach the gospel to all creation and signs showing His power will follow us. (Mark 16:15-18)

July 16th ~ Watch Your Mouth

Bill takes *The Desert Sun* newspaper while we are here in Palm Springs. I very rarely read anything but the weather report and a few headlines. (Not like my hometown newspaper where the first thing I read is the obituaries.)

The headline that caught my attention today was entitled, "Watch Your Mouth." I doubt the editors knew they were speaking a Biblical truth. I was surprised as I read that the California state legislature passed a resolution that the first week in March would be a "cuss-free week" throughout the state. Lawmakers to residents: "Clean up that language." This resolution was inspired by a teenager who started a No-Cussing Club at his Junior High School in 2007. He has since been promoting other such clubs in other states and even internationally.

Sounds like a great idea, but I think Mother was right when she said that it was impossible to legislate morals. Of course, she was speaking about Prohibition during the 1920s when all alcohol sales were prohibited. This caused a rash of bootleggers and illegal sales. So I doubt if this resolution about what we speak will work much better. However, the idea of having a money jar might help if a coin is placed in it whenever anyone forgets and uses bad language.

God has been telling us for years to clean up our language, to watch our mouths, and we still speak words that are unpleasing to Him. (Words of fear and doubt and worry are "cuss" words to Him.) Although it seems to me that the desire must come from within and that only with the Holy Spirit's help can we possibly be able to obey His commands.

We can pray as David did in Psalm 141:3, "Set a guard over my mouth, keep watch over the door of my lips."

July 17th ~ Tool of Strife

Proverbs 16:27-28 says that scoundrels create trouble, their words are a destructive blaze, a troublemaker plants seeds of strife and gossip separates the best of friends.

Starting quarrels and strife is like opening a floodgate, so we should always stop before an argument gets out of control. (Proverbs 17:14)

The word "strife" in these verses denotes discord, lack of agreement, or disharmony. It implies a struggling for superiority or pushing to get position. Strife arises from the fear that somebody is going to take advantage of you. It says, "I have to fight to get what's mine."

Most believers should know better than to jump into a quarrel. So the devil sneaks up on them. They don't have a fist fight with the pastor in the foyer, but some pious-looking deacon may come up to them and say, "What do you think of the decision the pastor made about the small groups program? Do you really think he did the right thing?"

The truly wise believer cuts off that conversation right then and there. He refuses to start arguing (EVEN IN HIS MIND) about what the pastor decided. He recognizes the devil is trying to punch a hole in the harmony of the church so that strife can leak in. If you stop and pray for him right then, it will stop contention and strife. The Bible says that being slow to anger is another antidote to strife.

Proverbs 15:18 says, "A wrathful man stirs up strife, but he that is slow to anger appeases strife."

Strife deadens our spiritual senses and keeps us from hearing from God. Remember this: God never stops talking to us. He's never an absentee Father. He is always speaking and counseling, encouraging and building us up. But when we're in strife, we become too spiritually dense to know it. That alone is enough to convince us to avoid strife at all costs!

Strife is as dangerous today as it always has been. We keep strife out of our hearts by acting on our love relationship with God.

July 18th ~ Cast Your Burdens

The Lord tells us to cast our burdens or cares on Him as He cares for us. (1 Peter 5:7) In Psalm 55:22 it says, "Cast your burden on the Lord (releasing the weight of it) and He will sustain you; He will never allow the (consistently) righteous to be moved, made to slip, fall or fail." (Amplified)

Wow, what great promises! But do you ever find yourself casting your cares or burdens onto other people instead of onto Him? For example we may tell another person: "Can you believe what she said to me? Let me tell you what he did to me" or "I just don't know how I can go on; so much is happening in my life." Yes, we have all done this sort of thing.

There is a great hymn that says, "I Must Tell Jesus." The chorus goes like this: "I must tell Jesus, I cannot bear my burdens alone. I must tell Jesus! I must tell Jesus! Jesus can help me, Jesus alone."

When we take our problems to Jesus, He keeps them to Himself. We need not be concerned even when we tell him our hidden secrets and our innermost thoughts that we sure don't want others to know. And best of all, He always understands, does not condemn, and even forgives us. How good is that?

Well, how do we do it? Cast our burdens, that is. The secret is in the word, CAST:

C - Commit your burden to the Lord. Give it over to Him who cares even more than you do and has the power to do what you cannot. (I just say it out loud, "I commit this problem to You." Sometimes I offer it up with outstretched hands.)

A - Ask for His help in prayer. Philippians 4:6 tells us to be anxious for nothing, but in everything, by prayer and supplication, with thanksgiving, let our needs be known to the Lord. This was one of the first verses I memorized and it has never failed to bless me when I obey, even in little things.

S - Search the Scriptures. God has a promise for every need. Speak it forth often. Our faith will rise as we do this. Matthew 19:26 says, "Jesus said, 'With men this is impossible, but with God ALL things are possible.'"

T - Trust Him for He does care for you!

(As I was working on this devotional, I had the opportunity to obey this Word and it really works. Immediately afterwards, I truly decided to trust Him in a bothersome situation and to quit trying to work it out myself. I felt the peace that passes all understanding.)

July 19th ~ "In Him"

When Bible reading was still new to me, I was fortunate to find a book entitled *Sit, Walk, Stand* by Chinese Christian author Watchman Nee. It was a study of the book of Ephesians and changed the way I looked at being in Christ. The author had the reader underline all the passages that said "in Him, with Him, in Christ, in the Lord Jesus, In His Name." This was so eye-opening and exciting to me. Since then, I have never doubted who I am in Christ. It was a wonderful lesson to learn early in my Christian walk.

The first three chapters of Ephesians are about the "sit" part of the book. Chapters four and five are the "walk" part and chapter six is the "stand" part.

Sit – Our position in Christ.

Walk – Our life in the world.

Stand – Our attitude toward the enemy.

These three key words clearly show us the way to victory in this life and for eternity.

It is neat to underline the "In Him" in all the Pauline epistles, especially the four together that include Galatians, Ephesians, Philippians and Colossians.

(Charlotte Clark, one of the darling ladies in our Joy Group Bible Study, told us a way to remember these four books: General Electric Power Company or GEPC. Is that cute or what?) I am now enjoying underlining these "In Him's" all over again in my new Giant Print New American Standard. And I am amazed at how many there are.

I also learned the order of sit, walk, stand. We first have to learn our position in Christ – sitting with Him in heavenly places; then we are able to walk – the practical outworking of that heavenly position here on earth; and then we are able to stand against all the wiles of the devil after we have put on the armor of God.

We cannot stand unless we know who we are "In Him."

July 20th ~ If You Want a Change, Make a Change

If we will give God a way into our lives every day, He can change even impossible situations. So, if we want a change, we need to make a change. Commit ourselves to do whatever it takes to maintain living contact with God and spend time with Him every day. Determine right now that by the strength and grace, if you have to get up earlier in the morning or go to bed later, you will do it. Decide to put God as number one in your life every day. He really means it when He says to seek Him first. (Matthew 6:33)

Basically I am a lazy person. I would really prefer to lie in bed, read a good book and eat bonbons. I would also like to stay up late reading and sleep all morning. It really was a change in my lifestyle to start getting up at 6 a.m. to spend quality time with the Lord. This was contrary to my nature.

God has given us all a supernatural nature and I realize that we can overcome being spiritually lazy by purposing in our hearts to rise up, march forward and get on fire for the Lord.

I probably have an addictive personality. I used to be addicted to alcohol and smoking, just to name a couple. Now I am addicted to spending time with Him. Addicted means to devote, to deliver over, to apply habitually. It can also mean an addiction for Jesus. I would love for people to say that about me.

I am purposing in my heart right now that I will change other things in my life to give more time to God and His Word. I am asking the Lord to show me how to simplify my life and eliminate the things that were stealing my times with God.

Growth always causes change, which is sometimes painful. But God always meets us more than halfway when we become serious about making godly changes.

Please rearrange and change me now, Lord. Amen.

July 21st ~ An Ax to Grind

This has come to imply someone having an ulterior motive. I was interested when I recently read that the saying originated when a man bragged on Benjamin Franklin's whetstone. Franklin offered to show him how it worked and the man promptly pulled out his own ax to see how it could be sharpened. It was not hard to realize that was the man's original intention.

I remember being very impressed that one of the grandchildren was so interested in our vacation plans. It did not occur to me till later that the grandchild only wanted to check dates so a pool party could be planned while we were gone.

Then I began to think what axes I had to grind. It could be thinking that my agenda is more important than other people's. Am I so judgmental about others with ulterior motives that I fail to see my own?

Lately I insisted on going places in my car so that I would have access to the big box of my books in the trunk, just in case anyone wanted to buy one. Laura Patterson was telling about how good the day's devotional was in the *Word for Today* and she fell out laughing when I immediately told her to read my devotional book as it was good, too. (Both devotionals were timely for the horrible hurricane Katrina situation we were watching on TV.)

Matthew 7:1 says, "Judge not that you be not judged." Good advice.

Colossians 3:12-13 says, "Therefore, as the elect of God, holy and beloved, put on tender mercies, kindness, humility, meekness, longsuffering; bearing with one another and forgiving one another, if anyone has a complaint against another, even as Christ forgave you, so you also must do."

July 22nd ~ ALL

Recently I heard a Bible teacher say something about her life verses. So I began to think of the ones that I want to live by. I have tons of favorites, but these seem to be the basic ones: Romans 8:28; Proverbs 3:5, 6; and Philippians 4:6, 7. The Lord showed me something that I had never noticed: These verses became so familiar that I just quote them quickly and don't take time to meditate on their great truths.

What I saw today was the word "ALL" and what they ALL have in common. Not some things, but ALL. When I was a new Christian, the very first verses that I memorized were Philippians 4:6, 7 because I was an anxious person. These really blessed me and changed my life.

The first time I gave my testimony to a small group, I mistakenly said Romans 8:38 instead of 28. Afterwards, my good friend David Morris corrected me and when I asked him how he knew that so well, he told me that it was a verse that nearly all Christians loved. And then Proverbs 3:5, 6 is one I use often, reminding the Lord that I am acknowledging Him in whatever I am facing.

So in reviewing them, we will see what they are saying to us. Romans 8:28 says, "ALL things work together for good to those who love God, to those are the called according to His purpose." Philippians 4:6, 7 says, "Be anxious for nothing, but in ALL things (everything) by prayer and supplications, with thanksgiving, let your requests be known unto God and the peace of God, which surpasses ALL understanding, will guard your hearts and minds through Christ Jesus." Proverbs 3:5, 6, "Trust in the Lord with ALL your heart, and lean not on your own understanding; In ALL your ways acknowledge Him, and He shall direct (make smooth or straight) your paths."

What precious promises!

July 23rd ~ Because the Lord is Faithful

When I was reading about the history of the Civil War, I was interested in discovering that General Richard Taylor was horrified when his orders from General Stonewall Jackson were to march his troops – who were totally exhausted – back over the mountain they had just crossed. Soon he realized General Jackson had a masterful plan: to come at the enemy from a completely different way than spies had informed the Union army they would come, and totally surprise them.

Sometimes we feel like General Taylor not understanding the reason for our orders from the Lord. Not realizing the Master's plan is so much better than anything we could ever dream of.

Isaiah 49:7 says, "...Because of the Lord who is faithful, the Holy One of Israel and He has chosen you." He chose me! Yea! I am so thankful

Recently as I was fretting and stewing in my mind at my quiet time, I glanced at this verse in 2 Thessalonians 3:3 that says, "But the Lord is faithful." That is really all I need to know. He's already got all my problems in His hands and, since He is faithful, I can rest in that promise and take it to the bank. He is faithful even when we are not.

1 Corinthians 1:9 says, "God is faithful, by whom you were called into fellowship of His Son Jesus Christ our Lord."

July 24th ~ Good Intentions

We all have them and all have regrets about the good deeds we have failed to do: the letters we did not write, the phone calls we did not make and the people we waited too late to visit. Most times we get away with our failures except from our own conscience.

But not me, I had an experience that made an indelible impression on me. It concerned one of my former high school friends, an only child who died early. Her parents were not in the best of health, especially the father who was home-bound. Each time I would see the mother, she would plead with me to drop by to see him as he was so lonely. She told me that a visit by me would cheer him up as he had always loved me.

I must have thought about going by to see him a hundred times as I passed by their home nearly everywhere I went. My excuse was busyness with children and their activities. I always felt a little guilty and would promise myself that I would stop by the very next time I possibly could.

What a shock when I read in the paper that he had died. I immediately went to the house to call on his widow. Imagine how I felt when she greeted me at the door with these words, "Well, now you have come when it is too late." Wow, how true and how sad. She was so right – it was too late and all my good intentions were for naught.

I wish I could tell you that I changed overnight and now never fail to obey the Holy Spirit's leading. However, I do try to be more sensitive to His nudgings to go by, call or write.

We've heard the statement, "The road to hell is paved with good intentions." Actually this is not a true one as the only reason a person goes to Hell is their unbelief in Jesus. They condemn themselves; God does not condemn them. But we do miss many blessings when we fail to show acts of love.

James 1:27 says, "This is pure and undefiled religion: to visit widows and orphans in their trouble." God is love and desires that we show forth His love.

July 25th ~ Small Gems

Sorrow looks back. Worry looks around. Faith looks up.
There are 3 kinds of people:
Those who make things happen.
Those who watch things happen.

Those who wonder what happened.

Are you in the Way or in the way?

Here's a nursery rhyme based on Biblical truth: "Early to bed, early to rise makes a man healthy, wealthy and wise." However, 3 John 2 says, "Beloved, I desire above all things that you prosper and be in good health even as your soul prospers."

I know I can't be all things to all people, but God can.

When God guides, He provides.

Law - Moses turned water into blood meaning death. Grace - Jesus turned water into wine meaning life and celebration.

There's no need to worry if we believe this promise: "My times are in Your hands." (Psalm 31:15)

(I especially needed to hear this one today as we cancelled our flight home due to fires around our East Texas area causing so much smoke that the kids thought would be bad for Bill's lungs. We have no idea when it will be a good time to go home BUT our times are in His hands.)

Proverbs 16:9 says, "A man's heart plans his way, BUT the Lord directs his steps."

July 26th ~ In the Blink of an Eye, by Bob Lowry, Friend, Los Angeles, CA

The pain started around 4:30 p.m. It was the kind of pain that caused me to think back and count the number of cups of bad, black coffee I'd had that day. Then a little nausea set in. As I walked to my car through the hotter than normal parking lot, I thought, "...chicken fried steak on a stomach full of black coffee, not good and I've got to stop ordering extra gravy on the side. I know better."

Have you ever prayed for something, received it and then forgot to thank God for it? I have. "Please, Lord, help me do well on the exam." And then an A comes in and family and friends praise you, but God is forgotten. "Please Lord, let my boss notice and appreciate the subtlety of my work." And then the boss calls you and basically tells you how much he values your work. You are special, unique, gifted. You leave his office ecstatic, because, after all, God has nothing to do with gifts. And even if you know He does, you forget to thank Him. After all, this is your moment of glory. You worked for this all by yourself.

It is now 5:30 p.m. and I'm driving on the freeway, doubled over behind the wheel and drenched in pain, struggling to keep my head high enough above the dash so I can drive in the traffic and not hurt myself or others in some needlessly uncontrolled accident. I'll be fine. Besides, God can't drive. And it can't be a heart attack, all of the pain is on the right, not the left. I'm not driving myself to the E.R. That would be absurd.

In addition to the times we pray to the Lord and forget to thank Him when all goes our way, there are the times that we don't thank Him for the things that don't go our way. After all, why would we thank Him for not getting what we think we want? It's called dodging a bullet, that's why. God can see the bullet coming when we don't even know the gun has been fired. Most of the time we don't even know there's a gun.

I finally get my doctor on the phone. Based on my history (which I forgot of course because it was over five years ago), he tells me I am in the middle of a severe gall bladder attack. He says that he would tell me to go to the Emergency Room but there is really nothing they can do for me. He tells me to 'ride out the night' because the stone has to clear the duct.

I am now curled up on the floor, soaked, literally screaming into a pillow. This is nothing for the neighbors to hear. Every breath feels as if my rib cage is being torn apart. I can only breathe an inch or two because any more forces the entire right side of my body to feel as if it's filled with burning charcoal briquettes. I cannot lay on my back, side or stomach for more than two seconds at a time before the pain radiates into new areas of my body. I crouch on all fours arching my back in an attempt to stretch the area and force the stone. I've even been told the pain is worse than childbirth. I would never DARE write that unless the person who told me had given birth to five children and also had gall bladder attacks.

And then, without even thinking, I cry out in the room, "Please Jesus, intervene, please!"

In two seconds it stopped. I said, stopped. It didn't just start to get a little better. It disappeared. It was like it was never there. My heart rate was normal. Tears were no longer in my eyes. There wasn't one position that was better than another. They were all good. It was just gone. Stones don't pass that quickly in this way. I knew it was because I cried out, "Please, Jesus, intervene please."

I still forget to thank Him for the traffic lights not run, the friends who don't abandon me, the roof over my head that has never disappeared or the stomach that has never been empty. But I've never forgotten the episode with the gall bladder because my prayer was answered like a rocket and relieved such horrific distress.

Why is it so easy to forget about all the others? Philippians 4:16-17 says, "Don't worry about anything; instead, pray about everything. Tell God what you need, and thank him for all he has done. Then you will experience God's peace, which exceeds anything we can understand. His peace will guard your hearts and minds as you live in Christ Jesus."

July 27th ~ Tree Climbing

Do kids still climb trees in this day of TV and computer games? I hope so. That was one of our favorite pastimes when I was growing up. We had a large chinaberry tree in our yard and I would spend many an hour perched on a high limb daydreaming and picturing my future. (Mainly I liked to think of myself as a bride.) But usually I was with a friend and we would play house or movie star or other of our favorite pretends.

In Luke 19:1-10, we read the story of Zaccheus climbing a tree so he could see Jesus who was passing through Jericho. There was such a crowd and because Zaccheus was short, he needed to climb a sycamore tree in order to see Jesus. (Sometimes we need to get above the crowd so we also can see Him more clearly.)

I notice several things about this story. First of all, we know that Zaccheus was a hated tax collector. In those days the tax collectors were despised even more than the animosity that we feel toward the IRS. As a group, they were thought to be corrupt and would take more than their due. And Zaccheus was very rich.

I also noticed that when Jesus saw him up in the tree, He told him to "hurry and come down for today I must stay in your house." (He also sees us wherever we are.) I think this is the only time I remember Jesus telling anyone to hurry.

Zaccheus obeyed and received Jesus gladly. Imagine his excitement when he was singled out by Jesus.

Jesus proclaimed that, "Today salvation has come to this house…for the Son of Man has come to seek and to save that which was lost."

The name Zaccheus means "pure and righteous." How wonderful that he was called pure and righteous even before he was saved. And that is how Jesus sees us - as pure and righteous.

July 28th ~ The Proof's in the Pudding

I had not heard that old saying in a long time, but someone on a news program said it today. So I suppose it isn't just us old folks that remember it. I guess it means that if what we are saying is true, it will be confirmed if the pudding is good. Waiting to see if the pudding sets up right or something like that. The news commentator was using it in the context of whether a politician's idea was going to be successful.

Isn't it wonderful that we don't have to wait to know

if God's Word is true? It is the only constant in this world. "Forever, O Lord, Your Word is settled in heaven" (Psalm 119:89).

One of the best sayings I have heard recently is that something may be a fact but not necessarily the truth. In other words, the doctor may tell you that an illness is terminal, which may be a fact, but the truth is that by Jesus' stripes you are healed. (1 Peter 2:24)

Your bank account on the brink of disaster may be a fact, but the Lord says He will supply all your needs according to His riches in glory in Christ Jesus. (Philippians 4:19)

Your family relationships in turmoil may be a fact, but the Word of God says that He will restore back to you the years the locust has eaten. (Joel 2:25)

The proof in the pudding is that God sent His only begotten Son to die for your sins so He could be reconciled to you. Jesus was wounded for our transgressions so that we could be made whole and live an abundant life in every way. (John 10:10)

We can always count on our faithful God to be more than enough for every problem or need we will ever have. "O, taste and see that the Lord is good" (Psalm 34:8).

"How sweet are Your words to my taste! Yes, sweeter than honey to my mouth!" (Psalm 119:103). This "Pudding" will never lose its flavor.

July 29th ~ The Names of the Lord

Psalm 20:7 says, "Some boast in chariots, and some in horses; but we will boast in the name of the Lord, our God." To boast means '"to have confidence in, to trust in." To boast in God's name means to have trust in Him. But if we don't know Him as we should, we can't boast in His name. To boast in His name is to have a settled confidence in everything He is.

As we study His many names mentioned in the Bible, we will always find one that meets our particular need. Proverbs 18:10 says, "The name of the Lord is a strong tower; the righteous run into it and are safe."

Is the Lord your strong tower? Is His name your fortress in a time of weariness, attack or great distress? If not, it may be that you don't really know your God, or you don't comprehend His fierce love and unspeakable tenderness and mercy toward you. None of us know enough about this wonderful God who loves us so! We could all profit by reviewing some of His names.

Elohim: The Creator
El Elyon: The God Most High
El Roi: The God Who Sees
El Shaddai: The All-Sufficient One
Adonai: The Lord
Jehovah: The Self-Existent One
Jehovah-jireh: The Lord Will Provide
Jehovah-rapha: The Lord Who Heals
Jehovah-nissi: The Lord My Banner
Jehovah-mekoddishkem: The Lord Who Sanctifies You
Jehovah-shalom: The Lord is Peace
Jehovah-raah: The Lord My Shepherd
Jehovah-tsidkenu: The Lord Our Righteousness
Jehovah-shammah: The Lord is There

July 30th ~ SOS

This morning the Lord whispered these precious words into my spirit: "Keep on believing my promises and I will bring them to pass. I, the Lord God Almighty say to you: never fear, I AM always near."

The great I AM loves me and is always near? How blessed and thankful I feel.

I love the words of the old hymn "Leaning on the Everlasting Arms." It says, "What have I to dread, what have I to fear Leaning on the everlasting arms? I have blessed peace with my Lord so near, Leaning on the everlasting arms."

It always reminds me of Song of Solomon 8:5 that says,

"Who is this coming up from the wilderness leaning on her beloved?" Many times my beloved Jesus has brought me out of the wilderness, even the wilderness in my mind. My thoughts can become pretty much of a wilderness - wild, I guess you might say, and the only way to change them is by leaning on Him.

SOS 2:4 says, "He has brought me to His banquet table and His banner over me is love."

When we are with Him, it is always a feast! As I was abbreviating SOS for Song of Solomon (an allegory of Jesus and His love for His bride: that's us, the Church), it struck me that we can always send up an SOS to Jesus. Of course, we know that SOS is the universal distress signal. Bill tells me it is three dots, three dashes, three dots.

Once he tapped this out on the horn of his scooter when he got stuck in the mud in our large side yard. At that time in his life he could not walk without help. I was working in another part of the yard and did not hear him. But a passerby saw him and stopped to help; a true good Samaritan. So all this reminds me that Jesus can hear us anywhere and anytime and will quickly answer our SOSs.

Praise His name!

July 31st ~ Sons of Korah

There are over 25 Psalms credited to the Sons of Korah who were among the song leaders appointed by King David. Wait a minute, wasn't it Korah who contended with Moses and Aaron in the wilderness? And the earth opened up and swallowed him and the others? I thought his family perished with him. But I looked it up in Numbers 26:11, that said, "Nevertheless the children of Korah did not die."

This makes us know that there is hope for anyone. There is another verse that reminds us that sons are not put to death for their fathers, or fathers for their sons. (2 Chronicles 25:4)

Yes, our Christian walk is a very individual thing. I

heard it said that God does not have grandchildren, but only children. We are each responsible for our own beliefs. Obviously, the sons of Korah did not agree with their father's rebellion. Many times throughout the Old Testament, they are listed with other Levites. Some were described as expert warriors, especially with the bow and sling, who joined David at Ziklag when he was being pursued by Saul. They are also mentioned as doorkeepers in the house of the Lord; what a wonderful designation to have.

David set them over the service of song in the house of the Lord and they are mentioned in bringing back the ark to Jerusalem. Many wonderful Psalms are credited to their account, but one of my favorites is Psalm 84:1, 2, that says, "How lovely is Your tabernacle, O Lord of Hosts! My soul longs, yes, even faints for the courts of the Lord; my heart and my flesh cry out for the living God."

Verse 10 says, "For a day in Your courts is better than a thousand elsewhere. I would rather be a doorkeeper in the house of my God than dwell in the tents of wickedness." I want this to be my testimony, too.

All of this shows that we can even overcome obstacles of unbelief or criminal lawlessness in our own families, for God sees us as new creations in Christ Jesus.

Praise the Lord!

August 1st ~ Mercy That Endures Forever

I certainly appreciate God's mercy. I desire it more than justice. And he has taught me to give grace to others. Matthew 5:7 says, "Blessed are the merciful for they shall obtain mercy."

I am always shocked to learn that some people are not very merciful. Our little town had a tragedy in 2004 when an automobile accident took the life of a precious girl going off to college for her freshman year. A 16-year-old girl driving the other car had been drinking. She was arrested, convicted and sentenced to nine years in prison! Most of the people I knew agreed that she should have been received probation to include alcohol rehab and community service like the others who were also involved in the accident.

I read a letter to the editor of the *News-Journal* saying that was not severe enough. Personally, I see nothing to be gained from this very sad and repentant girl going to prison. It seems to me that mercy was warranted. The prosecution wanted to make an example of her to discourage underage drinking but I don't think it will deter a single teen who wants to party. They all think they are bulletproof at that age and nothing will happen to them.

God's mercy endures forever. His willingness to act on man's behalf is still operating in the earth. His mercy never runs out. Neither has it abated or weakened. His mercy continues towards those who love Him and do His Word. He is faithful to keep His covenant and offer His mercy to those who call on Him. (Psalm 136, Deuteronomy 7:9, Psalm 86:5)

As you confess God's mercy, have faith and say, "Surely goodness and mercy shall follow me all the days of my life" (Psalm 23:6).

August 2nd ~ His Joy in Us

Jesus desires that His joy be fulfilled in us. In the High Priestly prayer to the Father in John 17:13. Jesus said "that we may have His joy made full in us." He also tells us in John 16: 24 "that if we ask anything in His name we will receive so that our joy may be full." And in John 15:11 He says, "These things I have spoken to you so that My joy may be in you and that your joy may be made full."

How clear are these verses that Jesus desires us to be full of joy. So exciting! So we should definitely wonder if for some reason we don't have joy since it is a fruit of the Spirit and His Spirit resides in us. (Galatians 5:22)

In the early Charismatic movement in the 1970s, we used to sing a tune that we would have joy like a fountain in our souls; bubbling up. Even in upsetting times, we can still have Jesus' joy in our soul.

I heard a preacher tell a funny story about having a fight with his wife. While they were arguing, the doorbell rang. He had scheduled an appointment for counseling but did not feel like talking to anyone. But in obedience to the Lord, he listened and then prayed with the lady to have guidance. She told him afterwards that she could see the joy of the Lord in him and what a blessing he had been to her. So our joy is there whether we feel it or not. Praise the Lord!

August 3rd ~ "The Best Things in Life Are Free"

The lyrics to this old song kept going over and over in my mind and I realized they were truth:

"The moon belongs to everyone.
The best things in life are free.
The stars belong to everyone.
They gleam there for you and me.
And love can come to everyone.
The best things in life are free."

In the first chapter of Genesis we read how God made the moon and the stars to light the night and to give light to the earth. Then Jesus said, "I am the Light of the world" (John 8:12).

I was thinking how certain celebrities are called 'stars' which, I guess, means they shine. Some are even known as 'superstars.' Of course, no earthly person shines like our Jesus. The musical, *Jesus Christ Superstar,* had beautiful music and I always hoped it was written by Christians. I am not sure, but hopefully it made people at least think about Him, as He is truly the only real Superstar and our very own Super Hero. With Him nothing is impossible.

God Himself is love and He will come to everyone who will allow Him. He sent His only Son to prove His love – what more can He do?

The best thing in life really is free: OUR SALVATION! Jesus paid it all with His sacrifice on the cross. It cost Him everything, but it's free to all of us. Praise His name.

August 4th ~ Little People of America

What a shock years ago, when Billy, Julianne and I drove into the Villa Capri Motel in Austin, Texas, and I saw the swimming pool filled with "little people." The marquee noted that there was a convention of what we called 'dwarfs.' We felt like giants in the land or maybe even a little like Gulliver must have felt in his travels. It was a very strange feeling. We had never seen so many tiny people all in one place at one time. Julie was afraid to swim as she would have been the only normal size person in the pool. (I think she was about eight or nine at the time and we were on our way to see Grace at Camp Waldemar in the Hill Country.)

The next morning at breakfast, we felt strange again since we the only big people in the crowded dining room. We stuck out like sore thumbs. I began to think how they must feel when they are the only 'little people' in a room full of us. This is the way it almost always is with them. Nobody likes to be different or to be stared at. It was a good lesson to understand how it feels to be the strangers in a group.

In thinking of the spiritual message here, I began to think of how the Bible calls us as believers to stand out, to be "peculiar" people. (KJV: 1Peter 2:9, Titus 2:14) Most of the newer versions call us "His special treasure, His own special people, His chosen possession." We are to be different from the world. We are "called out" to be His very own people. We are called to be separate from the things of the world. "Chosen" designates one picked out from a larger group for special purposes and privileges. How exciting is that? 1 Peter 2:11 also calls us "strangers, sojourners and pilgrims" here on earth. We are dwelling here as "resident aliens." (1 Peter 1:17)

Our true home is Heaven where we will not notice anyone's differences. We will all be together in Christ.

August 5th ~ Living Free From Strife and Offense

Strife is defined as: fighting, heated and often violent conflict; bitter dissension; a struggle between rivals; or contention.

Living free from strife and offense is not a suggestion but a command from Jesus Himself. (Matthew 22:37, 39)

Paul prayed for us and clearly believed it was possible for born again children of God to be rooted and grounded in love and then be filled with the fullness of God. (Ephesians 3:14-21)

Since God is love, when we comprehend and live completely in it, we reveal God in His fullness. The full comprehension of God's love doesn't just fall on us like an apple falling out of a tree. It must grow within us, starting with a seed. As we begin to meditate on it, confess it, and align our lives with it, the command to love begins to root itself in our minds and hearts. If we stick with it, eventually we will become so grounded in the commandment of love that we'll judge our whole lives by it. Hence, if somebody says something ugly to us, instead of lashing out at them, we search for a way to keep the commandment and respond to them in love.

It's actually a very simple process, so simple in fact that you might wonder why we seem to have such a difficult time with it. Why do we quickly, and so often, lose sight of this all-important commandment of a life free from stress and offense?

As our relationship with the Lord grows, we begin to strongly desire His peace. When we come to the point that we intensely hunger and thirst after peace, the Holy Spirit starts teaching us about the dangers of strife. We learn to recognize it and quickly resist the enemy. We need to treat strife as a dangerous enemy that will bring destruction to our life. The more we practice yielding to God's peace and love, the stronger His love is revealed.

August 6th ~ "Restore"

How excited I was to receive a good teaching about restoration from an email sent me from prayer partner Diane Gilbert. The teaching by a certain preacher really thrilled me by showing new meaning to a scripture in Isaiah 42:22, "But this is a people robbed and plundered; all of them are snared in holes, and they are hidden in prison houses; they are for prey, and no one delivers; for plunder, and no one says, 'Restore'."

He lists three keys to restoration.

1. Christians are anointed to declare "Restore!" It's like God is saying, "If somebody would have said, 'Restore!' I would have delivered those people who were robbed." The devil comes to steal, but God has provided a remedy so that we can reverse and restore those situations devastated by the enemy. Simply declaring, "Restore!" is powerful. Things change.

2. Stand in faith and be "Repairers" and "Restorers." We need to believe that we can rebuild the ruins and be repairers in the body of Christ. Isaiah 58:12 says, "Those from among you shall build the old waste places; you shall raise up the foundations of many generations; and you shall be called the Repairer of the Breach, the Restorer of streets to dwell in."

3. Prepare ourselves for the ministry of restoration. We can do this by remembering God's goodness to us in the past and by reminding God of His promises to us. "Remember the word to Your servant, upon which You have caused me to hope" (Psalm 119:49).

God wants you to know that He will restore what has been plundered and robbed by the enemy whether it is health, relationships, finances or whatever. Our part is to speak His Word to our problems and declare "Restore!"

August 7th ~ "Non-O-Ya"

One thing I notice as I get older is my tendency to speak my mind on things that are absolutely none of my business. Today I had to control myself from telling a young man, who was well dressed, that it is not correct to wear white socks with a black suit. Talk about "non-o-ya" - the phrase that our boys said to each other when they were young. It was short for "none of your business." I must have heard them say it a million times.

Right after seeing the young man's glaring white socks, I saw a woman walking across the street with a cigarette dangling from her mouth. I could hear my mother's saying ringing in my ears that a lady never smoked while walking and I wanted to share that with the woman on the street.

Back when I was growing up, and then as a young adult, almost everyone smoked. It was very accepted. (Easy to believe when you watch old movies and see them smoking - it actually looked glamorous to us.) But ladies had certain rules. Men could walk and smoke, but not us. Back then, we even carried small engraved 'silent butlers' to put our ashes in while at a tea or other stand-up parties. I still have a large silver 'silent butler' that I would use to empty the ash trays when entertaining at home. (This was before we knew cigarettes were not good for our health.)

Another thing that is almost more than I can bear is to see women and girls chewing gum at church and other inappropriate places. I do nag my own children and grandchildren about this habit. These taboos are certainly not sins and it is not my place to try to change people. I am called to show them the love of Jesus. He convicts, but does not condemn. (Romans 8:1)

My prayer is: "Set a guard, O Lord, over my mouth; keep watch over the door of my lips." Amen! (Psalm 141:3)

August 8th ~ "In the Garden"

This has always been a favorite hymn of mine. I read that the author of this wonderful hymn meditated on the scripture in John 20:14 "…she turned around and saw Jesus standing there…" The art of mediating on scripture involves using one's imagination. Instead of simply reading the passage, we must read it, close our eyes and visualize the scene; perhaps even putting ourselves in the picture. That's what pharmacist C. Austin Miles did before he wrote *In the Garden.* He actually felt like he saw Mary when she was sobbing at the tomb of Jesus. And then saw her joy when she turned and saw Him. Under the inspiration of this vision, he quickly wrote these stirring words and later the same evening he wrote the music:

"I come to the garden alone while the dew is still on the roses, and the voice I hear, falling on my ear, the Son of God discloses. And He walks with me and He talks with me and He tells me I am His own, and the joy we share as we tarry there, none other has ever known."

As we meditate on the scripture "…she turned around and saw Jesus there…" we can almost picture her excitement and wonder as she sees that her beloved is truly alive. She knelt in awe before Him, with arms outstretched, and looking into His lovely face she cried, "Rabboni!"

Kenneth Copeland teaches on how the Lord taught him to meditate on the Word beginning with the passage about the Pool of Bethesda in the fifth chapter of John. In obedience, brother Kenneth began to picture that scene with the multitude of sick people waiting for an angel to stir the waters. Suddenly the entire passage became alive for him and he has never read it the same since.

We, too, can do this with all the scriptures. They become so much more real and meaningful to us.

August 9th ~ "Immediately"

Mark's gospel is full of the word "immediately." I like Mark because he is like me and is in a hurry to tell his story (Bill says Burke and I want "immediate" gratification). I also like the fact that Mark believes our God is an "immediate" God. Once I started counting how many times Mark used that word and it was over 30 times. People were healed, made whole and all fed "immediately" by Jesus. Jesus was even "immediately" recognized by the people when He did these wonderful miracles.

Mark's is the shortest of the gospel (good news) stories and is a fast-moving narrative of the life of Jesus and tells of 21 miracles that He performed. It reads like a newspaper story and is very good for the new Christian to get into the New Testament.

Certainly I wish all prayers were answered immediately but realistically I know this is not always going to happen. But I am always touched at how quickly He does speak to me saying to trust Him when I am tempted to fear.

In Mark 6:47-50, we read the story about the wind on the sea causing the disciples to struggle at rowing their boat. Then Jesus came to them walking on the water and they thought He was a ghost and were afraid. But "immediately" He said to them, "Be of good cheer! It is I; be not afraid."

"Immediately" He calms our spirits, too, by telling us all is well and to trust him. He does not want us to have one moment of fear. He is so precious.

Then in Mark 6:51, we read that Jesus got into the boat with them and the wind ceased. When He gets into our boats, the winds of adversity coming against us cease, too. Praise His holy name!

August 10th ~ Singing a Hymn

In reading about the Last Supper in the Bible we see that the disciples would sing a hymn after they took the bread and the wine. I'll never forget when someone asked me if I knew which hymn they sang. I felt really dumb as I had never thought about it. Since I knew that the book of the Psalms was the Jewish hymnal of the day, I guessed correctly that it might be one of them. How excited I was to learn that the certain hymn that was sung after every Passover service was called the *Hallel* and was comprised of Psalms 115-118. I realized anew that it behooved me to learn more and more about the Passover service.

I began to think how rude it had been of Bill, the little boys, and me to leave immediately after taking communion at the Episcopal Church instead of staying for the thank-you prayer. (Talk about "eating and running.") I know we are forgiven but I still am sorry for the awful example we set for the children. I still am guilty of doing that in my prayer time; just getting up and leaving without really thanking the Lord for the blessing I had just received. I now take communion almost every morning and Bill and I take it together on Saturday. What precious times of fellowship with the Lord.

We are always careful not to make it into some kind of ritual that loses its significance, just something we do but not just to be doing it. No, I want it to stay meaningful to us as we remember Jesus' sacrifice. In 1 Corinthians 11:23-26 we are told to call Jesus affectionately to remembrance. (Amplified) Yes, we do this to be truly grateful for His sacrifice bought for us. Not only forgiveness of sins, but blessings of health, prosperity and every other good thing that we need for daily living. Thank You, Jesus!

August 11th ~ Tug of War, by Rev. Melanie Hart, Friend, Editor

"Therefore, prepare your minds for action; be self-controlled; set your hope fully on the grace given to you when Jesus Christ was revealed. As obedient children, do not conform to the evil desires you had when you lived in ignorance. But just as He who called you is holy, so be holy in all you do; for it is written: "Be holy, because I am holy." (1 Peter 1:13-16)

Society teaches us that we need to 'see it to believe it'. But in God's Kingdom, it's the exact opposite: we need to believe it first, and then we'll see it. This is where the tug of war begins! There is an ongoing battle inside of us. Our unrenewed soul and body is fighting with our renewed spirit: faith versus unbelief; flesh versus spirit.

In other words, our flesh (soul and body) wants to think ungodly thoughts of fear and unbelief. It wants to eat and say whatever it wants, but our spirit does not want to act like that anymore. Romans 12:2 says, "Do not conform to the pattern of this world, but be transformed by the renewing of your mind. Then you will be able to test and approve what God's will is - His good, pleasing and perfect will."

This constant struggle between the flesh and spirit is what Paul talks about in Romans and here is the answer: "I thank God that our Lord Jesus Christ rescues me! So I am obedient to God's standards with my mind, but I am obedient to sin's standards with my corrupt nature" (Romans 7:4). God is the only one who has the power to rescue us from the great tug of war of soul and spirit. As He does the work, attitudes change, values are rearranged, and our words reflect our new nature.

"No one can serve two masters; for either he will hate the one and love the other, or he will be devoted to one and despise the other" (Matthew 6:24a). He works from inside our spirit, taking all the good things that God gave us at salvation and works them through our soul until they're eventually seen on the outside, in our words, attitudes and actions.

August 12th ~ God Calling

God Calling is my all time favorite devotional book. It was written by two ladies in England who preferred to remain anonymous and be called "Two Listeners." The claim they make is that these messages have all been given by the Living Christ Himself. And I believe them. These two prayer partners were meeting daily for prayer in a time of turmoil and war in England. In their personal lives, they were facing sickness, poverty and a hopeless future unless the Lord intervened. As they prayed, the Holy Spirit comforted their hearts and cheered their spirits giving them new hope for the future. Their spiritual journey has blessed thousands and still blesses us today.

They stood on Jesus' promise in Matthew 18:18-19, "If two of you shall agree on earth as touching anything that they shall ask, it shall be done for them by my Father which is in Heaven, for where two or three or gathered together in My name there am I in the midst of them."

All the devotionals are inspired but a particular one touched my heart this week as our country is facing difficult times and this will encourage us to continue diligently in prayer.

Note: the following is from the devotional from *God Calling* entitled "Rule the World."

"Remember, no prayer goes unanswered. Remember that the moment a thing seems wrong to you, or a person's actions to be not what you think they should be, at that moment begins your obligation, and responsibility to pray for those wrongs to be righted, or that person to be different.

"Face your responsibilities. What is wrong in your country — its statesmen, its laws, its people? Think quietly, and make these matters of prayer. You will see lives changed, laws made at your request, and evils banished.

"Yes! Live in a large sense. Live to serve and to save. You may never go beyond one room and yet you may become one of the most powerful forces for good in your country, in the world.

"You may never see the mighty work you do, but God sees it, evil sees it. Oh! It is a glorious life, the life of one who saves. Fellow-workers together with Me. See this more and more. Love with Me, sharers of My life".

August 13th ~ Giving

Exodus 23:15 says, "None shall appear before Me empty handed." And in Verse 16 we are admonished to give our "first fruits" to Him. We should always give God our best and not our leftovers.

2 Corinthians Chapters 8 and 9 are both about giving. The Macedonia church excelled in giving; out of their poverty they gave to needy Christian brothers. But this scripture makes a point of saying that they FIRST gave themselves to the Lord and THEN to the will of God. He wants all of us committed to Him, much more than He wants our gifts.

Christ is our pattern for giving - He gave His all. (2 Corinthians 9:6-15)

It is possible to give away and become richer because we are building up treasures in Heaven. "He who gives to the poor will never lack" (Proverbs 28:27).

When we think of giving, we first think of money or material things. But we can give of our time in prayer, or acts of service, or encouragement, or whatever the Lord leads us to do. It will always be multiplied back to us. (Luke 6:38)

We need to free our hearts from our possessions; they all belong to God anyway and have no eternal value. Jesus tells us to not lay up for ourselves treasures on earth that can be stolen, but lay up for ourselves treasures in heaven that will last forever. (Matthew 6:20)

August 14th ~ "I Can Do All Things Through Christ Who Strengthens Me"

This has always been one of my favorite verses from Philippians 4:13 and I have quoted it often. But it never had much meaning to me until April of this year when I had bilateral knee replacement surgery. Many people were amazed that at 80 years young I had chosen to do both at one time; but not my very young and skillful Dr. Jordan Stanley in Longview. He said attitude was the most important asset and he could tell I had the right attitude in trusting the Lord. How secure I felt knowing I had a Christian surgeon praying over me and I knew I had the prayers of family, friends, and friends from Bible studies from California to Texas.

Horrors though when the very first morning after surgery they wanted me up and dressed! Daughter Grace was there to be my 'coach' and she just kept reminding me of this verse. She rolled me to the rehab room and I managed to do a few of the exercises, saying over and over and over, "I can do all things through Christ who strengthens me." And how excited I was to see that same verse on the placard in the room!

This routine continued for four days in the hospital and 10 more in rehab, with Christ strengthening me more, I realized how blessed I was to have such support from not only Grace, but all my family and the nurses and therapists that the Lord brought into my path. I felt such favor of the Lord. Daughter-in-law Donna and adopted son, nurse David Bruyere, took turns spending the night with me.

I could never thank everyone enough so I gave the Lord credit for the wonderful people in my life. They were so faithful, beginning with precious husband Bill, who went above and beyond in giving me special care.

Amazing, too, was our son Tim who came from Los Angeles to take over my home rehab. He stayed a month and was another wonderful 'coach.' Plus he took care of his dad when he had cataract surgery on both eyes. This was before I could drive or help; some ran and the grandchildren brought food. Again, how blessed I feel to have such a loving family! Special kudos go to Baby Grace and to Will and Amber who had our 17th great-grandchild, William Carson Payne, while I was in the hospital. What a blessing!

Tim took me to my first-month visit with the doctor

who raved that I was his poster child for doing so well; that many single knee patients were not as far along as I was. It was true that I could give all the glory to God. I was anxious to start driving but he told Tim to take me out on country roads to practice stopping fast and, when he wasn't scared of my driving anymore, I would be good to go. Tim said there was a slight problem as he had always been scared of my driving and was not sure that would change. Not funny.

It's been four months now as I am writing this and I hardly think about my knees anymore; certainly no more pain at all. God is so good and proves His Word over and over. It really is the truth: "I CAN do all things through Christ who strengthens me."

August 15th ~ Esther

In the book of Esther, Chapters 4-7, we read the story about how an evil man Haman had convinced King Xerxes to make a decree to kill all the Jews in the land. The King did not know that his wife Esther was Jewish. She was raised by her cousin Mordecai and he warned her of the problem and told her she must help save herself and all her people by asking the King to change the order. After prayer and fasting, she bravely went into the throne room, knowing that unless the King held out his scepter to her, she could be killed.

Instead of making her petition immediately, she only asked the King and Haman to come to a banquet that night. At the dinner, the King kept asking her what she wanted saying that he would give her up to half his kingdom, but she only requested that they come to another feast the next night.

It had always been a little hard for me to understand why Esther did not ask the king for her request at the first banquet. The Lord finally showed me that she was spending time in fellowship with him, instead of just rushing in and spilling out all her problems. What a lesson for us. We need to spend time with the Lord before we spew out our petitions.

It is difficult for me to go slow like this example as I am very pragmatic and always in a hurry. If I need something, I don't want to put off asking. I just jump right in. (I do this with my husband, too.) How much better to wait for the perfect timing!

After I finished writing these thoughts in my journal this morning, I quickly began listing all my prayer needs. The Lord actually laughed and said, "Sister, are you practicing what you preach?" He has really got my number and has such a marvelous sense of humor.

August 16th ~ Say My Name, by Julie Setzer, Daughter

My name is Julianne. I am named after my maternal grandfather Julian, who died when I was 10. I remember him as a fun, full-of-life man. I have a couple of nieces who are named after me so I understand the special feeling you get when someone is named in your honor. I imagine my grandfather Julian loved me very much and probably got a certain joy each time he said my name.

When I was about 14, I started introducing myself to others as Julie and now the only folks who still call me Julianne are a few family members and my childhood friend Gayle. A couple of my friends call me 'Jewels.' They write that on birthday cards, not Jules, which I think is so sweet.

When my very kind husband Frank (who has a very heavy East Texas accent as we all do around these parts) says my name it sounds more like 'jelly' than 'Julie' which cracks me up nearly every time I hear him say it. His nickname for me is 'Buttercup." Not sure when or why that originated, probably from a movie or something, but if you saw me, you would think 'butter-house' would be more appropriate if we are using it as a size indicator. He has been calling me that for years, even before I got fluffy, so it is definitely a term of endearment and I never tire of hearing him call me that. It literally brings a smile to my face and a softness to any situation.

The reason why my name is even on my mind today is that God said it to me this morning and it was an amazing moment for me. I had just walked out of my bathroom and was headed out the door to go to work. I had caught a glimpse of myself in the bathroom mirror and was, as always, thoroughly disgusted with myself and grossly disappointed in who I am and what I look like.

On the short walk from the bathroom to my back door, God said, "I love you, Julie. All the things you hate about yourself - I love those things. And all the things you don't like in other people, well, I love those things too!" Now bear with me, I'm not trying to say that God loves sin or that He wants us to live in sin. I'm just saying that He loves people no matter what. He totally knows you and loves you and He loves me! What a lovely thing to hear first thing in the morning and what a lovely affect it has on me and on my attitude towards other people.

It truly is music to one's ears to hear a loved one say their name and it is heavenly music to my ears to hear my Best Friend, my Lord, my Savior, my Redeemer say MY name with such love and grace. Hallelujah, God knows my name and not only that but Isaiah 49:16 tells me that He has it written on the palm of His precious, nail-scarred hand! The idea of MY name written on HIS hand is very exciting to me. I am beyond grateful.

August 17th ~ Bravo, God, Bravo

Reading this in Psalm 29:1-2 in the Message Bible made me want to jump up and applaud our fabulous God. "Bravo, God bravo! God and all angels shout, encore! Stand in awe before the glory, in awe before God's visible power. Stand at attention! Dress your best to honor Him. He has done great and mighty things for us."

These words sound so much more exciting than the traditional version of "Ascribe to the Lord, O sons of the mighty, Ascribe to the Lord glory and strength. Ascribe to the Lord the glory due to His name; Worship the Lord in holy array."

There have been times at the theater when an audience jumps to their feet and applauds the performance and shouts "Encore!" It has always been so thrilling. I can only imagine when we saints with all the company of Heaven shout 'glory' to our fantastic God who is worthy of all praise and honor and glory. I think I'll do it now!

I thought about being dressed in our best to honor Him. When I was growing up, we wore our 'Sunday best' to church: hats and gloves for the ladies and suits and ties for the men, even the children. When Grace was only about two, she had a tiny white leather purse with a gold chain about the size of my hand and I would put an extra pair of panties in there in case she had an accident at Sunday school.

Old-timers in the rural areas would call them their "Sunday go to meeting clothes" and would never dream of going in the sort of clothes we wear to church today: jeans, T-shirts, shorts, or whatever. In a way, today's informality is good as it gets people there who would never attend in more formal dress. However, I know this is not what is meant by this verse. The true meaning is to be dressed in His righteousness alone. (Isaiah 61:10)

August 18th ~ Peter

At least he got out of the boat and that's more than the other disciples did. We all know the story of how Peter walked on the water and only started to sink when he took his eyes off Jesus and looked at the wind and the waves. (Matthew 14:22-33) We need to focus on the positive here: he actually DID walk on the water! Wow, for a faith like that! 2 Corinthians 5:7 says, "For we walk by faith and not by sight."

How many of us would have held on to the boat or never gotten out to try to walk? What keeps us from making a step of faith when the Lord asks us to? What keeps us from getting out of our own boat? FEAR.

1. Fear of circumstances - waiting until everything is alright, until the water is smooth. Romans 8:15 says, "You did not receive the spirit of bondage again to fear, but you received the spirit of adoption by whom we cry out, Abba, Father."
2. Fear of failure - looking bad if we do not succeed. 2 Timothy 1:7 says, "God has not given you the spirit of fear, but of power and of love and of a sound mind."
3. Fear of what others might say - like she's crazy. Isaiah 54:17 says, "No weapon formed against you shall prosper, and every tongue which rises against you in judgment you shall condemn, this is the heritage of the servants of the Lord and their righteousness is from Me, says the Lord."
4. Fear of change - leaving our comfort zone. (This one gets me.) Proverbs 3:5-6 says, "Trust in the Lord with all your heart, and lean not on your own understanding; in all your ways acknowledge Him and He shall direct your paths."
5. Fear of losing control - so hard to give up the control of our lives. Matthew 11:28 says, "Come to Me, all you who labor and are heavy laden and I will give you rest."
6. Fear of our lives - we are called to live selflessly. Revelation 12:11 says, "And they overcame him by the blood of the Lamb and the word of their testimony, and they did not love their lives to the death."

August 19th ~ "I Have Decided to Follow Jesus"

What a wonderful hymn that I have always loved. But as I was listening to a Christian radio station, I heard the fascinating story of its beginning. It seems that in a small village in India a man was being persecuted for being a Christian. He was told that if he did not renounce his faith in Jesus that his children would be killed. He stood strong saying that he had decided to follow Jesus and would not turn back. So he had to watch as they shot all his children. Then they told him they were going to shoot his wife and he still kept saying that he had decided to follow Jesus and would not turn back.

So again he had to watch as they shot and killed his wife. Now it was his own life that was now at stake. The religious zealots attacking him stood amazed as he again repeated the words that he had decided to follow Jesus and would not turn back. As he was shot and died, one of the attackers was so impressed with this man's witness to his love for Jesus that he became a Christian and later wrote this hymn. It is attributed to S. Sundar Singh and is a Hindustan melody.

I guess you would say that this is a hymn of decision. (Luke 9:57) Naturally, I immediately wondered if I could possibly be that strong in my commitment if I was tested in this manner. Only Jesus could give anyone that sort of grace. Corrie ten Boom wrote years ago how her father explained grace to her. When she went to the train station, he gave her the ticket. So she understood that she would have the grace — like the ticket — when she needed it. What a good example.

"I have decided to follow Jesus, no turning back; Though I may wonder, I still will follow, no turning back; The world behind me the cross before me, no turning back; Though none go with me, I still will follow, no turning back, no turning back." These are powerful words to ponder.

August 20th ~ Wrong Sayings

Growing up I heard many statements about religion that I have since learned were misleading or even wrong. Thankfully I don't believe they are heard quite as much nowadays. To list a few:

1. To be so heavenly minded is to be no earthly good.

   I really want to be heavenly minded; keeping my mind stayed on Jesus and letting Jesus Himself guide me in good works. (Ephesians 2:10)

2. Any religion that helps a person is alright.

   I now know that many religions are dangerous with their wrong thinking so this one is wrong, too. Plus, Christianity is not a religion, but a relationship.

3. God helps those who help themselves.

   And this one is the most oft-quoted incorrect statement – actually God helps the helpless. God helps us when our strength is gone.

4. Every tub should stand on its own feet.

   Man is trying in his own strength and not depending on God

5. The devil made me do it.

   It's sorta nice to blame the devil for our own wrong doings, but it will not cut water with our Lord. We must resist the devil and he will flee from us. (1 Peter 5:8, 9)

6. I never trust a person who says they personally hear from God.

   All believers can and should hear from the Lord daily. He speaks to us in His Word, by the Holy Spirit whispering to our spirit (John 16:13) and sometimes even in an audible voice. He walks with me and He talks with me and He tells me I am His own. So let's be alert for the Holy Spirit speak-

ing. He is always more willing to talk than we are to listen.

August 21st ~ Lord of the Breakthrough

(Baal Perazim 1 Chronicles 14:8-17 and 2 Samuel 5:19-25)
How exciting it is when we truly believe that the Lord of the Breakthrough will act on our behalf. Here are some of the things we can expect when God comes through for us:

1. He brings us out of bondage. (Genesis 50:4)
2. He revives and refreshes us. (Job 12:10)
3. He preserves us from trouble. (Psalm 32:7)
4. He crowns our lives with bounty and goodness and supernatural increase. (Psalm 65:9, Amplified)

When I think of the Lord of the Breakthrough, I think of Jesus Himself coming to fight my battles. I always tear up when I read the passage in Revelation 19 that describes His coming again, our true Knight in shining armor: "Behold a white horse. And He who sat on him was called Faithful and True, and in righteousness He judges and makes war. He was clothed with a robe dipped in blood, and His name is called The Word of God. And out of His mouth goes a sharp sword and He has on His robe and on His thigh a name written: KINGS OF KINGS, LORD OF LORDS." Is that exciting or what? That is He who fights for us. The Captain of the Lord of Hosts is He! What problem can withstand that sort of power?

The truth is that God really loves us. We just need to believe and be totally convinced that He yearns to be the Lord of the Breakthrough for us personally and individually. There is such peace, assurance and comfort that God will see us through. He can and He WILL break through for us. Breakthroughs are on the way!

August 22nd ~ Boomerang

I just read something about what we send out – blessing or cursing — comes back to us just like a boomerang. I bet that is why Jesus tells us in Matthew 5:44 "Love your enemies, bless those who curse you, pray for those who spitefully use you and persecute you."

Bill reminded me of a silly rhyme we used to say as kids: "I'm rubber, you're glue; whatever you say about me bounces off me and sticks on you." This might be true! If we bless someone, the blessing comes back to us. So does the cursing.

We find this to be a principle throughout the Bible. In Matthew 10, Jesus sends out His disciples and empowers them to heal the sick and cast out unclean spirits and to preach the kingdom of heaven is at hand. He told them in Verses 12 and 13, "And when you go into a household, greet it and wish it well. If the household is worthy, let your peace come upon it. But if it is not worthy, let your peace return to you." (Amplified)

Proverbs 25:21-22 quoted in Romans 12:20 says, "If your enemy be hungry, give him bread to eat, and if he be thirsty, give him water to drink; for in so doing you will heap coals of fire upon his head and the Lord will reward you."

The notes in the Amplified Bible explain this is not to be understood as a vengeful act, intended to embarrass it's victim, but just the opposite. The picture is that of the high priest who on the Day of Atonement took his censer and filled it with "coals of fire" from the altar of burnt offering and then put incense on them for a pleasing, sweet-smelling fragrance. The cloud covered the mercy seat and was acceptable to God for atonement.

Sounds like reaping what we are sowing, doesn't it? (Galatians 6:7) Help me, Father, to remember to speak words of blessing. Amen.

August 23rd ~ Benefits of God's Favor

The Favor of God is for your success. That is the purpose. The reason is so He will look good and appeal to others. Someone may notice it and call it luck. But we don't confuse luck with favor. I don't live by luck but by the favor of God. Favor will help you to get a raise or find a discount while shopping.

There are magnificent benefits of God's favor. Here are a few:

Our petitions are more likely to be granted through the favor of God. Esther 7:3 says, "Then Queen Esther answered, 'If I have found favor in your sight, O king, and if it please the king, let my life be given me at my petition; and my people at my request.'" He granted her request.

We will receive life if we declare the favor of God over our lives and our families. "His favor is for life" (Psalm 30:5).

God will show mercy on your behalf. Psalm 119:58 says, "I entreated Your favor with my whole heart: be merciful unto me according to Your Word."

Our enemies will not triumph over us when we live in God's favor. Psalm 41:11 says, "By this I know that You favor me, because mine enemy does not triumph over me."

God will encompass us with a shield when we understand God's favor. Psalm 5:12 says, "For You, Lord, will bless the righteous; with favor as with a shield."

We can grow in favor both with God and with man as did the child Samuel (1 Samuel 2:26) and the child Jesus (Luke 2:52). Every one of God's people should desire and seek to have favor in the eyes of the Lord. We grow in that favor as we faithfully live for the Lord and believe His Word.

August 24th ~ Walk The Walk

A Christian speaker asked, "Are you walking the walk or just talking the talk?" How convicting. I know all the Christian 'buzz' words and talk a really good game. But the proof is in the pudding. Does your daily walk really reflect Jesus Christ? I need to check myself each day. Am I walking in love and forgiveness? Do I have peace and joy in the midst of trouble? Do I judge others before I judge myself? Do I show patience and self-control? Do I have faith and trust instead of worry and fear? My answer should be 'yes.' With God's help, I pray to walk this 'love walk' of His.

When daughter Julianne, 16, had her first car, a cute little Ford Pinto, she covered it with Christian stickers. I warned her that if she was going to 'advertise' her love of Jesus, she needed to be very careful always to act like a Christian because people would be watching to see if she lived up to her hype. When I discovered that she was letting some pretty wild boys drive her car, I suggested that she better stop or take off her fish and other Christian symbols. Thankfully, she now is a truly committed Christian who really 'walks the walk.'

By the way, for this reason I have never put any stickers on my car because I sometimes drive too fast or run a caution light or other infractions. I certainly don't want people to think Jesus would drive like me and break the law.

One good thing came of Julie's stickers. A new believer in town was passing by our house and saw her car and thought, "How nice, Christians live in this house." She ended up attending our weekly prayer group and she would not have known we were believers without Julie's witness. So there is a balance. We want to wear our crosses and other Christian symbols, but just be careful to always live up to His name; to 'walk the walk' not just 'talk the talk.'

"But be ye doers of the Word and not hearers only, deceiving yourselves" (James 1:22).

August 25th ~ When God's People Get Blessed

Think about it, when God's people are blessed, He receives the respect He deserves from the world. Religious tradition has taught that God gets glory when we suffer sickness or poverty nobly but that is not what the Bible teaches at all. It teaches that God gets glory when we're healed, healthy and blessed! God gets glory when we're plenteous in goods. He gets glory when we have a surplus of prosperity. (Deuteronomy 28:11)

He wants us blessed today, tomorrow and the future. Hebrews 13:8 says, "Jesus Christ is the same yesterday and today and forever." God is able and eager to bless us because He knows we will give Him glory when we're blessed. (2 Corinthians 9:8, Amplified)

He wants us to live and reign like kings. (Romans 5:17) And now, because of the covenant blood of Jesus and the power of the indwelling Holy Spirit, we can do it, not just physically but spiritually. Ephesians 3:20 says, "Now to Him Who, by the power that is at work within us, is able to do superabundantly, far over and above all that we ask or think…" (Amplified Bible)

He wants us to do what Abraham did to believe His Word and act on it. He wants us to walk upright before Him. He wants us to fully take advantage of His covenant of blessing so that we astonish the world. He wants us to be so assured of His blessings that we can stop being concerned about ourselves and start being a blessing to all the families of the earth.

And above all He wants us to give Him the glory, knowing that all our blessings come from Him.

August 26th ~ Joy In Christ, by Donna Payne, Daughter-in-law

As I spend time this morning in prayer and quiet time, I find myself reading the introduction to Paul's letter to Philippians. How the Spirit guides us, if we listen! This message is exactly what I need to pull out of the despair I let myself fall into. Although I have read this before, today God opened my eyes, talking directly to me through it.

Lately I have become overwhelmed by my circumstances and have allowed Satan to steal my joy. I have been depressed because things aren't working out this summer as I had 'trusted' they would. I now see I was not really trusting. I have been expecting happiness to come through my time on Vinalhaven Island in Maine.

Instead, here I am on this beautiful island, in this beautiful home, with my beautiful husband and sons, feeling blue and discouraged. I find myself neglecting to appreciate the gift I am given because of the lack of business here this summer. Yes, I was counting on a profitable summer season. But can't that 'profit' be in the joyous time together with my boys, having conversations that my usual schedule doesn't permit?

The introduction to Philippians opened my eyes to my mistake. "...often happiness flees and despair sets in. In contrast to happiness stands joy. Running deeper and stronger, joy is the quiet, confident assurance of God's love and work in our lives - that He will be there no matter what! Happiness depends on happenings, but joy depends on Christ."

Wow! It is as if God had to hit me over the head! I have been telling myself to "rejoice in the Lord always" but haven't been listening. I was searching for happiness in circumstances, rather than seeking the joy that is found in Christ that is here with me at all times and in all circumstances.

Thank You, dear Lord, for opening my eyes and revealing Your presence (and presents) to me. Help me as I rededicate myself to finding joy in Christ rather than seeking happiness in what the world can provide.

August 27th ~ Great Hymn Writers

Isaac Watts - 1674-1748 — is referred to as the father of English hymns and wrote over 600 of our most familiar ones. I first became interested in him when I was reading a biography of Robert E. Lee, the famous Confederate general. It seems that when the soldiers ran out of paper to use for wadding in their rifles, they would tear up hymnals from the churches. Then would shout a battle cry of: "Let's give them some Watts, boys."

In appearance, Isaac Watts was, well, odd. Standing five feet in his stockings, he had an outsized head and prominent nose and his skin was tallowy. One lady, having never met him, fell in love with him through his hymns and poems. But when she saw him face-to-face, she was unsettled. He fell in love with her, but she couldn't bring herself to marry him. She later said, "I only wish I could admire the casket (jewelry box) as much as I admire the jewel."

Well, I know we are all thinking how superficial she was because he was a brilliant man having learned Latin at age five and also was a magnificent preacher. We are all guilty of judging a person by outward appearance and looking at the wrapping rather than the gift. Thank the Lord - He looks on the inside, our heart condition. (1 Samuel 16:7)

I read a story about him and how even after his death he influenced another great hymn writer - Fanny Crosby. In 1851, at the age of 31, she attended a revival service at a Methodist church in New York City. They sang the Isaac Watts hymn "Alas! And Did My Savior Bleed." When they sang the third line of the fifth stanza — "Here, Lord, I give myself away" — she was saved. How fitting that Watts played a part in winning to Christ the author of a new generation of hymns and gospel songs!

August 28th ~ The Word

Truly I love the Word of God and read and study it often. But sometimes I do get a little bogged down in the book of Numbers when God tells the Israelites to take a census. After listing all the people, then the specific duties of all the Levite families are spelled out very carefully. (Numbers 4)

In Numbers 7, the same gifts given by each tribe are listed over and over. Since I remember that ALL scripture is inspired by God and is helpful to edify me (2 Timothy 3:16, 17), I ponder why this repetition is important to me personally. Finally, I get it - in Chapter 4, God is pointing out that each one of us has a specific task or place in the body of Christ and none is more important that the other. Then when it tells about the gifts, God is letting us know that our gifts are very significant to Him and He sees them all.

In Numbers 4, some of the duties assigned to the various Levite families seem a little unimportant to us but they are very essential to God. Some of them are responsible for only small parts of the tabernacle, such as the draperies, the boards or pillars. God tells Aaron, the head priest, that he must assign to each man by name the items he must carry when they move the tabernacle while they are in the wilderness.

God has chosen a specific task for each of us in the body of Christ, but we sometimes want to do another person's job which might seem showier and more prestigious. It would help us to be more satisfied with our lot in life to remember that it was chosen for us personally by God Himself and that no position or task is small in God's eyes.

He is just as impressed with the person working in the kitchen as He is with the person speaking in the pulpit. It is all the same in His eyes if it is done as an offering to Him for His glory. Colossians 3:17 says, "Whatever you do in word or deed, do all in the name of the Lord Jesus, giving thanks to God the Father through Him."

August 29th ~ Little Children

In thinking about how Jesus instructed us to become like little children, I pictured a small child worrying about how to pay the rent and realized how sad that would be. We certainly did not want our children ever to be concerned about bills or food or whatever. This thought rose up in my spirit and jumped out at me - GOD DOES NOT WANT US TO WORRY ABOUT OUR NEEDS, EITHER. I know this should not seem like such a big revelation, but do we really believe it? We are to become like little children simply trusting in the Lord to supply all our needs.

Why is that so hard? I guess because we in America have been taught to stand on our own two feet, to be independent, take care of ourselves, and trust in only what we can see, and so on. But Jesus tells us to become like little children for a reason — to make life easier for us.

In the Amplified Bible, we read in Matthew 18:1-4, "The disciples asked Jesus, who then is really the greatest in Heaven? He called a little child to Him and said, 'Truly I say to you, unless you repent (change, turn about) and become like little children (trusting, lowly, loving, forgiving) you can never enter the kingdom of heaven at all. Whoever will humble himself therefore, and becomes (trusting, lowly, loving, forgiving) as this little child, is the greatest in the kingdom of heaven.'"

Jesus says it twice, that we are to become trusting, lowly, loving and forgiving just like little children. I love to hear little children pray as they have such simple faith. As adults, our thinking gets so cluttered with all the problems of the world that we forget what a big Daddy we have who is more than able to take care of all our needs. And He will if we turn and become like little children, trusting a loving Father God.

August 30th ~ Haywire, by Delores Morris, Friend, Atlanta, GA

My life went haywire on August 30, 1975, as we were preparing for a 16th birthday party for my daughter Karen. That evening, with jukebox on the patio and badminton and ping pong table in place, my 17-year-old, first born, beautiful, blonde high school senior Katrina asked if there was anything else she could help me with.

I asked her to drive to a neighbor's house to pick up an additional card table we were going to need for the party. As she headed back home from my friend's home, a pick-up truck hit her car on a blind-sighted street. She suffered brain injuries and only lived several hours.

Of course, my world came crashing down and Valium became my best friend. If it had not been for God and the people He had placed in my life (my husband David, dear family, loving friends and inspirational Sister Payne), I could not be telling you this story today.

Even though I had always been a believer, Katrina, my precious daughter, introduced me to Jesus in a very personal way. I know that she wouldn't trade her life now for anything and she is happy with our Lord. A consolation to me also is that she only knows true peace and happiness, no more sorrows or disappointments this life can bring. We still terribly miss her, after almost 35 years.

I am 70 years old and have experienced many hardships (as well as many blessings) in this life. But I can truthfully say that God has always been there for me. I cling to His promises: "God is our refuge and strength, an ever-present help in trouble. Therefore we will not fear, though the earth gives way and the mountains fall into the heart of the sea, though its waters roar and foam and the mountains quake with their surging" (Psalm 46:1-3). Jesus told His disciples, "Surely I am with you always, to the very end of the age" (Matthew 28:20). And God has said, "Never will I leave you, never will I forsake you" (Hebrews 13:5). Hallelujah! Thank You, Lord.

August 31st ~ "God is There" Poem/Song by Katrina Petty, Age 15

All mankind are brothers seeking love and joy and happiness. All mankind are brothers seeking love and happiness for all.

Verse: Let the magic spell of God's touch bring the joy of love to all. Mankind are brothers seeking love.

Chorus: God is with you. Don't be afraid. He loves you; all of you so let's love each other, too. Let God help you seek love, joy, and happiness. He's always there, so just turn around.

Verse: Love your neighbor. Don't be afraid. He'll always be with you. If you need Him, He's there to take you by the hand.

Verse: DON'T BE AFRAID. He's with you. If you need Him, just call. He will take you by the hand and show you the way, Don't be afraid. Don't be afraid. He loves you; just ask Him so.

Chorus: He'll pick you up and show the way. He'll pick you up and love you every day.

Verse: He watches you. He loves you. Let Him into your heart: make you feel so good. Let Him in, Let Him in; feel so good. Let Him in, Let Him in: You feeling good. Let Him in, Let Him in; Feel so good. Let Him in.

Author's note: This is especially precious as Katrina was killed in an automobile accident at age 17. This was found by her mother Delores Morris in Katrina's own handwriting and was a tremendous comfort to her. What a blessing to know that your daughter knew the Lord in such a wonderful, personal way. I typed it just like she wrote it.

September 1st ~ Sitting by Jesus

God has invited us not to just stand in front of the throne but to come up close and sit down right next to Jesus.

What if you feel unworthy or have committed a sin? If you have, then deal with it. (1 John 1:9) Confess it and call that sin by its dirty, ugly name and get rid of it. Then believe God has already forgiven and cleansed you from all unrighteousness just like He said He would. And remember, you are the righteousness of God in Christ Jesus.

Act on your faith and not your feelings. Take authority over those lying emotions of guilt and boldly sit down beside Jesus, trusting Him as your merciful and faithful High Priest. (Hebrews 2:17) Dare to believe that God meant it when He said He had already settled the problem of your sin and completely blotted it out of His remembrance. (Isaiah 43:25, Psalm 103:12)

Throw aside the religious rags of unworthiness and sit beside Him. Start believing, really believing, that Jesus' precious blood has washed you clean of sin and robed you in

His righteousness. Start rejoicing that the Word has you covered and God's wisdom belongs to you. Jesus, your merciful High Priest, is inviting you now. Remember that He is waiting for you, expecting you.

You can sit down beside Him saying, "He is my refuge, my fortress, my God in whom I trust."

Why spend another moment pacing the floor or worrying when you can take your Heavenly Father up on His gracious invitation? Sit down at His right hand with Jesus in heavenly places and you will soon see your enemies under your feet!

September 2nd ~ Holy Spirit Conviction

Holy Spirit conviction means conviction of His love for people who may have sinned, for love covers a multitude of sins. (Proverbs 10:12) And when we get a revelation of God's unfailing love, we will want to give up any besetting sin.

In the midst of this wonderful teaching given me by the Lord, I began to think what to have for lunch. The Lord in His wonderful sense of humor quoted back the scripture about the Kingdom of God, it is not meat and drink but righteousness, peace and joy in the Holy Spirit. (Romans 14:17)

He said it was His goodness that leads to repentance (Romans 2:4b) and not harshness. I must send love to people like Jane Fonda and not hate. God sees these people with eyes of love and we should, too. He sees these people as already saved and we should not condemn them even in our thoughts. We only can do this with His help. He loves all the people in the world and desires that none should perish but all men be saved. (2 Peter 3:9)

After we had this great time together, everything else I read seemed to pertain to this message. One of my scriptures for the day was Proverbs 10:12 that says, "Hatred stirs up strife, but love covers all sins." Then Max Lucado's devotional was on the same theme. I guess the scripture was from the Message Bible. Romans 12:14 says, "Wish well for those who harm you, and do not curse them."

We are more familiar with the Word that says bless those who persecute you; bless and do not curse. And we are told to pray for those who despitefully use us, that the Holy Spirit, not us, would bring conviction on them.

Jesus tells us that "when the Holy Spirit comes He will convict the world of sin and of righteousness, and of judgment of sin, because they do not believe in Me" (John 16:8, 9).

So let's let Him do the work and not us.

September 3rd ~ Luke 15

Jesus tells three parables in this chapter. He was speaking to angry people - the Pharisees and scribes who were complaining about Him. (Interestingly in verse one, we see that the sinners drew near to hear Him as opposed to the religious folk who just wanted to find fault.)

All three stories are about the lost.

First we read about the shepherd looking for the lost sheep, second the lost coin, third is the story is about the prodigal son who was lost. All three tell about how there was rejoicing when they were found. They illustrate the three different reasons why people are lost.

1. The sheep was lost because of his own foolishness.
2. The coin was lost through no fault of its own; a person may never have had the advantage of hearing the gospel.
3. The prodigal was lost deliberately through his own rebellion.

In reading about the prodigal son, we see three stages in his life: 1.He came to the pigpen. 2. He came to himself. 3. He came to his father. And the father was waiting for him and, when he was still a long way off, welcomed him with open arms. (Verse 20)

I heard a preacher say that at one time or another we all are at one of four places: Safe and secure in the Father's house; on the way to the pigpen; in the pigpen: or on the way back from the pigpen

All of us probably have been in one of these four places at different times in our lives. We may even have acted like the self-righteous older brother. Hopefully, we can act like our Father God who grants us forgiving love even when we are a long way off.

September 4th ~ Words That Hurt

Sometimes it is better not to say something that is a put-down even if it is true or done in a teasing manner. A wise person said that we should never criticize anything about a person that could not be changed. Meaning - it might be alright to comment on a person's hat, but not their head. Right?

In grade school, we had what we called Slam Books where we would pass our books around to others and they would say something bad about us. What a horrible idea! I don't know how this got started but I can still remember the pain I felt when I learned that people did not like something about me. I was sweet and would try to put something in others' books that would not sound too bad.

Little girls can really be hateful to each other and some may have really been scarred from these hurtful written words. Thankfully, I always had so much confidence that I did not dwell on them. (Probably the word said most about me was that I "talked too much" and although I could have changed that, I did not. I still do - talk too much, that is.)

There are so many Scriptures about the importance of our words, especially in Proverbs in the Old Testament and James in the New. I had a hard time deciding which ones to use. Finally, I chose Proverbs 16:24, "Pleasant words are like a honeycomb, sweetness to the soul and health to the bones."

But one of the scariest is in Matthew 12:36-37, "But I say to you that for every idle word men may speak, they will give account of it in the Day of Judgment. For by your words you will be justified and by your words you will be condemned."

WOW is a good acronym for WATCH OUR WORDS.

September 5th ~ Freedom from Fear

Jesus warned us that in the end times men's hearts would fail them from fear and the expectation of those things which are coming on the earth. (Luke 21:25-26) However, there is glorious freedom from fear for Jesus' followers who trust in God's promises to preserve His children.

Our Father God desires us to be able to go about our daily business without fear or anxiety, totally trusting in His care. This resignation to Him has a very practical effect in our lives. The more resigned we are to God's care and keeping, the more indifferent we'll be to the conditions around us.

Before I was born again, my life was ruled by fear. My parents were not fearful people and I am sure they had a hard time understanding my nameless fears. When I first married at 19, Billy would leave for work early in the morning while it was still dark. I would sit with a butcher knife in a place where I could watch both doors until dawn. (I don't know what I could have done with that knife but this just shows how silly fear can be.)

At the time, we were living on the second floor of an apartment complex and an older couple without children lived across the hall. When they learned what I was doing, they insisted that I call them and come over and sleep in their guest bedroom as late as I desired. How precious of them to offer a refuge for me and how unfeeling of me to awaken them at five in the morning. (Daddy knew that the man was a heavy drinker. He laughingly said I was probably better off with my knife.)

What a joy and freedom when Jesus came into my life and delivered me from all my fears! (Psalm 34:4)

September 6th ~ "Pure D"

Where in the world did that saying come from? Bill and I were puzzled about that when we both said that someone was "Pure D crazy." That statement is "Pure D" crazy (besides being judgmental, too? Eh?). What could it possibly mean? "Pure D" what? We use it in lots of ways - Pure D dumb, Pure D fun, Pure D exciting and on and on. It probably is an old country saying and those not from East Texas may never have heard it.

There are many statements that we become so familiar with that we don't even stop to think what they really mean; even some from the Bible. It occurred to me that Ecclesiastes 11:1 says, "Cast your bread upon the waters, for you will find it after many days." Certainly I know what this is talking about - giving and it coming back to you. But when you think about actually throwing bread on the water, it seems strange. Is this where we get using bread or dough as slang for money?

When I looked up the Scripture in my old Amplified Bible, I had penciled a notation to refer to Isaiah 32:20 that says, "Happy and fortunate are you who cast your seed upon all waters [when the river overflows its banks; for the seed will sink into the mud and when the waters subside, the plant will spring up; you will find it after many days and reap an abundant harvest], you who safely send forth the ox and the donkey [to range freely]." This seemed to better explain the words 'casting your bread.'

I was reading this verse in Isaiah during the first week and aftermath of the horrible hurricane Katrina. It blessed me to think that even though the river overflowed its banks, when the waters subside, an abundant harvest of blessings will come up. God always brings much good out of any situation no matter how bad it seems at the time. Since this is the very worst disaster I have ever heard of, we can expect God to do many great miracles - a huge revival of souls saved, restoration of families, property and jobs.

September 7th ~ Restoration and Revival

God is in the restoration and revival business. He loves to do this in our lives. It is a principle we find throughout God's Word. We are the generation that saw the restoration of Israel and God is restoring all things we have lost during these end times. God is restoring everything back to the way it was before the fall: no disease, shortage, sadness, strife, or death.

He even restores to us the years the hopping locusts, stripping locusts and crawling locusts have eaten. (Joel 2:25, Amplified Bible) Some of us have had many years the locusts have eaten and we love God's promise that He will restore all back to us. And He always restores more than we had before. That is His style.

Exodus 22:1-4 says, "If a man steals an ox or a sheep, and slaughters it or sells it, he shall restore five oxen for the ox and four sheep for the sheep." Five for one ox and four for one sheep? That's at the very least double. We're always to receive better and more than was lost.

So we can go before the Judge and lay our case before Him, knowing what we have lost and claim it back. Don't just say, "Oh, I am not worthy to receive it back, or it's OK." It is not OK. God wants us to have all that Jesus bought for us on the cross. We should forgive any person who stole from us. But it is important to get back what the devil has stolen through them or someone else.

God wants us and our families to have heaven here on earth and restore to us all we have lost. I'm talking about everything! This is God's heart for us. And when He does this, He wants people to look at you and say, "Who is your God?"

September 8th ~ Waiting

No one likes to wait. But I was really convicted when singing from an old hymnal this morning and began to realize how many of the hymns are about Jesus waiting for us. Imagine the Lord of the whole earth having to wait for us! Is that wild or what?

In Fanny Crosby's great hymn "Jesus Is Calling," it suggests that He not only is WAITING for us, but is PLEADING for us to come to Him. "Softly and tenderly," begs the question, "Why should you tarry when Jesus is pleading, pleading for you and for me?... O for the wonderful love He has promised… though we have sinned He has mercy and pardon."

I was smugly thinking that I had asked Jesus into my heart over 36 years ago when the Holy Spirit nudged me saying, "You keep Him waiting still."

"Like when, Lord?" I asked.

"Every time you miss an opportunity to have fellowship with Him," He answered.

How convicting is that?

But He did not stop there, He pointed out other times I keep Him waiting - like when I fail to obey, when I pass a person by without a smile or a word of comfort, when I forget to pray for others, or even when I forget and try to do something in my own strength without looking to Him for His answer. And many, many more occasions, too numerous to name.

I eventually found several more times I keep him waiting. In the hymn "Jesus Thou Art Standing," the verses remind us that He is standing, knocking and pleading outside a fast-closed door in lowly patience WAITING. Shame on us for keeping Him standing there.

"Lord, with shame and sorrow, I open now the door."

The good news is that no matter how long we have kept Him waiting, we can still answer His call and run into His loving arms. Softly and tenderly Jesus is calling us TODAY!

Come, Lord Jesus!

September 9th ~ Worship, Response to God

We must worship before we serve, because worship produces in us two crops that are pleasing and beautiful to God: humility and kindness. Humility shows up in our response to God; kindness is evidenced in our response to others.

When we decide to enter into worship, we are no longer supposed to be focused on ourselves, but we are entering His turf and submitting ourselves to the worship of God. This is where true humility kicks in. It's all about Him.

True worship of God caused Isaiah to say, "Woe is me, I am a man of unclean lips" (Isaiah 6:5). He saw the greatness of God and he recognized his inability to reproduce it. But God is waiting for us to realize this truth and give up, acknowledge that He is God and trust Him. He is waiting for us to ask for His forgiveness for getting into pride and simply to worship Him in Spirit and in truth. (Isaiah 57:15)

The opposite of true worship is pride. When we keep trying ourselves to get our loved ones saved then He can't do His job. We cannot possibly save them or heal them, but He can and will. With man it is impossible; with God all things are possible. (Matthew 19:25, 26) We can't save ourselves or anyone else. Our job is to pray and believe He will do it.

Run to the Source, joyfully pour yourselves out at His feet, tearfully, humbly, and lovingly. Pour out everything you treasure — your trophies, your pride, your gifts, talents, ambitions, and ministry. Hold nothing back. Spend yourself completely on worshiping Him. Fix your eyes on Him until He gives you a new way of seeing. In heaven, we will all worship Him and no one will grow weary. Life here on earth is our rehearsal. Practice for heaven.

September 10th ~ "Don't Mention It Again"

I think Ray Charles recorded the song "I Won't Mention It Again" but this morning the Lord brought to my remembrance just the words "Don't Mention It Again." This was in regard to something He had already warned me not to do. In other words, I was to say no more about a certain matter to Bill. Good advice, I knew. If I mentioned it again, it was going to come under the heading of nagging and that never is a very good idea.

So I guess that will have to be my theme song as it keeps playing over and over again in my mind. It seems as though I need constant reminding not to try to force an issue. The Holy Spirit is so faithful to help me when I need special help with something hard for me to do.

My favorite Proverb about a nagging wife is about it "being better to live in the corner of an attic or a roof than in the house with a contentious woman." (Proverbs 21:9; 25:24)

Bill tells the true story about a family that he knew well in the town where he grew up. It seems that the man lived in one small back room in a large house to keep away from a "scold" as she would have been called in older times. Once Bill took papers for the man to sign and found him sitting in a straight chair in the tiny room all by himself. How sad was that?

I am reading a wonderful fictionalized history of England and it seems they would put "scolds" in the stocks for a day with that title written above them. Wow! Or, even worse, they would douse them in a lake or river over and over. Sometimes the "scolds" would even die from this ordeal if accidentally held under water too long.

Oh, I am so thankful I did not live back then. However, I really don't think I am that bad. Ha, who knows? I might not be able to see my own faults clearly but surely this one time, at least, I am able to obey God and I won't mention it again!

September 11th ~ The Times Are A-Changin, by Julie Setzer

After September 11, 2001, I really thought the hearts of Americans would change, that we would all realize how short our life here on earth is and that people who had never thought of entering into a relationship with God would begin to consider Him a worthwhile investment. I was wrong. I bet a number of people did come to Christ as a result of the attack and devastation, and I bet a lot of people did make major life changes, but the mass spiritual awakening that I envisioned didn't materialize. Several times since that day I've asked God "What was up with that?"

He didn't bother to answer that particular question but now that our economy has changed dramatically and is in a state of peril, I'm thinking this may be the thing that turns our attention to God. I don't know why I had not thought of it before but it stands to reason that when our pocketbooks are affected, we respond. Boy, do we respond. We jump out of windows, lose our minds, turn to medicine, prescribed or not, to alleviate our fears or to numb our pain, cry, freak out, worry, and try to figure out what got us here in the first place and try to fix it so it never happens again. We blame others for our misfortune, we hunker down and hope for the best.

I am not trying to make light of suicide or of taking necessary medication to help maintain a balanced attitude and outlook. I'm also not implying that the Spirit of God is not constantly moving and working on a daily basis in the hearts of individuals. I'm just trying to look at our nation's situation as a whole and I'm wondering what our response to God will be, how the people of our nation will handle the change in our economy. Only time will tell.

My first pastor Joseph Dearinger was an excellent Bible teacher. He is in Heaven now but when he was here on earth, he always said his main purpose in life was to lay a foundation of Biblical truths upon which we can depend.

As you know, if a foundation is weak or shaky, the house you build on it will not stand the test of time and circumstances. In wobbly times like these, I'm so grateful for the foundation that Pastor Joseph laid in my life.

Here's what I know for certain, no matter how much the economy or any other life circumstance changes:

1. God loves me. God loves you. Because He loves us with a perfect love, all fear is cast out of our lives. 1 John 4:17-18 says, "God is love. When we take up permanent residence in a life of love, we live in God and God lives in us. This way, love has the run of the house, and it becomes at home and mature in us, so that we're free of worry on Judgment Day - our standing in the world is identical with Christ's. There is no room in love for fear. Well-formed love banishes fear. Since fear is crippling, a fearful life - fear of death, fear of judgment - is one not yet fully formed in love." I can trust God's love to help me not be afraid of what's happening in the stock market.
2. God promises peace in every situation. Philippians 4:7 says, "And the peace of God, which transcends all understanding, will guard your hearts and your minds in Christ Jesus." I can trust that the peace that only God can give me will surround me when confronted with a scary financial future.
3. God will never leave me alone. Deuteronomy 3:18 says, "The Lord Himself goes before you and will be with you; He will never leave you nor forsake you. Do not be afraid; do not be discouraged." This verse promises me that whatever trials and tribulations I face in life, I will not have to face them alone. My Lord and Savior has not only gone before me to prepare a way for me, He will walk with me and allow me to feel His presence as I move forward.

There are many other wonderful truths from the Bible that have stood the test of time in my life. But those are just three that seem especially important right now. Thank You,

God, that You, unlike the Stock Market, are the same yesterday, today and forever.

September 12th ~ Peace and Joy

Romans 15:13 says, "Now may the God of hope fill you with all joy and peace in believing that you may abound in hope by the power of the Holy Spirit." If we don't have peace, we will be robbed of all the joy God has for us.

Satan wants to rob us of our joy and peace to keep us from enjoying all the good things God has given us and to keep us from enjoying our relationship with the Lord and the abundant life He died to give us.

One of the causes of anxiety is not being content with where we are or with what God is doing in our lives. We should know by now that outward circumstances don't bring true, lasting joy.

We are to rejoice in everything, not after everything is over. We are to bring the anxious thoughts to Him when they come - whenever they come. We are to tell Him what we need and thank Him for how He helped us before; recalling the details of how God helped us in the past, and helps us to trust Him now. It magnifies the Lord and minimizes the problem.

Remember, Paul wrote Philippians — the great joy book — from prison. He admonishes us to rejoice in the Lord always. This is a sure cure for anxiety.

Recently on a missionary trip, our 19-year-old granddaughter Julie Katherine was left behind all alone in London due to some problems with her visa into Ghana.

Thankfully she knew this truth and put it into practice. Sometimes even through gritted teeth, she would worship and sing praise to the Lord. I am convinced that is what made it possible for her to withstand the long trial of four days alone in an airport hotel. (She also flew from London's Gatwick Airport three days before the recent terrorist scare when all the planes were grounded.)

September 13th ~ Ironing

Shortly after his father died, Billy had to go to New York without me. The fragility of life had just become real to me as this was my first brush with a death of a close loved one. I was absolutely terrified that now something would happen to Billy. It certainly did not help when I got an envelope in the mail with the insurance policy he had bought before he got on the plane. I did not want money, I wanted Billy.

After I put the girls to bed, in my nervousness I started ironing, of all things - this was certainly not like me. Anyway, picture me at midnight ironing and crying. Very clearly the Lord spoke to my heart saying, "I am enough for you no matter what happens to Billy - you will always have Me."

At this point of time in my life, I did not know Jesus as my personal Savior but believed in a loving Father God. This simple statement brought such an overwhelming peace to me that I no longer feared. It has stayed with me all these years. It has been a real touch point in my life, even when I really did lose Billy and my parents as well. I knew that He would never leave me nor forsake me. (Hebrews 13:5) Yes, the great "I AM" is always enough for me.

How precious is the Lord - He always comforts us quickly. He never desires for us to be afraid. He meets us at the point of our need.

Sweet grandson John Crabtree is in the midst of a terrible tragedy - his best friend shot and killed his girlfriend and himself. My heart aches with yearning to comfort John. But I am unable to do anything but pray for Him to know the true Comforter and to lean heavily on Him. I believe the Lord will make Himself real to John at this time and he will come to know Him personally in an ever- increasing way. He is the God of all comfort. (2 Corinthians 1:3) He yearns, far more than I, to comfort John.

September 14th ~ Surplus Day

I had a dream in which the words Surplus Day appeared in my subconscious. Sounded good so I meditated on what the Lord had meant. I am always wanting more time and so the first thing I thought of was maybe an extra hour – a surplus day. Quickly I thought of Proverbs three which talks about a man finding wisdom and so finding length of days. (Verse 17)

But best of all, I looked up the word surplus and read that the synonym was superabundance! Surplus days are coming with superabundance of everything we need. Yea! I receive that prophecy.

Other meanings of surplus:

1. Something that remains above what is used or needed
2. Amount, quantity
3. Extra, excess, redundant, spare
4. Superfluous

These words remind me of the story of Jesus multiplying the loaves and fishes to feed the multitudes. We read these stories in all four gospels. (Matthew 14, Mark 6, Luke 9, John 6)

Our God does multiply blessings to us superabundantly above all that we can ask or think. (Ephesians 3:20) Giving us more than we can use or need, an extra amount, in excess so that we have much to spare to give to others. I truly believe that we are in the time of Surplus Days as Christ's return draws nearer; surplus for all who will receive God's superabundant blessings.

September 15th ~ Attitudes

We are told to be joyful. (1Thessalonians 5:16, Philippians 4:1) And we are responsible for our own attitudes. Some of us complain about everything – the weather's too hot, the weather's too cold or my own favorite gripe – spring forward, and on and on.

In an old Peanuts comic strip, Lucy announces, "Boy, do I feel crabby." Her little brother Linus, always anxious to relieve tension, responds, "Maybe I can be of help. Why don't you just take my place in front of the TV and I'll go and fix you a nice snack? Sometimes we all need a little pampering to make us feel better."

Then Linus brings her a sandwich, a few chocolate cookies and some milk. "Now, is there anything I haven't thought of?" he asks. "Yes, there's one thing you haven't thought of," Lucy answers. Then she shouts, "I DON'T WANT TO FEEL BETTER."

Do you know anyone like that? Some people don't want to feel better; they just want attention. We are all like that at times. Once you are willing to face the truth about your attitude and do something about it, your life will begin to rapidly improve. After all, to be joyful is a command and the joy of the Lord is our strength. That is what we all need at times. Joy is a fruit of the Spirit so we can have it all the time. We need to choose to be joyful and not be complainers who live in the past, nursing old wounds, refusing to forgive others and even ourselves.

When I first lost a loved one, someone told me that I could get bitter or better and I quickly chose better. God wants us to experience the abundant life, not the exhausted servitude into which we have wandered. And He has made a way, carrying us on His own shoulders. The same way we received salvation is the way we are rescued from slavery through Jesus Christ.

Listen for His voice, saying "Come to Me." "You will show me the path of life; in His presence is fullness of joy at Your right hand are pleasures forevermore" (Psalm 16:11).

September 16th ~ Angels

We all know that Angels are God's messengers but do we know how active they are in our lives?

Over and over again in the Bible, we see angels in the

role of God's messengers carrying the all-important message to Fear Not. God wants us to have peace of mind; He has charged His angels with the task of comforting and assuring us. The message they carried to earth 2000 years ago is more applicable to today's world - with its increased war, terror, crime and disease —than ever before.

David taught us the secret of working with angels in Psalm 103:20. He said that angels move at the command of God's Word. As we speak God's Word - not our opinions or our own words — angels move mightily on our behalf or on behalf of those for whom we have spoken the Word. They come to our assistance with a message of God's comfort, love and protection. As new covenant believers, we should Fear Not, knowing that angels will work to bring God's promises to life for us.

If you are born again, you are an heir of salvation and are in Christ. Therefore, the angels have one purpose - they are sent forth to minister to you and me, in the present time and in the eternal hereafter. (Hebrews 1:14) The Greek word translated 'minister' literally means 'to do service.' In other words, the angelic host has been commissioned to serve us.

Many times an angel intervenes in the normal course of somebody's life to rescue them from a disaster such as in the story of Lot. (Genesis 19:1-26) The ministry of angels is real and it is a vital part of our lives here on this earth and a part of God's supernatural provision for us as Christians. I daily pray Psalm 91 over myself and my loved ones that the Lord would send His angels to guard, guide and protect us.

September 17th ~ Send the Word

While I was still in bed this morning, the old World War 1 song "Over There" kept going through my mind. "Send the word, send the word... the Yanks are coming the Yanks are coming... and we won't be back till it's over, over there."

Of course, I got excited about the admonition to "send the word." That is what God is telling us to do. Send the

Word, His Word, Jesus, into every situation that we face. And don't quit sending it till the problem is over.

Imagine how excited the French and English were when they got the word that the Yanks were coming. They were so encouraged and felt they soon would have the victory.

How much more powerful is the Word of God? When it is sent, we can be assured of victory! Psalm 107:20 says, "He sent forth His Word and healed them and delivered them from all their destruction."

He promises in Isaiah 55:11, "So shall My Word be that goes forth from My mouth, it shall not return to Me void, but it shall accomplish what I please, and it shall prosper in the thing for which I sent it." Since we are His voice here on earth, we are the ones who send forth His Word.

Hebrews 4:12 says, "For the Word of God is living and powerful, and sharper than any two-edged sword, piercing even to the division of soul and spirit, and of joints and marrow and is a discerner of the thoughts and intents of the heart."

As I was writing this, I thought of several people with desperate needs to whom I could send the Word. Not just send it this one time but over and over till it is over, over there. Send the Word, Send the Word, the Lord is coming and victory is assured.

September 18th ~ Seeds or Weeds

Our wonderful pastor Jeff Walker of Victory Christian Center in Rancho Mirage, California, preached a great sermon on sowing seeds or sowing weeds. He titled the sermon "Your Deeds are Either a Seed or a Weed."

He began with Galatians 6:7-9 that says, "Do not be deceived, God is not mocked, for whatever a man sows, that he will also reap. For he who sows to his flesh will of the flesh reap corruption, but he who sows to the Spirit will of the Spirit reap everlasting life. And let us not grow weary while doing good, for in due season we shall reap if we do not lose heart."

Pastor Jeff said that we have two bags - one is of the flesh and one is of the Spirit. And we can choose one or the other to draw from. He told some really funny stories of his own experiences when he chose the flesh bag. We could all identify with his experiences as we have certainly done the same. But we need to ask ourselves before we react, "Are we sowing a weed or a seed?"

We read in Mark 4, Jesus' words about sowing seeds. The entire chapter is good but mainly we are interested in Jesus explaining that sowing seeds is sowing words. We are told in Philippians 4:8 about giving a good report. That is a reminder to speak encouraging words that build others up rather than tearing them down.

I've known many people that really take joy in giving a bad report about others. It excites them to 'get' something on another person, especially a real failure and then to let others know. That's so sad sowing so many weeds from the flesh bag. It actually makes them feel superior when really it makes them inferior. But surely we have all done this at times, hopefully not too often. I truly want to sow good seeds in the life of others as well as my own.

Help me, Lord. Amen.

September 19th ~ In a Hurry

The Hurst family was born in a hurry, especially me, my daddy and my brother. We never took time to read directions or do anything carefully. Slapdash was more our style.

Well, when Billy Patterson came into my life, he brought new meaning to being careful - doing things right. My brother J.G. was having trouble putting a fancy tire cover on the back of my convertible so Billy suggested that it might be wise to read the instructions. Then he gave the admonition, "Time spent sharpening the ax means time saved cutting the wood." My brother laughed over that saying for years.

One of my favorite wedding gifts was a musical door knocker. Since my brother could fix anything, I asked him to come over to attach it to our apartment door. The directions on the box said that even a child could assemble it. After working several minutes, J.G. said that the child would have had to have had a Ph.D. in door knockers. Again, he was forced to carefully read the enclosed directions.

I still have trouble doing things slowly but have learned to read the directions – especially those in the Word of God. Paul tells us in 2 Timothy 3:16, "All Scripture is given by inspiration of God, and is profitable for doctrine, for reproof, for correction, for instruction in righteousness."

When I need specific directions, I claim James 1:5, "If any of you lacks wisdom, let him ask of God, who gives to all liberally and without reproach, and it will be given him." It is very clear that the Lord wants to give us all the wisdom we need to fix the things that need fixing in our lives.

September 20th ~ Blessed to Be a Blessing

How good is that title? The more we give out, the more we receive. We will have abundance to share. (Matthew 13:12) One of the first Scriptures that I read was in Luke 12:48, "To those whom much is given much is required." I have never known anyone who has been given more than I have; more love, more joy, more fun, more friends, more everything.

This morning when Bill and I were having our regular Saturday morning communion, a large plane flew over and I had a vision of packages of provision floating down to us (similar to the Berlin airlift in the 1950s). And we knew it was provision for every need we could ever have: health, wealth, abundance, joy, peace, comfort, and so on. In other words, it was showers and showers of blessings; blessings to give out to others with lots to keep for ourselves. We gratefully believed and received it.

As a new Christian back in the 1970s, the Lord gave

me a Word for our blended family that at the time seemed impossible to be fulfilled: "I am in control of this family, saith the Lord and My will shall be done. I will continue the good work I have begun and nothing will thwart My plans. I brought this family together for My glory and I will complete My work. The zeal of the Lord of hosts will accomplish this.

"I will perfect that which I began and the least shall become a great clan. I, the Lord, will be their God and I will make them and the places around them a blessing and I will cause showers of blessings to come down on them. They will be secure in the land and they will know that I am the Lord when I break the bars of their yokes and deliver them from the hand of those that enslaved them. Then they will know that I am the Lord, their God, I am with them and they are My people, declares the Lord God!"

How good is that? We are blessed to be a blessing, overflowing with love and promises from the Lord.

September 21st ~ "Bringing in the Sheaves"

Do you remember the old hymn "Bringing in the Sheaves?" It says, "They shall come rejoicing, bringing in the sheaves." I got excited singing this old hymn and began to think what "sheaves" mean. So I looked it up in the dictionary and learned it means a shaft of wheat or a gathering together of several shafts.

I know the song is speaking of the harvest of souls, but it also is speaking of the Feast of First Fruits where after the harvest the people brought their First Fruits offerings with great joy.

All through the Bible we read about people bringing their offerings with joy. God really does love a cheerful giver. And I was reading about acceptable sacrifices and offerings which made me think that some are unacceptable; those that are made out of duty, to show off or given begrudgingly are clearly unacceptable to the Lord.

I saw in 2 Chronicles 24, how King Joash put the chest with a hole in it for the people to bring their gifts to restore the temple. They came with such rejoicing and so much giving that they were eventually restrained from bringing anymore! (That is a lot different from our rather reserved passing of the plate.)

To bring in a harvest of souls, to bring in the sheaves, we must have money to make it happen. That is why our offerings are so important and bless our Lord so much. Knowing all that, we get joyful and excited about giving into His work.

"Bringing in the Sheaves" was written by Knowles Shaw, a singing evangelist who lived in the 19th century and credited with bringing over 12,000 souls into the kingdom in 19 years of preaching. He was killed in a train wreck but entered heaven rejoicing, bringing in the sheaves.

"Bringing in the sheaves, bringing in the sheaves, we shall come rejoicing bringing in the sheaves."

September 22nd ~ Hold Fast to the Word

For a few generations, Abraham's children held onto the word God had given to their father. As long as they kept that word, they were blessed just as he was. Eventually that word slipped away from them and, since it is the only means of escaping the curse that came on the earth through Adam's sin, the Israelites began to suffer the effects of that curse.

Instead of living in affluence, freedom and power as their forefathers did, they were afflicted as slaves in the nation of Egypt. But that did not change God's will. His will for the nation of Israel was the same as it was for Adam and Eve in the Garden of Eden. It was the same as it was for Abraham. God wanted them all to live a life of blessing and abundance. He wanted His people to live like kings and He still does.

So what did He do? He sent them His Word. Deuteronomy 28:1 says, "Now it shall be, if you diligently obey the Lord your God, being careful to do all His commandments which I command you today, the Lord your God will set you high above all the nations of the earth." He told them to be diligent about His Word. The curse was out there diligently working 24 hours a day. So they had to be diligent about the things of God.

He promised to bless them, not just a little here and a little there, but in every area of their natural lives. Their children would be blessed, their crops and livestock, and so on. (Deuteronomy 28:9-13) He did not leave anything out of that blessing. God made a way through His Word for His people to live the most wonderful life anyone could imagine here on earth. He desires for His people to be so blessed that the whole world would know just by looking at them that they belong to a loving God.

So grab on to the Word in faith and hold onto your hat because you are about to be BLESSED.

September 23rd ~ Don't Forget to Log-In, by Donna Payne, Daughter-in-law

Once again I showed up for an event that had been postponed. I explained that my busy work schedule does not allow me the opportunity to regularly check my email. But this did not change the fact that once again I had to rearrange my schedule. I began to think how my day might have started differently if I had taken the time to log-in.

This made me wonder how many blessings I have missed when I have been too busy to 'log-in' with my Creator, God. How would my day have proceeded if I would have taken more time in the 'chat room' with my Counselor? Would I have been more of a blessing to others? Would the mishaps of my day been avoided? What am I missing out on?

I do make it a habit of waking up with a thankful heart and praising God every morning. But, as I get busier and busier trying to make ends meet in these difficult economic times, I find that I do not as regularly 'log-on' to His Word. I might say my morning prayers, sing a song of praise along with the radio, but did I take time to listen to His Message for me this morning?

I guess this has been a wakeup call for me. No matter how hectic things are these days, they are less so when I open the Good Book and align my will with His will for me this day. I will start fresh today with a new commitment to myself to make the time to start my day not only in His presence but in His Word.

Psalm 119:105 says, "Your Word is a lamp to guide my feet and a light for my path."

September 24th ~ Songs in the Night

Psalm 77:6 says, "I call to remembrance my song in the night; I meditate within my heart, and my spirit makes diligent search."

God, our Maker, always gives us songs in the night no matter how dark our night may be. Remember how Paul and Silas in the dark dungeon at midnight were singing songs of praise to God? And even in the book of Job, we read that God, our Maker, gives songs of rejoicing in the night. (Job 35:10)

The secret is to call to our remembrance the many times the Lord has seen us through a dark night and then meditate on His faithfulness. Knowing He will never leave us or forsake us and remembering that weeping may endure for a night, but joy comes in the morning. (Psalm 30:5) And morning always follows the evening.

I prayed often with a dear friend when she was going through a dark night in her life that seemed to be lasting quite a long time. Her husband had a serious problem with alcohol. But she kept singing songs of praise and crying out to the Lord to bring about His deliverance.

Finally after all the weeping, the morning came and her husband was completely delivered from his problem and is now a much sought-after speaker at AA meetings. She is, too, for Al-Anon programs. The Lord honored her faith. Joy really did come to overflowing. Their marriage is stronger than ever.

Thankfully, He Himself GIVES us songs in the night to help us in our midnight hours.

September 25th ~ Ours

Oh, how exciting this morning as I was praying during what I had been calling my quiet time. But the Lord spoke very clearly to me and said that it was not just 'my' time, but 'ours.' How wonderful is that?

Then it occurred to me that it is not always a 'quiet' time but a time of singing and praising Him and us both talking back and forth. Guess I better rethink what I call the special set-apart time for prayer early in the morning. It is always a blessed time of fellowship with Him. This morning he called it a 'love-in' or 'love feast' where I seek His face and we feel each other's love. He especially wants me to let Him love me instead of just doing all the singing and talking myself.

Zephaniah 3:17 shows what His heart is for us, "The Lord your God is in your midst, a victorious warrior. He will exult over you with joy, He will be quiet in His love, He will rejoice over you with shouts of joy." That is a picture of what happens when we spend time with Him.

The Hebrew Bible says, "The LORD thy God is in the midst of thee, a Mighty One who will save; He will rejoice over thee with joy, He will be silent in His love, He will joy over thee with singing."

What a blessing to think of bringing Him joy! That He sings over me is almost too much to comprehend. This verse even speaks of His being silent – another component of our time together. It isn't always talking and singing; sometimes it's just being still and quiet. But I guess I like the shouts of joy best. That makes me realize anew how very much He loves me. He rejoices over me with shouts of joy. O how He loves you and me!

September 26th ~ Houses They Did Not Build

There is a phrase that keeps going over and over in my mind: "Houses they did not build and wells they did not dig." This expresses my thoughts when I look around our new, to us, vacation home with wonder. I looked up the Scripture references and found two: Deuteronomy 6:11 and Nehemiah 9:25.

I am very excited about what God has made possible for us to enjoy. There is even a grapefruit and a lemon tree and a very nice pool which I guess is the well we did not dig. Oh my, I do hope we don't forget to be appreciative to the Lord as the Israelites were prone to do.

God warned them in the sixth chapter of Deuteronomy, verse 12, to not forget the Lord who gave them houses full of all good things. Yes, it is hard to imagine but when things are going well, seems to be the time it is the easiest to forget the Lord who made it all possible.

I just heard a marvelous teaching on Isaac digging wells in the time of famine. The story is in Genesis 26 where we read about the Philistines having stopped up all the wells that his father's servants had dug, filling them with earth. However, this did not stop Isaac. He just dug them again and found running water. But other herdsmen quarreled with his servants as they were digging so he left that first one and named it Quarrel. Then he dug another and they argued again so he left that one and called it Enmity.

He could have camped at Quarrel or Enmity and become bitter but instead he just moved on from there and dug another well they did not quarrel over. He called this one Spaciousness and declared, "For now the Lord has made room for us, and we shall be fruitful in the land."

What a tremendous lesson for us just to keep on digging without getting bogged down when someone stops up our wells or quarrels with us. When we move on, we become fruitful.

September 27th ~ It's ALL Good

Our children the Pattersons have a slogan: "It's ALL Good." I Love to hear Burke and Laura say it often. They even have the words written on a large wooden plaque over the door that goes into the garage so they see it every time they leave the house. Of course they are speaking scripturally as they are quoting Romans 8:28, "And we know that God causes ALL things to work together for good for all to those who love God, and who are called according to His purpose." I love that word ALL. Do I really believe that, though? In Jesus it is ALL good.

I also found a hymn: "All Things Work Out For Good." The first stanza says, "All things work out for good; we know such is God's great design. He orders all our steps below for purposes divine."

The fourth verse says, "Someday the path He chose for me will all be understood, in heaven's clearer light I'll see all thing worked out for good."

In re-reading Romans 8, I got excited thinking that ALL things really do work for GOOD for me and mine personally because we are called according to His purpose. Whatever His purpose is for us, it is good. We can completely trust Him in every way, all the way, in His way.

It's all good, it's all good, it's all good. I am blessed, blessed, blessed. Always, always, always.

September 28th ~ God Loves Me

How exciting to think that this morning in our quiet time the Lord told me to go get my laptop. He knows my handwriting is pretty awful so I guess He wanted to tell me something important. I now wait expectantly to see what He has to say. Here's what he said:

"How about Me just telling you how much I love you, Sis? That's pretty important. In fact, nothing is more important for you to understand than that. Till you get that truth firmly in your spirit, your walk with me will be lacking in the most basic foundation.

"Actually, you will never be able to grasp the depth of My unconditional love for you, but I do want you to realize that it was enough to die for you. That it is everlasting, unchanging and never failing. It is a solid rock to stand on in any storm of life. My love for you knows no boundaries. No limits. No conditions. It is just pure unadulterated love. After all, I AM love."

1 John 4:9-10 says, "By this the love of God was manifested in us, that God has sent His only begotten Son into the world so that we might live through Him. In this is love, not that we loved God, but that He loved us and sent His Son to be the propitiation for our sins."

I think the beloved disciple John got this truth and I want to be like him and say as he did in 4:16, "We have come to know and have believed the love which God has for us, God is love, and the one who abides in love abides in God, and God abides in Him."

The tune of the old hymn "O, The Blood of Jesus" keeps going over in my mind. But instead I say "O, the LOVE of Jesus." How true - His love caused Him to shed His blood for our sins. I do know and believe when I survey the wondrous cross.

Help me, Lord, to know daily Your love more perfectly. Amen.

September 29th ~ Hearing God's Words

John 8:47 says, "He who is of God hears God's words." Glory! I know I am of God so I know I am able to hear His words. This is written in red letters so it is Jesus speaking. (I once heard Larry Lea, a well-known pastor, say that when he was a new Christian, all he knew to do was "read the red and pray for power.")

Jesus also says in John 10:27, "My sheep hear My voice and I know them and they follow Me." He also promises it again in that same chapter where He tells us that He is the good Shepherd and He knows His sheep and is known by His own. How precious it is to be known by Jesus and to know His voice. (Verse 3-4) Also, how fantastic that He promises He will go before us wherever we go!

John 10:16 says, "And other sheep which are not of this fold; them also I must bring, and they will hear My voice and there will be one flock and one shepherd." How great is that? We can pray that our unsaved loved ones will hear His voice and also come and follow Him. They are all coming in according to the promise in Acts 16:31: "Believe on the Lord Jesus Christ and you and your entire household will be saved." I am standing on that promise.

When I was a new believer, one of the first promises the Lord gave me from His Word was, "I could have ALL sailing with me." (Acts 27:24) This was the promise given to Paul when he was being brought to Rome as a prisoner and it looked as though all on board would be lost in a shipwreck. I quickly realized that "all sailing with me" personally included all my family and all my friends.

I immediately started a list of all those I knew well and even those I only knew casually. It ended up being over 400 and now I know it is even larger. I am believing that all 1000 of the people that have bought, or to whom I have given copies of my first book, will be counted as those sailing with me. As the angel told Paul, not one of them will be lost. And this includes all the ones who continue to buy the first book as well as those that buy this new book.

September 30th ~ Fighting

Oh Lord, how it must grieve You when we fight with our Christian brothers. Bill and I lately have been so grieved when our two little Shih Tzu puppies Happy and Doc have started fighting all the time, trying to see who will be the Alpha dog - the boss. This is extremely upsetting, destroying the peace in our home.

We go around claiming that the brethren dwell together in unity from Psalm 133:1 and know the Lord will watch over His Word to perform it. We give the problem up to the Lord, but then as usual take it back trying to think of a way to solve it ourselves.

Our son Tim came in from Los Angeles one Saturday morning and when he saw the situation and me all but in tears said that he would take Happy. This turned out to be a big blessing for us and also for Tim. Bill had laughed and asked Tim if he could leave right then (just as he arrived). He did take Happy the next day and it has worked so well. Now when they get back together, they are not fighting and are no longer jealous of each other. We do love them both and are thankful it has all worked out.

James 3:16 is such a scary scripture: "For where jealousy and selfish ambition exist, there is disorder and every evil thing." Every evil thing? That sounds as though it behooves us to live in peace with all our brethren - always walking in forgiveness.

It does seem to me that unforgiveness on one side or the other is the real issue and sometimes causes a root of bitterness like we read about in Hebrews 12:14-15, "Pursue peace with all men, and the sanctification without which no one will see the Lord. See to it that no one comes short of the grace of God; that any root of bitterness springing up cause trouble, and by it many be defiled."

Good advice.

October 1st ~ The Living Word

It really is the Living Word. I am constantly amazed at how I learn something new each time I read it. There are times when the Holy Spirit will prompt me to take another look at a familiar passage and there will be a fresh insight for me on which to meditate.

This morning, my regular New Testament reading for the day was John 6:1-14 which is about the five thousand being fed. My new thoughts on the story began in Verse 2 where I noticed that a large crowd was following Jesus because they saw the signs He was performing on those who were sick. People follow signs and wonders, don't they? Also, it was such a large crowd because the feast of Passover was near.

Then as I read the story of a boy who had five loaves and two fishes, it dawned on me that although the disciple Andrew did not think the boy's lunch would be enough, at least he brought it to Jesus' attention. This makes us wonder how the boy must have felt when he offered his lunch to Jesus. What a sacrifice that would have been for him. It revealed a childlike faith like we are supposed to have.

Jesus tells the disciples to have the people sit down. All of us can receive so much more from the Lord when we are sitting down, even reclining. Not striving and worrying about where our next meal is coming from, but trusting Jesus to supply our need.

After giving thanks, Jesus distributed the loaves and fishes to those who were seated. He gave them as much as they wanted. Do you suppose some did not want as much as others? I want lots, don't you? Verse 13 tells us that there was plenty leftover. Jesus always provides more than enough for us. He came to bring us the abundant life. Praise His name!

October 2nd ~ Sensors

My new 2006 Ford 500 has the neatest innovation — there are sensors on the back bumper that warn me when I am too close to anything. This keeps me from backing into objects or even people. I am delighted with them. I didn't even know the car had the sensors until my son Jim told me all about them. What a surprise! (Bill says he wishes I had them all over the car. Maybe they will add those next.)

My niece Grace Anne says she also has them on her Ford Expedition. But recently she was talking on her cell phone and not paying attention to the sensors and backed into something.

We, also, can ignore the Holy Spirit's warnings. He is constantly speaking to us – those small checks in our spirit and urging us to be more sensitive to other's feelings. He is a true Sensor. But we don't always listen and just go right on and 'back' into someone's feelings.

Bill's brother- and sister-in-law Alec and Carol Bridges said they did not like their sensors and laughingly said that even a blade of grass would set them off. So, of course, they do not pay much attention to them. Again, this is what happens to us – we get so used to hearing the Holy Spirit's admonitions that they become 'old hat' to us. The more we ignore the still, small voice, the easier it becomes to close our ears.

My car sensor's sounds get stronger and faster when I get really close to hitting something. They start out rather easy and then become louder as I get into more and more danger. The other day at church, I was backing up and suddenly they started beeping furiously and I was spared from running into a small child that I did not see. I was more thankful than I can express.

The precious Holy Spirit will keep us free from danger, too, if we will listen carefully to His early warnings signals. "He will convict us of sin" (John 16:8).

October 3rd ~ Some Thoughts to Meditate On

The Beatitudes are simply what our attitudes should be. (Matthew 5:2-12)

Your own self sufficiency can keep you from experiencing God's sufficiency. (2 Corinthians 12:9)

We have the power to make life easier or harder by the words we speak. (Proverbs 12:18; 13:3; 18:21; 21:23 and many more.)

Snakes eat chickens, eagles eat snakes. Are you a chicken or an eagle? (Isaiah 40:31; Psalm 103:5) This summer David Donovan (our beloved handyman) found a snake in an outside storeroom in our backyard. He suggested that we put mothballs all around the house to protect us from the snakes. I thought about how we need to put the blood of Jesus all around our homes so that Satan cannot get in. (It was days before I would venture near that storeroom.)

An apology is a good way to have the last word. (Proverbs 15:1)

I heard Joyce Meyer say, "If we would only be more desperate for God, there would be less desperate situations in our life."

God says we can't be all things to all people, but He can and will if we let Him. (As a mother, I have a particularly hard time not trying to do the Holy Spirit's job in the lives of my children.)

Remember in the dark what God told you in the light.

The Acronym ACTS may be used as a guide to specific prayer:

A - Adoration
C - Confession
T - Thanksgiving
S - Supplication

October 4th ~ "Open Your Mouth Wide and I Will Fill It"

This quote is from Psalm 81:10, "I, the Lord, am your God who brought you up from the land of Egypt; open your mouth wide and I will fill it."

Once I saw a picture of five small birds with their mouths wide open waiting to be fed and I thought of this verse. Then I remembered the words of Jesus in Matthew 6:26, "Look at the birds of the air, that they do not sow, nor reap nor gather into barns, and YET your heavenly Father feeds them. Are you not worth much more than they?" How comforting that verse always is to me!

But this morning I asked God how to pray better for other people, and he led me to this verse, "Open your mouth wide and I will fill it." He will put His words in my mouth. Yea! Sort of like how He puts His heavenly language in my mouth as I am obedient to open it. Then I am able to speak in tongues to Him alone and He then can speak through me. I must have faith for this and the many other ways He leads, guides and provides for me just as he feeds the little birds.

So this is talking about spiritual as well as physical food. If we will open our mouths wide in trust to Him, He fills it with everything we need. Job 8:21 says, "He will yet fill your mouth with laughing, and your lips with rejoicing." I love that thought.

Lord, fill my mouth with gracious, loving, kind and encouraging words, truly Your words. Don't let me be like the Israelites who God said did not listen to His voice and did not obey Him. (Psalm 84:11) In Jesus' name. Amen.

October 5th ~ Key to Courage

A key to the courage of David, called a man after God's own heart, is that He knew firsthand of the goodness of the Lord. He wrote Psalm 23 from that revelation. The more deeply we understand the truth of those words, the more we will be able to trust God in every circumstance of life. Our confidence in Him will make us bold when others are timid.

That is what happened to David. It made him bold and daring in dangerous situations. When a lion came after the sheep in his flock, he single-handedly caught that lion by the mane and killed it and a bear, too. (I Samuel 17:37) The knowledge that it was the Lord who delivered him is what made it possible for him to fight the giant. He had seen the victories that God's goodness had won for him and just thinking about them made him bold.

But we don't have to wait till we get there to start thinking that way. We can start thinking of Jehovah the Good right now. We can start thinking of Him the way He really is – full of joy and full of love. Then we can have days of heaven right here on earth.

Psalm 16:11 says, "In His presence is fullness of joy." Those religious artists who painted all the people looking sad were wrong. God's people are not sad. Heaven is not sad. It is glorious with everyone dancing and singing and shouting for joy. Ever since the Garden of Eden, the devil has been devising schemes to separate people from God. And the one scheme that has worked really well is to cause them to doubt God's goodness.

Psalm 145:8-9 in the Amplified says, "The Lord is gracious and full of compassion, slow to anger and abounding in mercy and loving-kindness. The Lord is good to all, and His tender mercies are over all His works – the entirety of things created."

October 6th ~ CHOOSE TO REFUSE

This morning it seemed as though the Lord was telling me that my joyful spirit blessed Him. So I said, "Why would you be impressed with that since YOU gave it to me?" He quickly answered that I could "CHOOSE TO REFUSE" it. In fact, I could CHOOSE TO REFUSE any of His gifts. This really touched me. I realized it was true. Like when I "CHOOSE TO REFUSE" His help with my overeating. I know He is there, always ready, willing and able to help me resist temptation as I reach for another cookie or whatever else I don't need.

The title of the book *Happiness is a Choice* really made a big impression on me. My best friend Boopy swears I gave her that book when I thought she had grieved long enough over the loss of her husband. Maybe I did, anyway she examined herself and chose to be happy again and let Jesus bear her grief. (Isaiah 53:4) She exchanged a spirit of mourning for a spirit of joy. (Jeremiah 31:13)

After God brought the Israelites out of the bondage of Egypt, He told them that they could CHOOSE to obey Him or not. Deuteronomy 30:19 says, "I call heaven and earth to witness against you today, that I have set before you life and death, the blessing and the curse. So CHOOSE LIFE in order that you may live, you and your descendants." To paraphrase some of the rest of this passage, God is telling them (and us) that choosing life is not too difficult or out of our reach as the Word is very near to us – in our mouth and in our heart, that we may observe it and speak words of life.

We can receive His many gifts of love, joy, peace, health, prosperity – the list goes on and on. Or we can CHOOSE TO REFUSE and wallow in our own self pity. I want to receive from His open arms with my arms open.

October 7th ~ Impossible Situations?

Have you got anyone or anything in your life that seems to be a hopeless case? I think we all do. Many are problems that we have prayed over for years and nothing seems to change. There just doesn't seem to be a solution to the situation. The truth is we all have a secret graveyard in our lives. I'm talking about someone or something we gave up on long ago and wrote 'dead and buried' on it.

We need to remember that there are no impossible situations with our God. He can even raise up what we thought was dead. In Matthew 29:26 Jesus said, "With men this is impossible but all things are possible with God." Genesis 18:14 says, "Is anything too hard for the Lord?" We need a faith that refuses to give up on anyone or anything, no matter how hopeless the situation seems. We can trust Jesus to astonish us by His power.

Paul's specific prayer in Ephesians 1:19 is: "That you may know…what is the exceeding greatness of His power toward us who believe, according to the working of His mighty power." We often gloss over these words without realizing that they are meant for us today. We need to know Jesus as the God who still works miracles every day in the natural world we live in and as the Lord over our home, children, marriage, job and bills. He wants to display the power that has been given to Him - all power on Heaven and earth.

Indeed, if we will hold on to unswerving faith, we are in for a glorious manifestation of His resurrection power. (Romans 8:11, Colossians 2:13, Ephesians 2:4-5)

John 6:63 says, "It is the Spirit who gives life." How clear His message is to us: the Holy Spirit dwells in us to bring forth His constant life. That is Christ's present greatness. YOUR SITUATION IS NOT HOPELESS – KEEP THE FAITH!

October 8th ~ Waiting for Burke, by Julie Setzer, Daughter

If you are a Christian, you probably have figured out that a lot of your time is spent waiting for God to speak, move or act. The first thing I waited for in life was Burke, my baby brother. He was born when I was 10 years old and I had pretty much wanted him for as long as I could remember. I already had a big sister so I certainly didn't need another one of those. A brother was what I wanted.

I loved him from the moment I saw him and held him. He was the best baby, so good-natured, so loving, happy, and content. My best friend Gayle Vaughan and I thought he was our very own live doll. We played with him and he was our entertainment. Yes, I had waited for him to be born.

Next thing I knew, my brother was an alcoholic, consumed with self and addicted to that upwardly mobile lifestyle. My heart was burdened for him and I could not bear the thought of him not being in heaven with me for all of eternity. One day in church we were singing a song that stated "all nations will come and worship" and God said to me, "Julie, that includes Burke." I felt like the Lord was giving me the faith to believe that Burke would someday give his life completely to the Lord. And so, I waited for him to be born again.

In February 1999, Evelyn Christensen spoke at the annual Women's Conference at my church (East Paris Baptist). She challenged us to commit to pray for our loved ones who needed salvation. The following Friday at the 5 a. m. prayer group, each of us wrote down three names of loved ones who needed to be saved. We put all the names in a basket (we called them our "basket cases") and each Friday we passed the basket around, drawing three names out to pray for that morning. It was so cool to hear different people pray for my loved ones. At the conclusion of each Friday's meeting, the names would go back in the basket. And so, I waited.

On October 8, 1999, my mom sent an e-mail to me that said Burke had gotten saved! It was one of the happiest days of my life! I went to the prayer group that Friday morning and announced, "We get to take a name out of our basket!" The girls were so excited they cried. I took the piece of paper with Burke's name on it, had it framed and gave it to Burke at his baptism. He wept as I told him the story. I no longer have to wait for Burke to be saved! I am so grateful to God.

But I'm still waiting for other things, other loved ones – there will always be something or someone, until Jesus comes back. I don't mind waiting. Lots of divine things happen while waiting. It is worth every minute.

October 9th ~ Burke's Testimony, Son

From the moment I laid eyes on her at the TCU freshman orientation, I knew Laura was 'the one.' She was drop-dead gorgeous, sweet, smart and funny. Although we were from different towns, our families went way back. My grandmother and her great-grandmother were best friends.

She was 'perfect.' I had to date her, the problem was –

she didn't feel the same way. She had a serious boyfriend back home. For a very moral, mature, Christian girl with an evangelical boyfriend, a wild and crazy frat boy like me wasn't that appealing! Now I don't have too many natural talents, but I definitely have the gift of persistence, so after a year and a half of constant pursuit, I finally succeeded – she broke up with the preacher to go out with me – the party guy!

We fell madly in love. Those first few months together were awesome. I was so happy to have her, and so wanting to keep her, that my drinking and partying came to a screeching halt. I felt complete with her. We had each other and I didn't need anything else.

However, soon after, I dove back into going out with my drinking buddies. Laura always believed the best in me and would allow me to do my thing in hopes I would "grow out of this." We were married in a big ceremony and set off on our lives. Again Laura was hopeful that I would grow out of my immature ways, but I had no such intentions. I was in love with drinking, and didn't think I had a problem.

We managed to build a life together and, in 1998, something really miraculous happened. I landed a dream job that I thought was way out of my reach. We found ourselves moving to Sugar Land, Texas, with our beautiful three-year-old girl Mary-Margaret, a baby boy on the way and high hopes for the future. Life seemed so optimistic – Laura was able to stay at home, her lifelong dream. We bought our dream house. Our son Payne was born just a week after we settled in. Life was great. We were able to check off all the things the world would describe as 'signs of success.'

Laura even convinced me to join a church and I reluctantly went along. I still thought church was for 'weak' people. I was in control of my life and didn't need any 'church.' But I thought it would be good for our 'image.' That's what good people do, right? They go to church on Sunday.

However, it was only from the outside that we looked like the perfect little family. This 'perfect' picture wasn't so pretty on the inside. My drinking was worse than ever. I worked hard during the week but, come Friday afternoon, all I wanted to do was catch a buzz - as soon as possible. The way I looked at it, I worked hard and deserved to relax and enjoy myself on the weekends. Simply put, I was a lousy husband and father.

October 9th ~ Burke's Testimony Continued

This pattern of neglect finally culminated in Laura asking me to move out. I was shocked! How could she be so upset? Yeah, maybe I drank a little too much, but I wasn't abusive or anything! What about all this Christian stuff and what the Bible said about marriage.

Our marriage couldn't be that bad. Besides, we were the couple that everyone thought was happy. My friends couldn't believe it. You see, Laura wasn't ever the nagging, get-mad and throw-stuff type. She always presented a happy face, and defended me in public. Even to my family that was concerned about my drinking. To the outside world, she was always smiling, but on the inside her heart had been ripped apart. She was deeply hurt and scarred.

I immediately started trying to dig myself out of the doghouse. I knew I was in big trouble this time - she'd never gone this far, but I was always able to 'patch her up' whenever she had been upset with me. But this time a simple charm routine wasn't going to cut it. I was out of the house.

I rented a little room in a house in Sugar Land and started living out my worst nightmare. Laura was completely 'shut down' to me, cold and distant. And as much as I didn't really like myself, Laura had always been there to lift me up. As crazy and out of control my life had become, I always had held on to Laura as my foundation. As long as I had her, this perfect, beautiful, sweet lady, I must be OK. As long as our image was OK, I was OK. Now I was alone, devastated, and petrified. She had been my rock - and I had lost her.

I reluctantly entered an AA meeting. As I walked into the room, I saw a sign that jumped out at me as if it were in neon — Expect a Miracle. I latched onto that promise as I desperately wanted another chance. (That day was October 8th, 1999, and by the grace of God I haven't had a drink since.)

But after a particularly depressing and painful conversation with Laura the week following that first AA meeting, I hit my knees in my bathroom crying out to God for help. I was at the end of me and took down my hand that had been holding God at bay for so many years. I asked Jesus to take over my life and surrendered to Him. The words came out naturally as I had heard the prayer of salvation all of my life growing up in a Christian home. I was born again and felt a peace over me and a voice saying, "I've got you and I love you."

Life was so different now. I immersed myself in the Bible and into worship music. I read spiritual books and relationship books. God was so good to me – sending people from my church that carried me through this difficult time. My family, many of whom had been praying for my salvation, were ecstatic about my transformation and were a tremendous support system.

October 9th ~ Burke's Testimony Continued

I prayed constantly. I was growing spiritually by leaps and bounds. Even though I had peace for the first time in my life, I was still sad about losing Laura.

What about reconciliation? Couldn't she see I was a new man? My faith was so high for restoration in our marriage. I knew God was in the miracle business, for I had seen that on the sign at the AA meeting. I wanted my miracle, but in the natural it didn't look possible. Laura was way too damaged and way beyond me.

After one of our conversations where I thought I really had my 'pitch' down well, it backfired. She was running further away. I called my Dad and was crying to him; devastated that she wasn't responding. He paused for a moment and I remember vividly his words, "Burke, you have to let her go." Those words really spoke to my heart. So I did. I laid Laura on the altar and again felt such a peace wash over me and joy as God revealed to me how much He had done for me, how much I now had.

"Think about it, Burke: your misery is now joy," He said. "I've replaced your panic attacks with a peace that passes all understanding. Instead of drinking buddies, you have fellow friends in Christ that love you and support you. Your desire for the 'next best thing' is now a feeling of contentment. A strained family relationship has been restored. Your constant mindset of 'woe is me' is now replaced with praise and worship. Your self-loathing is now self-respect. Instead of avoiding people, you now want to connect with people. Your self-absorption has turned into compassion and from dreading having to do any activities with your children, to now loving every second of time with them."

When I laid her down and let her go, I could actually hear Him ask me, "You were miserable when you had her. Would you rather go back to that – or have what you have now?" Then He said, "I'll be with you - always. I'll heal your pain. You will be OK." I had lost her, but I had gained so much more. During our separation, I kept a little prayer on my bathroom sink. I still have it. It says:

"Dear God, Thank You for all You've given me.
Thank You for all You've taken away from me.
Thank You for all You have left me."

Note: Burke and Laura were reunited after five months and their marriage is now stronger than ever! Glory be to God!

October 10th ~ What Makes You Stand Up and Shout?

Is it an exciting sports play? A job promotion? When

you hear a good report from the doctor? Or, best of all, is it when you are praising and worshipping the Lord?

Sarah Schriener, one of our Bible Study members, asked us this question when she taught recently on Praise and Worship. I loved the various answers in the group. My favorite one may have been, "It is when I hear about a salvation." That is certainly shouting ground. Several answered that they wanted to stand up and shout when they heard a testimony of a miracle deliverance. Mine was just simply when I think of all God has done for me. I want to jump up and down and praise Him for His goodness. (At my age it is a little hard to jump up and down, but my spirit leaps anyway.)

Celebrate God because He is worthy of all honor and glory. I do love to raise my hands in praise to Him and shout "Hallelujah—Glory to His name!"

Psalm 134:2 says, "Lift up your hands in the sanctuary and bless the Lord."

1 Timothy 2:8 says, "Therefore I want the men in every place to pray, lifting up holy hands, without wrath and dissension."

When my son Tim was on the swim team, I would be literally screaming, yelling and waving my arms as I cheered him on. O mercy me, should I not be even more excited watching God as He works daily miracles in my life and in the lives of my loved ones?

Besides, we are told to make a sacrifice of praise. The only sacrifice we are called to bring in the New Covenant. Hebrews 13:15 in the Amplified says, "Through Him, therefore let us constantly and at all times offer up to God the sacrifice of praise, which is the fruit of lips that thankfully acknowledge and confess and glorify His name."

October 11th ~ "Jesus, I Am Resting, Resting"

I found this old, but new to me, hymn in my wonderful book *Then Sings My Soul — 150 of the World's Greatest Hymn*

Stories by Robert J. Morgan who tells all about the author of each hymn and usually what the song was based on. This one was written in 1876 and was from a poem by an Irish woman named Jean Pigott.

It was a favorite hymn of J. Hudson Taylor, the great missionary to China. Once when Taylor was overwhelmed with weariness and worry, a fellow missionary, John McCarthy wrote to him about abiding in Christ. "Abiding not striving or struggling" wrote McCarthy "looking off unto Him for present power....This is not new, and yet 'tis new to me.....Christ literally all seems to me now the power, the only power for service, the only ground for unchanging joy." This letter truly lifted Taylor's failing spirits.

The quote from the hymn that meant so much to me was "But how to get faith strengthened? NOT BY STRIVING AFTER FAITH BUT BY RESTING ON THE FAITHFUL ONE." Abiding in the Vine; resting on the Faithful One. Was this from Taylor or the hymn?

John 15:4 says, "Abide in Me, and I in you. As a branch cannot bear fruit of itself unless it abides in the vine, neither can you unless you abide in Me."

The first verse of the hymn: "Jesus, I am resting, resting in the joy of what Thou art; I am finding out the greatness of Thy loving heart. Thou hast bid me gaze upon Thee, and Thy beauty fills my soul, for by Thy transforming power, Thou has made me whole."

The hymn closes with the prayer, "Keep me ever trusting, resting; fill me with Thy grace." Amen, me, too, Lord.

October 12th ~ Growing Weary in Doing Good

"So let us not allow ourselves to become fatigued doing good. At the right time we will harvest a good crop if we don't give up, or quit". (Galatians 6:9 The Message Bible) But today our churches are full of fatigued people. Are we so exhausted because Christ requires so much, or because we don't understand what He truly requires?

Let's take a closer look at Galatians 6:9. It does not say "doing church" it says "doing good." This word "doing" comes from the Greek word *poieo* which means "producing" as in "bringing forth," "bearing a result" - the way a tree produces fruit. Does a tree bear fruit because it tries really hard? Of course not! The fruit and flower are the result of what the plant is - how God created it. The resulting crop is determined by the nature of the seed that is planted. Apple seeds produce apples, and so forth.

Jesus asks the question in Matthew 7:17, "Do people pick grapes from thorn bushes or figs from thistles? Likewise, every good tree bears good fruit but a bad tree bears bad fruit." The word "good" comes from the Greek word *halos* and means pleasing or beautiful.

The word here has nothing to do with deeds. It has to do with God's nature. His nature reproduced in us is beautiful and pleasing to Him. The fruit of the Spirit listed in Galatians 5:22-23 are love, joy, peace, patience, kindness, goodness, faithfulness, gentleness and self control. The bad news is that in our human nature we are not any of those things. And we become fatigued trying to act lovingly and patiently, when we can no more produce these qualities than a thistle can produce grapes.

So since our old nature cannot do this, we need to get a new nature and that is what Jesus said to Nicodemus in John 3:3 about being born again. Then we get a wonderful new nature and the Holy Spirit residing in us causes His fruit to grow in us.

Paul says, "I no longer live; but Christ lives in me" (Galatians 2:20). In fact, I have been set free from being busy for God. Instead, God is busy in me. Glory! This takes a lot of the pressure off of us. Philippians 3:13 says, "It is God who works in you to will and do His good pleasure." Who's doing the work here? God! He is doing the good - not us.

October 13th ~ Public Speaking

Public speaking is one of my favorite things to do, especially when I get to tell the Good News, the Gospel, about Jesus. But several years ago, one of the ladies in my Bible Study thought it would be good for me to bring the program for the Daughters of the American Revolution. My assigned topic was "Cooking in Revolutionary Days." All I knew about this subject was a Martha Washington cake. So I had to do lots of research. What was really funny was that I rarely ever cook.

While speaking, I thought I was doing pretty well till I noticed that one of the elderly ladies seated on the front row was sound asleep. This was a little disheartening. I guess I was more boring than I knew. A speaker can usually gauge the interest of the audience, but I have never had a clearer sign to shift gears. If I had been talking about the Lord, I could have been more flexible in changing directions, but with this speech, I really had to go by my prepared notes. Truthfully, it was boring to me, too.

My family teases me about saying wrong things with the wrong pronunciation of words, so they are always amazed when I speak under the anointing of the Holy Spirit. The Lord Himself speaks through me and it is never boring. 2 Samuel 23:2 says, "The Spirit of the Lord spoke in and by me and His word was on my tongue." How great is that?

My daughter Grace prays that scripture for me every time I go out for a speaking engagement. How blessed I feel that all my family prays for me and I know this is what makes the difference. My extended family prays for me, too: my Bible study group Longview Christian Fellowship's prayer line and the Love Overflowing ladies. I truly feel these prayers and I sure don't want to go out without them.

I did not ask for prayer for my DAR speech, so I learned that in the natural I am not a gifted speaker. "Apart from Him I can do nothing" (John 15:5).

October 14th ~ Seasons of Life

When my mother was in her 60's, I remember hearing her say that she did not feel any older - she still felt the same as she did when she was a 19-year-old bride. Well, at 78, I know exactly what she meant. I am still me and it is so hard to look in the mirror and see an old woman instead of a young one. Bill says he feels the same way. We are just in a different season of life and it is great. Lots more time to rest and relax and enjoy our lives together.

We do feel that we still have lots to offer our large family as we can draw on our experience in the other seasons of our lives. We try not to give them too much unsolicited advice but we do feel needed when they ask for our input. But sometimes it seems that we are out of step because of all the new technology and we really aren't 'with it' anymore.

So it is nice to read the story in Exodus 18:17-27 about Moses listening to his father-in-law Jethro's good advice. Moses was trying to judge all the people's disputes and Jethro saw what he was doing and told him that was not good as he was wearing himself out. So Jethro counseled him to choose several able men and let them judge the people except in major disputes which could be brought back to Moses. He did as Jethro suggested.

The older we get, the more wisdom we have. '"Older and Wiser" is an old saying. I wish that when I was younger, I would have known some of the things I know now. I would have made better choices, especially in spiritual matters. I wish I had received Jesus as a child instead of at age 39. But the Lord tells us not to look at the past, except to learn from our mistakes, but to look to the future. And the nearer I get, I realize I can hardly wait to be with Him in glory.

October 15th ~ Words, Words, Words

Words are spiritual triggers. They are little things that produce big results. Words trigger faith or fear, joy or despair, courage or discouragement. This is a spiritual principle.

We must become conditioned to saying the right words. If you start listening to yourself, you will discover that you have many, many wrong phrases and expressions that you use automatically, without even thinking.

Examples: "Blue Monday;" "If it wasn't for bad luck, I wouldn't have any luck at all;" "My memory gets worse each year;" "I feel like I'm catching a cold, I always get flu this time of the year;" "That just tickled me to death;" "I thought I would die laughing;" "I am getting so old and feeble;" and so on. Proverbs 18:21 says, "Life and death are in the power of the tongue."

I want to challenge you to begin turning those expressions around. Start conditioning yourself to respond to every situation with words of faith instead of words of unbelief. It takes work but it can be done. Make a decision right now to begin this spiritual conditioning. Remember this is how Jesus defeated the devil in the wilderness - WITH THE WORD OF GOD.

We must try to remember to stop speaking words that bring us into agreement with the laws of sin and death. Talk instead about the law of the Spirit of life in Christ Jesus which has made us free from the law of sin and death. Every time you do, your spirit will get stronger. Your spiritual muscles will get in shape. If you keep on exercising faith responses when challenging situations come, you'll be ready with the Word. You will be able to resist the enemy and he will have to flee from you.

Faith is a law that is more real than the laws of physics and the chemical laws that are at work in this earth. Faith is the law of the Spirit of life. It works when it is put to work. You need to continually and consistently exercise it so that when the devil sends some deadly situation your way, you'll be ready for it. You will be able to deliver the knockout blow that will put Satan on his ear.

October 16th ~ The Rapture

We read about this wonderful 'snatching away' to Jesus in 1 Thessalonians 4:13-18.

Verse 16 says, "For the Lord Himself will descend from heaven with a shout, with the voice of an archangel, and with the trumpet of God." How exciting is that? I can hardly wait and truly believe it will happen in my lifetime.

Bible expert Jack Van Impe always gets me excited when he talks about this soon-coming event. He explains that until May 14, 1948, when Israel became a state, and June 1967 when Jerusalem was again in the hands of the Jews after the Six Day War, there was no chance for the rapture to take place. But now, all has come into position for Jesus' soon return. Jesus could come any day now. Other generations that thought He was coming in their day did not have those two huge signs of His appearing.

Jesus tells us all about His return in Matthew chapters 24 and 25. Whenever He says, "Watch the fig tree," He is speaking of Israel. We certainly see events happening even now that point to the end of the age.

This morning as I was singing the hymn "Near the Cross" by Fanny Crosby, one of the phrases jumped out at me: "Till my raptured soul finds rest beyond the river." O, it will be rapturous in Heaven with Jesus and my loved ones.

What exciting red-letter words we read three times in Revelation 22:7, 12, 20: "Behold, I am coming quickly." I say, amen! Even so, come Lord Jesus! Maranatha!

October 17th ~ Kids Say the Darndest Things

Our youngest grandson Scott LaMaster is the youngest of daughter Grace's seven children. Some children are just naturally funny and he is one of them. He is sort of a sober little boy which makes his pronouncements even funnier. The other day when his mother was fussing at him, he told her, "I NEED you to be nice to me." Of course, she laughed, and started being nicer.

When asked why he thought a neighbor dog bit him, he suggested, "Maybe he was hungry?"

He announced to his mother when they were going to a birthday lunch that he did not want to talk to anyone while there. Since then Poppy his grandfather teasingly asks him if he chooses to talk this time.

My friend Anne Gassaway tells about taking her five-year-old granddaughter Kerry Anne to lunch at Neiman Marcus for her birthday. Her daddy could not wait to call his mother to tell her about little Kerry Anne's team winning their soccer game. They were going to be treated to a meal following the victory so the coach asked where the players would like to go. McDonalds was the first choice, but Kerry Anne suggested Neiman's. Go girl!

I realize our family's over developed 'funny bone' is a gift from God. In my life, I have only known a very few people who are humorless and I can't help but feel sorry for them.

Billy and I had a friend who once asked us, "What are you all laughing so hard about? I really would like to know." It was difficult to explain why we had thought some joke was so hilarious, it just was. It is a blessing from God to see the humor in life and especially not to take ourselves too seriously. Remember the old saying, "Laugh and the world laughs with you, cry and you cry alone." Not true. Jesus cries with us and dries all our tears. We are never alone. He promises He will not leave us comfortless. (John 14:18) He also laughs with us. (Psalm 2:4)

October 18th ~ Songs

Bill has a habit of having a song, usually an old one, on his mind and he keeps humming or singing it for days. Of course, it will then stay on my mind, too. Recently, it was the phrase, "I know a little bit about a lot of things, but I don't know enough about you." I wanted to think of the spiritual application to the song since I could not stop thinking about the words. It did not take me long to realize that the 'you' should become 'You.' How true. I know a little bit about a lot of things about my faith but I certainly don't know enough about my Jesus.

I could spend a lifetime and not know enough about the Lord. He is so precious. The closer I become to Him, I realize I need more of Him. I know that the more I stay in His Word, the better I know Him.

"To know" – the Greek word *ginosko* – means to perceive, understand, recognize, realize, come to know. It is the recognition of truth by personal experience. Well, I certainly had a personal experience with Jesus when I was born again, but now realize that I need to personally experience Him daily.

Just like the wedding ceremony is not all there is to a marriage, there must be a daily striving to know each other better.

Philippians 3:10 says in the Amplified, "For my determined purpose is that I may KNOW Him – that I may progressively become more deeply and intimately acquainted with Him, perceiving and recognizing and understanding the wonders of His person more strongly and more clearly."

This is my prayer. How great is it to understand the wonders of His person? A lifetime would not be enough to experience them all.

October 19th ~ Excuses

One of our favorite family stories happened when Grace was about 17 and would spend literally hours fixing her long hair. One day I asked her to run an errand for me and she quickly replied, "I can't possibly as Mike (her boy friend) will be here in four hours." Of course Bill and I laughed hysterically. She had the grace to laugh at herself and realized how absurd that statement was. We still tease her about it unmercifully.

Bill always cuts to the chase and can pull my chain in a quick minute. It seemed that I had the busiest week ever after our return from a 16-day Hawaiian cruise. There was something Bill had asked me to do and I had put it off for two or three days.

One night in bed, I piously told him that I had never been busier and simply had not had the time to do what he had asked. He immediately said, "That's right you were very busy clear up to the time I awakened you from your nap so you could get ready for your 5:45 p.m. meeting." We both fell out laughing and kept on laughing every time we would think about his remark.

Some of our excuses to God are just that ridiculous. But it makes me feel better when I read that certain Bible heroes used such bad reasons for not wanting to obey the Word God gave them. Like Moses saying he could not speak well, although he had been reared in Pharaoh's palace. (Exodus 4:10-16) God assured him that He had made his mouth and would be with him and teach him what to say. But Moses still insisted that he needed Aaron to speak for him. God was angered but agreed.

I am sure God gets very disgusted with us, too, when we tell Him we are unable to accomplish something He asks us to do. After all, He already knows we can't do it. And He does not expect us to do it in our own strength. He will do it through us. All He needs is our obedience and our willingness to be an empty vessel.

October 20th ~ What's Your Name? by Rachel Rice, Friend

Talk about bleak and black! I remember one day being so distraught and down. I was sprawled out on my hands and knees, nose dripping and mopping tears in the middle of the bedroom floor, screaming out to the Lord, "God, don't You care? You're so far away! Why aren't You speaking to me? Let me hear Your voice. Tell me what to do and

I will do it. How am I ever going to know what You want if You don't speak to me? You say I am chosen; You say You call Your sheep by name!"

Today I don't even remember what the huge dilemma was. I just remember how undone, hopeless and helpless I was. My whole world had stopped, disintegrated into dirt and debris. It was a melting point beyond anything I had ever known before. Void in complete dejection – a total pit experience. Was this how Joseph felt when he was down in the pit, or maybe even a small bit of Jesus' feelings in Gethsemane's garden?

"Lord, You say You know everything about me, that You have counted the hairs on my head and even numbered them. Where are You now? Lord, Your Word says You plan my every step and You know right where I am."

Again, the Lord asked me to consider my name. "Rachel," I yelled back! "And what does Rachel mean?" Oh, Lord, it means sheep, little ewe lambs, little sheep!" I blurted out the Hebrew definition.

"Ahhh, Lord!" I 'saw' it suddenly in my heart! He had named me 'Rachel,' His 'sheep.'* He had named me before the foundation of the world, and chosen me so I could be His sheep. He was right there at that moment, in the middle of my mental morass, with His love waiting for me to hush up and let Him whisper my name into my ears.

Oh what joy! I jumped up and ran throughout my house weeping tears with the revelation "I'm His sheep!" I was laughing so hard; what an about turn. The joke was on me! The Lord was waiting there with me, just trying to find a way to slip His Word in sideways. Needless to say, I have never allowed myself another pitiful, dark day. He is with us always, all ways, and He will not leave us or forsake us. Hallelujah!

"...His sheep hear His voice and He calls His own sheep by name and leads them out...for they know His voice" (John 10:3-4).

October 21st ~ A Mighty Fortress

Martin Luther based his famous hymn "A Mighty Fortress is Our God" on Psalm 46. While meditating on the first verse, "God is our refuge and strength, a very present help in time of trouble," I happened to glance at the footnote which says, "An abundantly available help." This really excited me. Of course, He is always a very present help but abundantly available sounds even better. Not just available, but ABUNDANTLY available. How good is that?

Psalm 46:2 goes on to say, "Therefore we will not fear, though the earth be removed, and though the mountains be carried into the midst of the sea." Sounds like an earthquake to me.

In California we hear much talk about earthquakes. It is said that it is not a matter of IF but WHEN a big one comes. On the news, they mention that people should get the supplies they would need in case there is a quake. The newscasters are always such prophets of doom, but I do think Palm Springs is right on the fault line. So is Los Angeles and I would worry about my son Tim if it was not for this special promise to believers - we will not fear if the earth is shaken. I believe that with all my heart. We will not fear. God is our refuge and a bulwark never ceasing.

In the last two verses of Psalm 46, we are told to be still and know that He is God, He is in control and is our high tower and stronghold. Even when the mountains are shaken, God is in our midst and we shall not be moved. The Lord of Hosts is with us. As the hymnist says, "Did we in our own strength confide, our striving would be losing, were not the right man on our side, the Man of God's own choosing."

October 22nd ~ Govern Your Tongue

"For we all often stumble, fall and offend in many things, And if anyone does not offend in speech (never says the wrong things), he is a fully developed character and a perfect man, able to control his whole body and to curb his entire nature" (James 3:2 - Amplified).

The word "govern" means to exercise authority, to rule, to direct and control; a regulating device for controlling motion. Your tongue is a regulating device for your body and your life. You must govern your own tongue.

"The tongue is a fire. The tongue is a world of wickedness set among our members, contaminating and depraving the whole body and setting on fire the wheel of birth (the cycle of man's nature), being itself ignited by hell (Gehenna)" (James 3:6 - Amplified).

Whenever you say anything that is the opposite of what God has said in His Word, it is evil. Remember the 10 spies in Numbers 13? God called their report "evil" because it was contrary to what He had said.

A scripture can be found that will cover any problem and so you need to keep confessing God's truth until it comes to pass. Your question should always be, "Well, Lord, how are You going to work this out for my good?" Not, "Woe is me." With every temptation and trial, God has made a way of escape and that comes by knowing and confessing God's Word. This is what I mean by governing your tongue; speaking God's Words and not your own.

In Mark 11:23, Jesus said that you can have what you say if you believe what you are saying will come to pass and do not doubt in your heart. It is based on God's provisions. Jesus defeated Satan with the Word and we can, too, if we govern our tongues and align our words with God's Words.

October 23rd ~ God of All Comfort

2 Corinthians 1:3-4 says, "Blessed be the God and Father of our Lord Jesus Christ, the Father of mercies and God of all comfort, who comforts us in all our tribulations that we may be able to comfort those who are in any trouble, with the comfort with which we ourselves are comforted

by God."

Yes, He is the God of all comfort. I always like to think of His loving arms around people who are grieving. He certainly did comfort me in my times of great sadness. Yes, He used people, too, but He was my main source of comfort, joy and strength.

In an old hymnal *Great Songs of the Church* given me by Florra Sorrels, my faithful Bible study friend, I came to a hymn I had never heard before, "Come, Ye Disconsolate" by Thomas Moore. The phrases that particularly struck me were talking about coming to the mercy seat of God:

"Here bring your wounded hearts, here tell your anguish; earth has no sorrow that heav'n cannot heal".

"Here speaks the Comforter, tenderly saying, earth has no sorrow that heav'n cannot cure."

"Come to the feast of love, ever knowing earth has no sorrow but heav'n can remove."

How true! God can and will 'heal, cure and remove' ALL sorrow IF we will only come to Him at His mercy seat and let Him. I often think about the time I was disconsolate with grief over my brother's death and went to the Word to read again Isaiah 53, the truth that Jesus bore my grief on the cross. So I simply said to Him, "Why am I still bearing it if You did it for me? I am giving it up to You right now." (Or putting it down or whatever, but something like that.) Almost immediately, I felt that heavy burden of grief lift off of me. He really DID take it away. He is the God of all comfort. Praise His name.

October 24th ~ Turned Around

John 20:14 "…she turned around and saw Jesus." Yes, sometimes we have to turn around to see Jesus. Like Moses who turned aside to see the burning bush, he could have ignored it. We may be so focused on worldly things that we don't see Jesus. Imagine having our backs turned to Him; how sad.

To repent means to turn around. This is what we need in our lives so we can see Him clearly. Letting go of our old way of doing things is easier said than done. We really don't like to give up our old, comfortable ways.

Recently I ordered a new Bible cover online as my old soft leather one was falling apart. But I hate this new one. It's stiff. I will just have to get used to it, I guess. I know the old sayings "like an old shoe' or 'old hat' and they are true. We settle for the comfortable. We resist change. I also just got a new cell phone but wish I had my old scratched up one back. It wasn't so hard to figure out.

I asked the Lord if I was doing this same thing in my spiritual life as well as my physical – that is, clinging to my old routine of prayer time or whatever and He assured me that I was. He said I tend to resist when the Spirit tries to lead me in a new direction, a different order in my usual quiet time with Him.

I think I must finish one part before I begin another. He showed me the reason I resist – ugh! It is because I want to be in control! I thought I had repented of and given up that old spirit of control. Guess it was not really dead as it keeps popping up.

All I need to do is 'turn around' and see Jesus in my situation and ask Him to help me let Him be in control. He will always set us in the right direction. Have Thine own way, Lord. Amen.

October 25th ~ Glory

Some of my grandchildren are taking sign language classes this summer and are very excited about all they are learning. Jane Anne, 8, showed me how to sign 'glory' and it really blessed me. Place your hand in the palm of the other and then raise it up with a shaking motion all the way to the other side. It makes you really think of the glory of the Lord. I also love 'forgiveness' which is shown by brushing your hands together with a finishing motion – all done.

There are two words for "glory" in the Bible. Isaiah 60:1 says, "Arise, shine; for your light has come! And the glory of the Lord is risen upon you."

"Glory" - *chabod* (in the Hebrew language) — means weightiness, that which is substantial or heavy; glory, honor, splendor, power, wealth, authority, magnificence, fame, dignity, riches and excellency." *Chabod* is God's glory, but not only His honor, renown and majesty, but also His visible splendor. (1Kings 8:11) From *chabod* are derived the names Jochebed (*Yahweh* is Glory) and *'Ichabod'* (Where is the Glory?"

"The word glory (Greek *doxa)* is found in John 2:11. It says, "The beginning of signs Jesus did in Cana of Galilee, and manifested His glory; and His disciples believed in Him." The word also means splendor, radiance and majesty, absolute perfection residing in Christ and evidenced by the miracles He performed.

Oh how I yearn to see and feel the heaviness of His presence, His glory, in all His magnificence like the people felt it at the dedication of Solomon's Temple. The priests could not continue ministering for they were unable to stand when the glory of the Lord filled the house of the Lord. (1 Kings 8:11) Just think, soon and very soon, His glory will cover the whole earth. Come, Lord Jesus.

October 26th ~ Faith, the Key to Unlimited Treasure

Faith is the doorway to abundance. It's the key to unlimited treasure. Jesus has given us His faith; not just a portion of it, but all of it. Neither did he give us only a portion of Himself. Everything He has and is has been given us in full measure.

Colossians 2:3 says that all the treasures of wisdom and knowledge are hidden in Him. Well, that's where we are, in Him. (Verses 9, 10)

We can use the faith of God as Jesus does. After all, He is

as much your Father as He is Jesus' Father. You're as much His child as Jesus is. The Word says all things are possible to the believer.

It is up to you and me to decide how far we go with the faith He has given us. The only limits placed on the growth of our faith are determined by us for the Father has not limited the faith in any way.

The growth of our faith is in direct proportion to the time spent developing it. It's not like the growth of natural things that have built-in limitations. Faith will continue to grow however large it has to be to overcome the storms of life that seek to destroy us.

Satan is limited. Everything, thank God, in this world of sin and death is defeated. Faith is unlimited. Why? Because it's Source is unlimited.

Faith is born out of the Word Himself. "Faith comes by hearing and hearing by the Word of God" (Romans 10:17). That's why faith is so easy for the person who spends time in the Word. It's what we were born to do – BELIEVE.

October 27th ~ Fear

God does not always tell us why bad things happen to good people, He just tells us to trust Him. He really means it when He tells us that "all things work together for our good to those who love Him" (Romans 8:28). Sometimes this seems very hard to believe when we see disasters like Hurricane Katrina. Only God could possibly bring some good out of a situation like that. Satan comes to steal, kill and destroy but Jesus came that we may have an abundant life. (John 10:10) I even read that Katrina means purifying.

Our job is to trust and not be afraid when there are disasters. It is probably good for us to realize that everything we have is temporary and of no eternal value. I walked around my house just looking at my stuff and thinking how it could all be gone in an instant. That helped me put my life in perspective and appreciate the important things – God, family, country.

Still, the devil tries to put fear on me - reminding me of the hoodlums with stolen guns from New Orleans now loose in Baton Rouge looking for money to buy drugs. With Burke, Laura, Mary-Margaret and Payne living there, I pray extra hard. The Lord reminded me that I claim Psalm 91 for them every night so what do I have to fear? The angels are surrounding them with protection.

I truly believe this promise and come against even the tiniest bit of fear. I just heard Charles Stanley on TV say that fear is a landmine that Satan puts in our paths and we must uncover it and disarm it.

Franklin Roosevelt often said during the Great Depression that all we had to fear was fear itself. How right he was. God says in Isaiah 41:10, "Fear not, for I am with you; be not dismayed, for I am your God. I will strengthen you, yes, I will help you. I will uphold you with my righteous right hand (His sovereign, ruling hand)." He is still on the throne. Thanks be to God.

October 28th ~ Cherish

Ephesians Chapter 5 tells husbands to love and cherish their wives and I am very, very grateful that Bill definitely obeys those commands. He has always made me feel loved and cherished.

The year that our great nephew Jay Hurst was quarterback for the Lobos, I decided that I had lost enough weight to buy some blue jeans. One night when we were dressing for a game, I surprised Bill with my new jean outfit. He all but stuttered in trying to be tactful. These were his words that I still laugh about: "I am not sure that is how you would like to look." In other words, "You are way too fat for those jeans." I immediately got his meaning and changed into clothes more fitting to my mature body. How thankful I was that he told me the truth in such a loving way.

There are countless other ways that he shows me that I

am very valuable to him and this makes me ashamed that I don't obey the commands to the wives in Ephesians 5 such as: "Wives submit to your husbands in everything." Duh. In EVERYTHING? How about some things? How about in hardly anything?

Through the years, the Lord has shown me that submission is a heart attitude. (I bet Bill would like to see it get into my actions, also.) The example He gave me was that I should turn off my reading lamp at night at the same time Bill does. I know this seems like a little thing, but I look back in shame at how my first husband Billy needed to go to sleep, but I would keep reading with my light on till all hours. (Now it is Bill who mostly reads later than I do and I have to wear a sleep mask. Talk about reaping what we sow.)

At least, I do obey Ephesians 5:33 about respecting my husband. I think he is the most wonderful, fantastic man in all the world. I do have him on a pedestal in my thoughts. (Bet he had rather have my submission.)

October 29th ~ Sports

Our eight-year-old great-grand daughter Allie is very athletic and loves all kinds of sports. When she first began softball, she reported that she would get to play the 'behind catcher.' Besides that, they play 'endings' and 'double hitters.' It sounds good to me.

I was never athletic and was the last one picked when teams were chosen. Thankfully, I was very confident and knew I was well liked even though I would not be an asset to either side. So my feelings were not hurt but I am sure many children really suffered from being overlooked. I did not care because I did not want to play.

This makes me think that we all have different gifts and we should never be upset if we do not do all things well. God does not want us to compare ourselves and our gifts to others; just to be the best 'me' I can be. Stay in the place and use the talents He has chosen for me. He always chooses us for something - we are never left out of His plan. Jesus tells us in John 15:16, "You did not choose me, but I chose you and appointed you that you should go and bear much fruit and that your fruit should remain, that whatever you ask the Father in My name He may give you." The fruit He wants us to bear is His character. The fruit of the Spirit is love, joy, peace, patience, kindness, goodness, faithfulness, gentleness and self-control. (Galatians 5:22, 23)

We can all bear this fruit because it is in us when we are born again. We just need to let it grow with the Holy Spirit's help. Not straining - an apple tree just naturally grows apples - or pushing or trying but just abiding. That's our secret, too; just abiding in the vine. (John 15:1-8) Abiding is making our home with, dwelling, just hanging out with Jesus. It's hard to imagine that the Lord of Lords and King of Kings lives in us and we in Him. He's always with us and is our 'behind catcher.' When we get behind in anything, He says to us: "I've got your back."

October 30th ~ Worry

My first child Grace was born on October 30th and I started almost immediately worrying about whether to send her to school early. I asked everyone I could think of what they thought. Billy finally told me not to mention it to him ever again, as I completely wore us both out worrying about it. I was literally frantic trying to decide right up to her kindergarten age. My excuse for my concern was that I had gone to school early and when my peers were ready to ride bicycles, skate or whatever, my motor skills were not up to theirs. Well, I finally decided to just let her go at the regular time.

Worry is to strangle or choke. This worry and many other concerns over the children's health and other less-important things choked out much of my joy and peace. I now realize that I must not get into the world of 'what if's' and vain imaginations. (2 Corinthians 10:5)

Psalm 55:22 (Amplified) says, "Cast your burden on the Lord – releasing the weight of it…" Burden means load, weight borne or carried, oppression. A burden not released to the Lord will strain your shoulders or your back, but YOU have to cast it off. God will not take it unless you give it to Him. Literally hurl the weight off.

"Be anxious for nothing" is a command not a suggestion. (Philippians 4:6) And John 14:27 says, "Do not LET your heart be troubled." He bequeaths peace to us but worry will choke it out. There is no peace when you are walking in anxiety. What we all need is a revelation of God's unconditional love; then we never have to be anxious. Praise the Lord!

1 Peter 5:7 (Amplified) says, "Casting the whole of your care, [ALL your anxieties, ALL your worries, ALL your concerns, once and for ALL] on Him, for He cares for you affectionately and cares about you watchfully."

October 31st ~ Singing Over Me

Some scriptures are so utterly fantastic that they seem hard to believe. Zephaniah 3:17 is one of those. It says, "The Lord will rejoice over you with singing."

Wow! I run out of adjectives thinking how marvelous that is. The Amplified Bible says, "He will exult over you with singing." And best of all, the Hebrew Amplified says, "In fact, He shouts and sings and triumphs joyfully proclaiming the gladness of His heart in a song of rejoicing all because of you! Hear the voice of the Lord as He sings over you, His child." How good is that? Wow, again.

At a Love Overflowing meeting, Pat Salisbury gave me a word that I should just be still and let Him rejoice over me with singing and hear His voice. Well, since then I have been listening and expecting. But I admit that I have been patient and quiet enough to hear Him only a few times. Why in the world would I deny myself this wonderful privilege?

My only excuses are becoming distracted or feeling that I need to fill the quiet with prayer requests or just plain not wanting to spend the time it takes to listen closely. Forgive me, Lord, and give me more chances to let You bless me.

This verse never fails to inspire me with wonder and awe. "The Lord your God is in the midst of you, a Mighty One, a Savior [Who saves]! He will rejoice over you with joy; He will rest [in silent satisfaction] and in His love He will be silent and make no mention (of past sins, or even recall them); He will exult over you with singing." I keep thinking it is I who should be exulting over Him in singing.

My resolve is to meditate over and over on this one verse till I believe it deep in my spirit. Then I will be still and know the voice of the Lord is singing over me.

November 1st ~ Continually

We are told in Psalms 70:4 "And let those who love Your salvation say 'continually' let God be magnified." Oh, I do love Your salvation, Lord, so help me to 'continually' say, "O magnify the Lord with me and let us exalt His name together" (Psalm 34:3).

I think the Bible likes the word 'continually' as it is used often. Just in Psalm 71 we are told three times in Verses 3, 6, 14, "Be to me a rock of habitation to which I may 'continually' come." And, "My praise is 'continually' of You." Finally, "But as for me, I will hope 'continually' and will praise You more and more." Also in Verses 15 and 24, we read that we are to think of and tell of His righteousness all day long. That sounds like 'continually' to me.

The heading on Psalm 71 in my New American Standard Bible is, "Prayer of an Old Man for Deliverance." So now at my age I pay close attention to it. Verse 18 has long been a favorite, "And even when I am old and gray, O God, do not forsake me, until I declare Your strength to this generation, Your power to all who are to come."

This is my desire and Bill's. We truly want to bless our

many children (eight) and grandchildren (23) and great-grandchildren (17) and lots more to come. We feel humbled to be called Matriarch and Patriarch of such a large group and take our responsibility seriously, praying for them all by name every night. Certainly, prayer is the most important investment we can make in their lives, but we also desire to declare His wondrous works to them.

Actually, we realize there is no way we could possibly relate ALL the miracles He has done for us personally in our 80-plus years but we can 'continually' tell them of His goodness, power and love.

November 2nd ~ Time

Most of us long for more time each day to get all we need to get done. I just read a story about the small town of Crimond, Scotland, which is famous for its unusual clock in the church tower. The clockmaker accidentally put six marks into one of the five-minute sections on the face of the clock. As a result, each hour in Crimond is 61 minutes, making a day there 24 minutes longer than anywhere else on earth.

Well, I guess we could all move to Crimond or trust in the Lord's promise to add length to our days. Proverbs 3:16 says, "Length of days is in her right hand, in her left are riches and honor." (The 'she' spoken of here is God's Wisdom.) I realize this verse is referring to long life, but when I am frustrated with lack of time, I claim it for the particular day I am experiencing.

Certainly we have all heard the old saying, "Time marches on." Well, as I grow older, it seems time is doing the quickstep. I heard Evangelist Kenneth Copeland say that we are in that funnel of time before Jesus' return and that time really has sped up. It is not our imagination. Even young people feel that it is going faster than usual. Well, I say yea, come, Lord Jesus. Amen.

Ecclesiastes 3:1 says, "To everything there is a season, a

time for every purpose under heaven." This means to me that there is enough time to do all we need to do each day. Thank You, Lord. You never give us more to do than we can accomplish with Your help. But You need to show us the difference in what You would have us do and our own ideas. Amen

November 3rd ~ Apples to Oranges by Julie Setzer, Daughter

A friend of mine and I were having a conversation the other day when the topic of comparisons came up. She was dismayed because she didn't have certain qualities that others had. She wondered aloud why she wasn't likeable as everyone else.

Her wonderings reminded me of a profound moment in my life that happened years ago. In the early 1990s, I had the privilege of going on several mission trips to Del Rio, Texas, and Mexico with some wonderfully gifted people.

If you have never been on a mission trip, let me tell you they can be very enlightening and revealing as well as very humbling. On a mission trip you are generally in uncharted waters. You are usually way out of your comfort zone and are ministering to people in need on an intense level. One of the coolest things about God is that you normally end up being ministered to more than doing the ministering. Like I said, it can be very humbling.

In our case, as in a lot of cases of ministry, we were ministering to people who not only didn't speak the same language as we did, but who lived in a completely different world. That type of ministry takes a lot of creativity and spunk. The people I had the pleasure of ministering with had plenty of both. So much so that one night as I lay in my bunk bed surrounded by about 30 other women and girls, I started complaining silently to the Lord. I had just spent several days watching my close friends shine as they ministered and I was feeling pretty much the dullard.

I said, "Look, Lord, why can't I be as funny as Paul or as smart as Susan or as charming as Kathy? Why did You make me like this? I've got nothing to offer these people. I've got nothing that will draw people to You. Why did You even let me come on this trip?"

This is what He said in response: "Are you through with your list of complaints against the way I made you?" To which I rather sheepishly replied, "Uh yeah, I suppose so."

Then He said, "The trap of deceit you have fallen into is the most common and stifling of all the traps of the enemy. Julie, I gave you the talents that I want you to have just like I gave everyone else their own talents and you need to appreciate them. You have no business comparing yourself to others. It is a dangerous trap, don't fall into it. The only thing you need to do is be aware of how much I love people; you need to feel it and share it. That is the main thing. You can be certain that I love all people and you can operate from that certainty. That will keep you from looking at yourself."

I lay there in stunned amazement. For the next few minutes I felt like God was washing me, nearly drowning me, in His love for others. What a wonderful freedom that brought to me in the area of reaching out to people in my own way. I quit hating myself for not being like everyone else. Periodically, we are all tempted to compare ourselves to others, but it is as fruitless (no pun intended) as comparing apples to oranges.

November 4th ~ Make-Up

One day when I drove up in my daughter Grace's driveway, I saw granddaughter Leslie sitting in her car. So I asked her where she was going and she said, "Nowhere, I am just putting on my make-up out here as I can see better in this light." I thought that was really funny, but perhaps also had a spiritual meaning: That we can see more clearly in the light of God's Word? Or that the Word is a mirror to us?

In the Message Bible, James 1:22-25 says, "Don't fool yourself into thinking that you are a listener when you are anything but, letting the Word go in one ear and out the other. Act on what you hear! Those who hear and don't act are like those who glance in the mirror, walk away and two minutes later have no idea who they are, what they look like. But whoever catches a glimpse of the revealed counsel of God - the free life! - even out of the corner of his eye; and sticks with it, is no distracted scatterbrain, but a man or woman of action. That person will find delight and affirmation in the action."

It seems we can look in a mirror and go away without seeing the real person we need to be. In my day we wore nothing but lipstick and sometimes a little powder. I was blessed with a nice complexion and did not wear any foundation or eye makeup until I was 31. That was when I was made up by a professional while performing in one of our Junior Service League's Red Stocking Revues. I could not get over how much better I looked, so I started wearing all the extra stuff. And now that I have looked into the mirror of God's Word and have stuck with it, I see the real changes I daily need to make in my life. My foundation is built on nothing else than the Rock of my salvation, Jesus Himself, and my eyes are made up as they are flooded with the light of His truth.

November 5th ~ Busy and Overwhelmed

Keeping busy in the non-essentials of life and inventing schemes to occupy our minds, we become busy and overwhelmed. Cluttered minds cannot hear the still, small voice of God. (Colossians 3: 2)

We're always playing the radio, iPod or talking on the cell phone when driving and keeping the TV, DVDs, CDs and PCs going constantly at home cluttered with noise. Pounding our minds with the news 24 hours a day. Flooding our mailboxes with junk mail, mail order catalogs, and every kind of Christian newsletter and promotion offering free products, services and false hopes. Being seduced by glitzy advertising that will lure us away from God, tempting us to spend, spend, spend, and borrow, borrow, borrow. Busy! Busy! Clutter! Clutter!

It is no wonder we become busy and overwhelmed. But Jesus said to Martha, "Martha, Martha, you are anxious and worried about many things. There is need of only one thing. Mary has chosen the better part and it will not be taken from her" (Luke 10:41-42).

Martha was too busy to spend time with Jesus. There was no quiet time with her. Sometimes we can be so busy and noisy, there is no time to spend with Jesus. A day without Jesus is a day wasted.

We live in a privileged time. God could have decided for us to live in Old Testament times before the coming of Jesus, but He has given us the honor of living here and now. Before Jesus' time, many would have longed to live in our time, with all our graces.

Do we give God time, attention and space in our lives every day? Do we welcome Him into our homes, lives and hearts every day?

Don't be so concerned about perishable things like food. Spend your energy seeking the eternal life that the Son of Man can give you. For God the Father has given me the seal of His approval. (John 6:27)

November 6th ~ Revelation Knowledge

Daughter Grace drew my name at our family Thanksgiving where each year we draw names of family members for whom we pray during the coming year. I was thrilled, as Grace is a strong and faithful pray-er. Right after the New Year, the Lord told her to pray for me to have more and more revelation knowledge. How exciting is that?

Well, the Lord asked me early this morning if I believed

her prayer would be answered. I replied that I certainly did believe and receive it. He quickly began to speak to me that as sure as I was seeing the sun on the horizon, He was coming soon. Jesus said He was standing ready to come whenever Father God says it is time.

He added, "So you stay ready to fly in the sky. Soon and very soon you will hear the trumpet sound and the angels will come to gather you. Look for signs that My coming is near – look up, your redemption is drawing nigh. Whenever problems arise, meditate on that truth and look up, look up to Me, look up to Me, look up to Me. For every answer, solution, direction, comfort, peace, provision, healing and everything you have need of.

"Don't look for the world to give it all to you for all blessings come from Me. Expect a great overflow of miracles and blessings as you rest and relax in Me. Looking unto Jesus the Author and Finisher of your faith, the Alpha and Omega, the beginning and the end, the way, the way, the way."

And He began showing me a wonderful picture of an escalator moving steadily toward heaven. (Like Jacob's ladder, but with 21st-century technology—ha.) It seemed that I was about three-fourths of the way up looking at Jesus standing at the top waiting with His loving arms wide open to receive me. Of course, the closer I came to the top, the clearer I could see Him.

And He said to me, "Sometimes it may feel as though the escalator is stuck, but I promise you that I will keep it running smoothly all the way to the top. You don't have to worry about it stopping or even slowing down. It's coming and you are on it and it is right where I have you in My perfect plan for your life. The enemy cannot stop it. You are riding to glory with more and more blessings as you get nearer and nearer to the top. You are being brought to Me with no effort of your own.

"Your only move was to come to Me in the beginning and so now I'm allowing you to come on and on. Don't you feel as though you were being carried upwards and upwards into my loving arms? The escalator is already in my Kingdom. No wonder you feel so much excitement lately.

"And I am taking care of your body, too. You will have all the strength and energy and knowledge that you need for the last one-fourth of the ride. Relax, relax, relax, enjoy the scenery, it's beautiful. Look up, look up, look up. You are almost there!"

(Thank You, Lord! This revelation seems to be for all true believers, so I am adding it to the book).

November 7th ~ Out of the Mouth of Babes

Our son Tim loves his Hollywood Presbyterian Church for many reasons, but he really enjoys it when the pastor gathers the children around him at the front of the church to tell them, in simple words, a story that relates to his sermon for the day. The children often ask insightful questions.

One day the pastor was telling the story from John 21 about Jesus appearing to His disciples by the lake. The disciples had fished all night and had no success. So the Lord told them to cast their nets on the right side and they hauled in a huge catch.

But when Peter heard that it was the Lord, he jumped out of the boat to swim to Jesus on the shore. One of the little boys raised his hand to asked, "Had Peter taken swimming lessons?" As the lesson continued, another child lifted a hand and said, "That light is in my eye." At least they were not asleep!

But my all-time favorite is when the pastor was talking about the first words that Jesus spoke when He came out of the tomb. He was excited to learn that in modern-day language it was equivalent to a familiar "Hi." So he asked the children what they thought Jesus' first words were and a little girl raised both hands and quickly replied, "Ta-da!" Pretty right on, eh?

Oh, that we would all have the simplicity of little children! In Matthew 18:1-4, we see Jesus using a child as an example to the disciples and He told them and us to become as little children to enter the kingdom of heaven. He goes on to say that whoever humbles himself as this little child is the greatest in the kingdom of heaven. Wow. I guess that we need to obey His command to become as little children. This makes me think of the admonition: "Keep it simple, saints."

November 8th ~ Encouragement

A lady from Kilgore, Texas, called to tell me how very much she was enjoying my book and it really encouraged me. How precious of her to take time to call just to tell me that it was blessing her. I had not been feeling very well all day and this lifted my spirit so much that I instantly felt better. It only took a moment for her to be kind to me and I still feel the glow of knowing I am appreciated.

Proverbs 27:2 says, "Let another man praise you, and not your own mouth; a stranger and not your own lips."

Wow! I began to think how seldom I do something like that. I am so selfish with my own time that I hate to give some of it up to make an encouraging phone call. Or even to write a note to let someone know they are being thought of, or just to pat them on the back for a job well done. I know we should look to the praise of God and not man, but it sure feels good when we get both. (John 12:43)

How stingy we are sometimes with our praise, when just a little word lifts others' spirits. I don't mean flattery, but sincere praise. We can always find something good to say about someone. (I don't mean like the old joke —you don't sweat much for a fat girl.) Just like simple praise can raise spirits, cutting words can break them.

As Christians, we are called upon to watch our words. Again, not being dishonest and lying about our feelings, but being careful not to deliberately hurt anyone. We hurt others enough without meaning to do so.

I was given a book that I did not care for at all, in fact, I did not agree with the premise; too liberal for my taste. But I did appreciate being thought of and so I stressed that in my thank-you note and also how clearly the author made his points.

Philippians 4:8 says, ".......If there is anything worthy of praise, meditate on these things." We can always find something to praise.

November 9th ~ His Eye is on the Sparrow

Psalm 33:18 says, "Behold, the eye of the Lord is upon them that fear Him, upon them that hope in His mercy." How much do you hope in His mercy? Do you really believe God loves you and yearns to be merciful toward you? Unless you have a very firm understanding that God loves you, you will never be convinced that His greatest desire is to bless you.

You must know, that you know, that you know, that He loves you. We are His most loved children and He loves us with an everlasting love. Nothing will ever change that fact, no matter what we do. God's focus is on every circumstance, every single detail in His children's life.

In Christ's day, sparrows were the meat of the poor, sold two for a penny. Yet, Jesus said, "Not one of these small creatures falls to the ground without your Father knowing it."

"Fall" in this verse signifies more than the bird's death. The Aramaic meaning is "to light upon the ground." In other words, it indicates every little wounded hop a tiny bird makes. He is concerned over every detail of its life even when it falls from the nest and begins to hop on the ground. (Matthew 10, Luke 12)

Matthew 10:31 says, "Fear not, therefore, are you not much more value than many sparrows?" Or in Verse 30, "The very hairs on your head are numbered." Simply put, the One who made and counted all the stars and keeps the galaxies in their orbit, has His eye fixed on you. Glory to

God.

In spite of all the glorious words from Christ, many Christians, in their times of crisis, cling to doubts about God's concern for them. Christ described the last days as a time so troubling and frightful that men's hearts would fail them in fear. (Luke 21:26) Yet, Jesus tells us three times in Matthew 10:26, 28 and 31 to "Fear not!"

And He gave the disciples the antidote for all fear: The Father's eye is always on the sparrow. How much more will it always be on you, His beloved child?

November 10th ~ Sure Way to Happiness

William Law was a 17th Century English scholar who said, "If anyone would tell you the shortest, surest way to happiness and all perfection, he must tell you to make a rule to thank and praise God for everything that happens to you. For it is certain that whatever seeming calamity happens to you, if you thank and praise God for it, you turn it into a blessing."

Paul tells us the same thing and when you think of all his hardships, that's an even more remarkable statement. He was persecuted, often hungry, shipwrecked, beaten, imprisoned and finally beheaded. He also said he had learned to be content in whatever state he found himself. (1Thessalonians 5:18, Ephesians 5:20)

Certainly the Pilgrims, too, were cold, hungry, sick and many were dying but when harvest came, they had a celebration to give thanks to God for His blessings. It was truly a *holy day* rather than a holiday as it is today.

Fretting can take away our joy and gratitude. We need to be overflowing with gratitude.

Philippians 4:6-7 in the Amplified Bible says, "Do not fret or have any anxiety about anything, but in every circumstance and in everything, by prayer and petition (definite requests), with thanksgiving, continue to make your wants known to God.

"And God's peace [shall be yours, that tranquil state of a soul assured of its salvation through Christ, and so fearing nothing from God and being content with its earthly lot of whatever sort that is, that peace] which transcends all understanding shall garrison and mount guard over your hearts and minds in Christ Jesus."

Then after you've prayed with thanksgiving, you wait with thanksgiving. Giving thanks is a simple concept; it does not require a doctorate in theology to grasp it. (Matthew 11:25)

Practicing the art of thanksgiving today will prepare you for heaven's courts of praise.

November 11th ~ "The Open Doors", by L.F. Payne, Grandson, Age 12

I see a door of opportunity Hanging open
Hanging open –
It read, All you want is in this room
Calling for me
And I open it
It will lead me to the other side
A world is shone
A world beyond my wildest dreams
There was a chance for me to do whatever I wanted
Let it be being in the majors, going through middle, high school and college with straight A's, whatever!
It seemed perfect
I said to myself, "What am I to do?"
I needed to get back to real life
I started to panic, the door was closing
What was I to do?
I ran towards the door, but it was closed tight
I thought hard about what I wanted to do
To hide and be sorrowful or to want a chance to get to life
I pleaded to get through the door

It opened and I walked through
Suddenly I saw another door, right next to the one I came out
There this time said, "What do you really want to do?"
I said, "Whatever God wants me to do."
It opened and on the other side I saw nothing like before
I saw many doors
I knew I could return out of the rooms because
These words were shone above the doors
ANYTHING IS POSSIBLE THROUGH GOD !

Author's note: L.F. was salutatorian of his graduating High School class at the age of 17.

November 12th ~ Overcoming Evil

Many of us are very concerned about the evil in our nation, the media, the government, the entertainment business and the world in general. We sometimes reach the point of not only of hating these things, but also the persons responsible for these things evil. Experience has shown, however, that hate by itself eliminates no evil. God tells us, "Do not be overcome by evil, but overcome evil with good" (Romans 12:21).

Along these lines, I read this statement that really stuck with me: "A PERSON CANNOT GROW FLOWERS SIMPLY BY HATING WEEDS." Isn't that good? The flowers become the main purpose. Eliminating weeds becomes a secondary thing.

Jesus counseled us to love our enemies, to do good and pray for those who despitefully use us. (Matthew 5:44; Luke 6:26, 27) We do win our enemies more often with love than in any other way. Lately, as I listen to my own conservative talk-show hosts, they talk an awful lot about the weeds and instead of speaking hope they speak hate. This isn't helping our cause. We do not produce good simply by hating evil. Doing good should be our main purpose.

What the Lord has been showing me is to remember that He is sovereign, that the battle is His and my job is just to pray.

This morning as I was outside praying and looking at the gorgeous mountains that He created, I thought, "God's in His heaven, all's right with the world."

Then I went on to think all is right in my world because I know the God of the universe and He turns the king's heart wherever He wishes. (Proverbs 21:10) These are not my problems. I am to look at an all-powerful God and not at the wrongs in the world. In other words, look at the flowers and not at the weeds.

O, God, in a world abounding in evil, make us aware of that which is good. Amen.

November 13th ~ Restoring the Walls

The word "restore" means to reestablish, replace. Revive means to bring back to life. In Nehemiah 4:2, the Samarians were taunting the Jews who had come with Nehemiah to rebuild the walls of Jerusalem and they mockingly said, "What are these feeble Jews doing? Are they going to RESTORE it for or by themselves? Can they REVIVE the stones from the dusty rubble even the burned ones?" (What a joke, they thought!)

No, they were not trying to restore it by themselves. They were looking to their God and constantly praying to Him, asking for guidance and help. God answered and they were able to completely restore and rebuild the wall.

Many were against them so they set up guards to protect them from their enemies day and night. Even their own people tried to discourage them. Nehemiah 4:12 says, "And when the Jews who lived near them came, they said to us ten times, You must return [to guard our little villages]; from all places where they dwell they will be upon us."

But they overcame discouragement when they remembered that their God would fight for them. How many times have people tried to discourage us from believing a promise of God or from continuing a mission we know we have been called to do for Him?

God says, "DO NOT FEAR—DO NOT BE AFRAID OF THEM, remember the Lord who is great and awesome, and fight for your brothers, your sons, your daughters, your wives and your houses" (Nehemiah 4:14). We are still fighting for our families in prayer today and rebuilding walls that have been torn down.

How do we fight for them? If you want to restore something lost in your life, start the restoration process by praising and worshipping God. He will not force blessings on anyone, so we need to believe His love and willingness to restore and then receive. God makes all things new.

November 14th ~ Doxology

This morning, the doxology kept going over and over in my mind. I grew up in churches where it was sung in every service and I miss it in the charismatic churches that I now attend. I love the words but realize that they had become so routine I didn't pay enough attention to the actual meanings.

The Doxology says, "Praise God from whom all blessings flow, Praise Him all creatures here below, Praise Him above, ye His heavenly hosts, Praise Father, Son and Holy Ghost." ALL blessings! And just think, we are praising Him with all the hosts of heaven. How good is that? Ephesians 1:3 is the inspiration for this, I believe.

So I decided to look up the origin. I learned that it was written in 1674 by Thomas Ken, a chaplain at a boy's school in England, who wrote it for the boys' devotionals. There are other doxologies, but Christians sing this one more than any other in the world.

The word Doxology comes from the Greek words: *doxa* – glory – and *logos* – word or speaking. Sometimes it closes with "As it was in the beginning is now and ever shall be, world without end. Amen." (NOW and EVER shall be! World without END! How good is that?)

Thomas Ken is known as England's first hymnist. Hymns were revolutionary in his time, as only the Psalms were sung in public worship.

He later became chaplain to King Charles ll. It was a thankless job as Charles kept a variety of mistresses. Once the king asked Thomas to lodge a mistress in the chaplain's residence but he refused saying, "Not for the King's Kingdom." This thankfully amused the king and He later referred to Thomas as "that little man who refused lodging to poor Nellie." That sort of character is needed in our clergy today. In us lay people, too.

November 15th ~ Jehovah Jireh — Our Provider

When we feel totally helpless and defeated, our answer may be right in front of us or perhaps even behind us. Like Hagar in Genesis 21:19: "God opened her eyes and she SAW the well of water." Just the minute before, she thought she and her son were going to die and then, right in front of her, was the provision they needed! God always has provision prepared for us, but when we are worried or anxious, we don't see the answer to our need.

Hagar prayed in Verse 16 that she would not see the death of her son. Although she was talking about physical death, we don't want to see our children's spiritual deaths, either. God is saying for us to draw water from the well of salvation for them. We can pray that their eyes be opened that they see their need for the Living Water. Hagar and her son Ishmael drank of the water and were refreshed and God was with her son. He will be with ours, too.

In Genesis 22, we read about Abraham and the sacrifice of his son Isaac. When Abraham thought all was lost, the Lord called to him and he lifted up his eyes and looked, and there behind him was the answer to his prayer, a ram to substitute for His son. So He named this place, "The-Lord-

Will-Provide" – Jehovah Jireh.

God has already prepared our provision, but we haven't looked to Him to show us what and where it is.

This morning in church, I was disappointed that a certain adult grandchild, who Bill and I pray for diligently, was not present. Church was almost over when I looked up and there he was. He had been there all the time, but I had not seen him. I realized that God is constantly working with our families even when it does not look like it. Jehovah Jireh provides for all our needs whether physical or spiritual. Praise His Name!

November 16th ~ In All His Ways, by Bob Lowry, Friend, Los Angeles, CA

My grandfather was the only man I remember who ever told me he loved me. We called him "Bumpa." One time that I'll somehow never forget was when I was about 12 years old. I was lying on the couch and he came up to me and patted my chest and said, "You have no idea how much your Bumpa loves you." He was right. I didn't. Not until many years later after he was gone.

We lived in a very small farming community and on Sunday afternoon, after church and noontime pot roast, we would drive out into the country in his '57 Chevy. He would put me on his lap and let me steer. When I was a young boy, he would take me fishing. He'd make his own bait out of corn flakes, vanilla and some other odd thing that was his secret recipe. We'd go to a pond full of carp and he'd bait my hook and fix the bobber. We'd always catch fish and, at the end of the day, he would wrap them in a newspaper and we'd take them to the only black family in town.

He was a gentle Christian who read the Bible every day. He was a chiropodist, foot doctor, and on Saturdays he would treat people in the town who couldn't afford to pay him.

A month or two ago, my brother passed away unexpectedly at the age of 65. He died in his sleep. He had absolutely none of his affairs in order, and being the only surviving member of the family, the job fell upon me. Going through the boxes, I found letters that Bumpa had written him in college. His letters were playful, full of nothing but love. He would end with, "God bless you and keep you in all His ways."

Thank you, brother Steve, for saving all of Bumpa's letters and for reminding me that he is still with me, urging me to "live in all His ways."

November 17th ~ Inheriting the Promises

Hebrews 6:12 says, "That you do not become sluggish, but imitate those who THROUGH FAITH AND PATIENCE inherit the promises." Often it seems to take forever for our prayers to be answered. Abraham patiently endured until he received the blessing. We, too, must patiently endure. Patience is a fruit of the Spirit (Galatians 5:22) so we can't say we don't have it - we do. Admittedly, it does have to grow with practice.

I think of the father whose daughter was dying in Mark 5:21-43 and Jesus promised to go to the girl, but then was stopped and delayed by the woman with the issue of blood. I can only imagine the father's impatience and frustration. I would have been climbing the wall. Worse still, the servant came to say that the daughter was dead! At that moment, Jesus said, "Fear not, only believe." How hard was that for the father?

Then I thought of us. Like this father, we also have Jesus' promise that He will come and take care of all our problems. But sometimes it seems as though He will never get there. The situation may even seem dead. This is when we must have the faith and patience to endure and trust Him to come and take care of whatever needs we have. He comes and says to our situations, "Arise and live." Like Ezekiel and the dry bones. Hallelujah!

When Jesus arrived at the house where the little girl lived, the professional mourners were crying and moaning. He said, "Why all this commotion and crying? The child is not dead but sleeping." (Like our dead in Christ, we will see them again.)

Many times we act like professional mourners, cry and carry on instead of staying steady and believing and especially not becoming fearful. Fear robs us of our peace and sometimes keeps Him from acting on our behalf. Even when the answer delays, we are to have faith in what He said He would do. He WILL do what He promises in His Word. Thank the Lord!

November 18th ~ Consider Your Ways

The book of Haggai is a short book of only two chapters, but has powerful messages for the Israelites about the rebuilding of the temple and meaning for us today.

The Lord tells us in Haggai chapter one to consider our ways. He says it twice which certainly should get our attention. Haggai the Prophet along with Zerubbabel had begun to rebuild the temple after the Babylonian captivity. The Lord had told him to ask the people the question: "Is it time for you yourselves to dwell in your paneled houses while this house (His temple) lies desolate?" (Verse 4) In Verse 5 and again in verse 7, the Lord of Hosts says for them to "Consider your ways!"

What are you telling us in particular to consider, Lord? Since You are talking about Your temple, I am thinking you may want us to consider the condition of our bodily temples. Do we need a little rebuilding? In Verse 8 He says to rebuild the temple that He may be pleased with it and be glorified. O, I certainly want to please You and also for You to be glorified in me, Lord. Sweet Holy Spirit, show me how!

Maybe this is the answer: for He comforts the people, and us, by telling them to "take courage, and work; for I am with you, declares the Lord of Hosts" (Haggai 2:4). Don't you feel much better immediately when the Lord says He will be with you? The Lord of Hosts, no less!

The Prophet tells the people twice to "consider from this day onward" in 2:15, 18. I am certain He is speaking to us, too, to "consider our ways" from this day onward. The book of Haggai closes with the wonderful promise, "I will make you like a signet ring, for I have chosen you, declares the Lord of Hosts" (Haggai 2:23)

November 19th ~ A Good Place

God cares about our places here on earth, our churches, our homes, and also our families. He loves beauty and wants us to have lovely surroundings. He made so many gorgeous mountains, oceans, flowers, and other things, showing that He wants us to be blessed by beauty. He has provided all his sons and daughters a blessed, peaceful place that is theirs to enjoy!

He had a garden for Adam and Eve and, even though they messed up, He still had a place for them. When the Jews were forced out of Israel, He promised them that when they returned, the wilderness would be glad for them. It would blossom abundantly. (Isaiah 35:1-2) We have seen this promise come to pass in our day as the Jewish people turn Israel from a wasteland into one of the most fertile, productive nations in the world.

Psalm 16:6 says, "The lines have fallen for me in pleasant places; yes, I have a good inheritance." And Psalm 24:1 says, "The earth is the Lord's and all its fullness." He created it all to bless His children.

God gives us richly all things to enjoy. (1Timothy 6:17)

The Lord created the earth for His family to enjoy. In the beginning, He put His people in a garden. Of course sin came in and messed up the environment, but it did not change His heart. He wants us to have a good place to live, too. (Genesis 2:9) This tells me that God cares about beauty as well as practicability. I believe that beautiful surroundings encourage fellowship with Him, too.

It is fun to think about Him having a special place for us. (Psalm 16:5-6) He has chosen our inheritance, our lot in life. Pleasant places. He leads us by still waters. (Psalm 23) Thank You, Lord.

One translation says that the man who fears the Lord will "lodge in His goodness" (Psalm 25:12-13). I love that. We can all do that if we only believe for it.

November 20th ~ Middle Verse of the Bible

Since this verse just about says it all, I don't think it is a coincidence that Psalm 118:8 is the middle verse of the Bible. "It is better to trust in the Lord than to put confidence in man." Wow – that is wonderful! The Message Bible says, "Far better to take refuge in God than to trust in people." Then Psalm 119 is the longest Psalm, actually the longest chapter in the entire Bible.

The hymn sung at the Last Supper in Matthew 26:30 was called the *Hallel* which means praise and consisted of Psalm 113-118. These were the Psalms always sung at the Passover meal, while Psalm 92 is still recited every Sabbath Day by the Jews.

Another truth that interests me is that Psalm 18 and 2 Samuel 22 are almost exactly the same. The Psalm was written by David as a song of praise to the Lord who had delivered him from the hand of all his enemies and from the hand of Saul and, in one of my Bibles, the chapter title is "God the Sovereign Savior."

David's last words are found in 2 Samuel 23:1-7, prophetic words about Jesus being like the light of the morning. In Revelation 22:16, Christ looks back to David and declares, "I am the Root and the Offspring of David, the Bright and Morning Star."

Although it is fun to know these facts, unless I concentrate on the meaning of them, it does me little good. I truly desire to trust in God more than people and for the most part believe that I do. I also want to learn to praise like David did and to remember that without God's blessing, everything I do or have would be as naught. It is always better to trust the Lord. He will never let us down.

November 21st ~ Grandchildren

If children are a blessing of the Lord, then grandchildren are a double blessing. Since they are not our responsibility, our only job is to love and pray for them.

When our children were young, we spent much of our time trying to solve their problems in our own strength. But it's a lot better now with the grandchildren since we have learned by experience that it is safe to trust the Lord to work things out in His own timing. Plus, there is nothing we can personally do about their situations. It is not our responsibility - what a freedom this is.

Sometimes we know the problems are really just training or testing grounds and when we try to get in the way, the process has to begin over. As I said, we did not learn this overnight. In fact, we had many sleepless nights tossing and turning trying to think of solutions. We did not adhere to the great AA saying that we should not do for others what they could or should do for themselves.

We were chief among enablers. Daughter Kathy said about one of her brothers that God would put him in a fix and her daddy would fix the fix. Yes, I guess we could call that playing God. Although it was done in love, it still was not the answer. It is always better to let God change our children. Both Bill and I have mellowed as we have learned from trial and error.

Just read a comment by Joseph Prince, senior pastor of Creation Church in Singapore, who said that it is not the trials that make us strong, but our responses to those trials. The devil wants us to respond, "Where is God in this?" But God wants us to respond with faith being secure in

His love. This is the truth we want to be our legacy to our grandchildren: that Jesus is the Truth and that He loves us unconditionally and will never leave us nor forsake us.

November 22nd ~ Thanksgiving Releases Power

In the Old Testament, we see that Daniel was prepared for the lion's den because he was in the habit of praying and giving thanks. He knew that when you give thanks, you release God's power and that power took him through the lion's den.

Now is the time to prepare for the lions that you may face. Give thanks daily: then when life's lions are let loose, they'll lie down and roll over like kittens. "Thanks be to God, who gives us the victory through our Lord Jesus Christ" (1 Corinthians 15:57).

When Jesus was faced with feeding the 5000, He did not wring His hands or rebuke the devil but thanked His Father in advance. (John 6:11) The disciples understood the miracle. It wasn't just the miracle of the multiplying of the bread that was so wonderful, but the fact that Jesus performed the miracle by giving thanks. If you gave thanks for the money you have in the bank, might God multiply it? Or for your job, might God promote you? Yes, thanking God can bring your miracle.

Jesus also used thanksgiving at the tomb to raise His friend Lazarus. (John 11:23) He even faced His suffering on the cross by giving thanks. (John 11:41)

Psalm 50:7-15 in the Living Bible says, "O My people, listen! For I am your God. Listen! Here are My charges against you: I have no complaint about the sacrifices you bring to My altar, for you bring them regularly. But it isn't sacrificial bullocks and goats that I really want from you. For all the animals of field and forest are mine! The cattle on a thousand hills! And all the birds upon the mountains! If I were hungry, I would not mention it to you – for all the world is mine, and everything in it. No, I don't need your sacrifices of flesh and blood. What I want from you is your TRUE THANKS; I want your promises fulfilled. I want you to trust Me in your times of trouble, so I can rescue you and you can give Me glory." (Our family reads this Psalm every Thanksgiving Day)

November 23rd ~ Good King Hezekiah

I love to read in 2 Chronicles 29-32 about Hezekiah, one of Judah's most Godly kings. In the first month of the first year of his reign, he ordered the doors of the temple to be opened and the temple repaired. What a great way to start his 29-year reign. He told the priests to sanctify themselves and carry out the rubbish from the holy places. We, too, are to seek Him first, open the doors of our own temple, repair them and carry out the rubbish. He continued to seek the Lord and he prospered wherever he went.

In 1 Kings 18-20, we read that Hezekiah did what was right in the sight of the Lord. He trusted in the Lord God; held fast to Him; and did not depart from following Him, but kept His commandments.

Once the Assyrians were surrounding Judah and sent him a message saying they were going to destroy his kingdom. Hezekiah spread the letter out before the Lord and prayed to Him to save them. He knew his mighty God and trusted completely in Him and God was faithful to answer.

Hezekiah also prayed not to die when he was very ill and the Lord granted him 15 more years. As a sign that the Lord heard his prayer and would heal him, the Lord caused the sundial to go backwards 10 degrees. Talk about favor from God. Wow!

2 Chronicles 32:7 says, "And the people were strengthened by the words of Hezekiah, king of Judah."

How wonderful to think our words would strengthen others. Yes, I believe there are many lessons we can learn from Hezekiah's life, but possibly the main one is to seek the Lord first.

November 24th ~ Thanksgiving - The Gratitude Attitude

More than anything else, thanksgiving ushers in the power and presence of God into every situation. Psalm 100:4 says, "Enter into His gates with thanksgiving and into His courts with praise: be thankful unto Him and bless His holy name." Thanksgiving opens the pathway to God, and it unlocks the supernatural power of God, as well.

The Greek word used for thanksgiving is *eucharisto* which is the root word for GRACE. Eucharist means giving thanks. Hebrews 12:28 says, "...let us have grace, whereby we may serve God acceptably with reverence and godly fear..." Grace here means thanksgiving. When you enter into thanksgiving, you enter into grace. If you are constantly complaining about your spouse, children and job, you will not activate God's grace or His supernatural power.

Colossians 3:15 says, "And let the peace of God rule in your hearts and be ye thankful." If you want to have the peace of God, start thanking Him for each person and situation in your life. The more we thank God, the more He wants to do for us, just like we feel when our children thank us.

Only one of the 10 lepers who was healed returned to thank Jesus. They all received the physical healing but only one was truly made whole, in spirit, soul and body, because he gave thanks. (Luke 17:11-19) Thanksgiving will put you into the grace of God.

Happiness and gratitude cannot be separated. Do you know any happy person who is not grateful? Or any unhappy person who is?

Thank God for every good and perfect gift from above and the indescribable gift of Jesus. Thank Him for who He is and watch things change in your life.

November 25th ~ Central Heat

Each morning when I get up on these cool November mornings, I am thankful for central heat. Just to push a button and have the heat come on is such a blessing. I remember how my daddy used to get up before all of us on cold winter mornings to light the stoves so it would be warm before we woke up. It would take him quite a while to build a fire and even longer for the stoves to get warm.

Yes, I am thankful for the simple luxuries that we sometimes now take for granted. Our children have never even known a day without central heat, or air conditioning, or TV, or many of the other conveniences we think we could not do without nowadays.

I still remember the first new home that Billy and I bought in October 1954, right after he was discharged from the Army. It was all of 1,300 square feet, a little red brick doll house with wall-to-wall carpeting, another new luxury. We were bowled over to have central air and heat. It had one very tiny bath and three bedrooms, a living/dining combo and kitchen with barely room for a table and chairs; but real pine paneling. It really was adorable for the times. Since then I've had lots bigger and prettier homes, but I still remember the excitement I had over this first one.

Especially at this time of Thanksgiving, I remember to count my blessings. I could never name them all, they are too great, but one of the main things I am thankful for is my grateful heart. All my blessings are from the Lord including that special one. I can always find something to be thankful for.

1 Thessalonians 5:18 says, "In everything give thanks; for this is the will of God in Christ Jesus for you."

In everything? That is what it says. I think He tells us to do that so He can bless even the not-so-good things in our lives. He does not say *for* everything but *in* everything. Since He is always in everything with us, we can be thankful all the time.

November 26th ~ Shaking

Have you ever known such fear that you were literally shaking? I guess we all have at one time or another. Sometimes we feel like the psalmist in Psalm 60:2-3 who says, "Oh, restore us again! You have made the earth tremble; You have broken it; heal its breaches, for it is shaking. You have shown Your people hard things; You have made them drink the wine of confusion."

I was thinking that the antidote for the "hard things" and the "wine of confusion" could be the communion wine. What better way than the Eucharist to get back in touch with the Lord? I am a great believer in taking the symbolic bread and wine as often as possible in remembrance of Him who died for all our "hard things" and "confusion." God is the author of peace not confusion. (1 Corinthians 14:33) So focusing on Jesus and all He did for us with His sacrifice on the cross is the perfect solution for all our shakings. (1 Corinthians 11: 23-26)

The answer for fear and trembling and the wine of confusion is Psalm 60:4-5 which reminds us, "You have given a banner to those who fear You, that it may be displayed because of the truth. That Your beloved may be delivered, save with Your right hand, and hear me."

One day when our dog Tippy arrived home from her daily walk without Bill, I was literally shaking with fear that he had been in an accident. I looked all up and down the road for him on his scooter and he was nowhere in sight. So I jumped in the car and backed out so fast that I ran into his car parked in front of the extra garage. If I had only slowed down and prayed, the Lord could have whispered "Trust Me" and I would have been fine, as Bill was.

I have heard, "Fear God and you will have nothing else to fear." Of course, that fear is talking about a reverential awe of the great and mighty God, remembering that "His banner over us is love" (Song of Solomon 2:4).

November 27th ~ Therefore Do Not Worry

The Lord hates worry. He commands us three times in the Sermon on the Mount not to worry. (Matthew 6: 25, 31, and 34 Wow! I used to be the queen of worry, the chief among worriers, before Jesus came into my life. I was such a worrier that I would worry if I was not worrying. When my daughters Grace and Julianne were five and two years old, we moved into a new house.

When they were older, I wanted a gaslight at the end of the sidewalk so there would be a light when they came home from dates. Talk about borrowing trouble way in advance. So Billy enrolled me in a Dale Carnegie class on How to Stop Worrying and Start Living. It was fun and I learned a lot, but nothing really helped till I asked Jesus to come into my life as Lord and Savior.

The things we worry about stop our blessings in some areas of our lives. Contrariwise, we are most blessed in the areas we worry least about. For instance, if I worry about money, that will stop the flow of provision in my life. I think I probably worry the least about my health and I have the least problems in that area (which is pretty amazing at my age).

Joseph Prince had a vision of soft golden pipes filled with oil of blessings flowing down to believers. But the pipes would be constricted if the believer began to worry in the areas of money, health, relationships, whatever. In this vision, the flowing of the oil of blessings would stop to a trickle when fear or worry came in. The Lord's blessings are always flowing to us, but we must receive them by faith.

Worry is unbelief in God's love and unbelief keeps us out of God's rest. We read in Hebrews chapter four about entering God's rest and the lack of faith in His goodness that will keep us from that rest.

Lord, I do believe, help Thou my unbelief. Amen. (Mark 9:24)

November 28th ~ Lava Lamp

My niece Tweet Hurst is a fantastic home decorator. She especially loves to decorate her entire house for each holiday. She arranges everything to perfection. Her husband, Jim, loves to tease her. So he will place something in the house that does not fit the décor. She usually finds it and quickly gets rid of it. But this Thanksgiving, after telling her guests of several days goodbye, she turned and gazed in horror at one of those blue lava lamps, popular in the 60's. It was nestled among her lovely antiques in a very prominent place in the living room. Talk about sticking out like a sore thumb. Her husband Jim really got her this time.

One day he put an old ugly wooden duck in with her elegant glass vases. One day the duck disappeared and he never found it. I am sure the lava lamp will be the next to go and be gone forever.

In the same way, one discordant note in our Christian walk will make a loud sound to the world. If we don't act in love in every part of our lives, people will see it and our witness will be spoiled. Picture being in a grocery line with a Christian that very piously asks you, "Do you love Jesus?" Then that person turns around and berates the checker. This action sticks out like a lava lamp among priceless antiques.

The world will never accept our message if our walk does not line up with our talk. Jesus accepts us just as we are, but He then begins the process of making us more like Him. People are watching to see if we are manifesting the love of Jesus in our lives. John 13:35 says, "By this all will know that you are My disciples, if you have love for one another."

Jesus tells us in the Sermon on the Mount in Matthew chapter five that we are to be lamps to give light to all who are in the house. Sounds like we need to show our love walk at home, too.

November 29th ~ Praise

The Lord inhabits our praise. The enemy is turned back, falls and perishes at the presence of our God. (Psalm 9:1-3) Praise not only honors God and empowers our faith, it is a powerful weapon. When we praise God, it works deliverance for us.

Abraham grew strong and was empowered by faith as he gave praise and glory to God. (Romans 4:20) As I praised God this past Thanksgiving, I felt my faith well up inside and I was empowered.

We were having a wedding for Julie's oldest daughter Beth here at the house on the Saturday following the big day. I was very concerned about having enough strength to make it through the whole week of company, Thanksgiving Day AND a wedding. But He promised me that I would have strength according to my days. (Deuteronomy 33:25)

I claim this scripture for Bill and me daily, but I always thought of it as for our days on earth, but that Thanksgiving Day He used it to bless me for the short term, too. (And I had more than enough strength for what turned out to be a very lovely wedding for an adorable couple with around 80 guests. Making it even more special, was that our precious Reverend Billy Flowers officiated.)

Proclaim His mercy! Mighty and powerful things happened when Israel proclaimed these words. They are words of praise and adoration to God. Remember that King Jehoshaphat appointed singers to proclaim "His mercy endureth forever" and their enemies destroyed themselves. (2 Chronicles 20:21-23)

Great things happen when you continually confess the mercy of God. Faith rises up inside you. The reality that God loves you begins to sing through your spirit. We are admonished to confess God's mercy in Psalm 118:4. Put these words constantly on your lips. You will begin to experience the thrill and joy of realizing God is indeed "rich in mercy" because of His great love for us. (Ephesians 2:4)

November 30th ~ Staying Hooked Up to Heaven

Perhaps the greatest challenge we face as believers is learning to correctly discern the voice of the Holy Spirit. God has always expected His people to do that. Even in the Old Testament, we see that God told Israel not only to obey His written Word, but also to obey His voice. (Jeremiah 7:23) He wanted them to know His will in specific situations. And He does us, too.

When the army of Israel invaded Jericho, they had to hear God's voice. Where else would they have acquired the strange battle plan they used? A seven-day march around a city as the most effective form of invasion did not make much sense in the natural. But Joshua listened to God's voice and heard His plan for victory. Then he obeyed God's instructions.

How do you cultivate such discernment and sensitivity? By staying hooked up to heaven, spending time in prayer daily and meditating on the written Word of God. THE MORE FAMILIAR YOU ARE WITH THE WRITTEN WORD, THE MORE EASILY YOU'LL BE ABLE TO RECOGNIZE HIS VOICE IN YOUR OWN HEART.

We need to maintain such an awareness and living contact with God that when He needs us to know something, He can reach us quickly. (I still think of the time that I was speeding and the Holy Spirit told me to slow down – I obeyed and shortly had a huge blowout.)

Remember though that the Holy Spirit is a gentleman and will not force Himself on you. If you want Him to be active in your life, you must give Him a place. We draw near to Him and He draws near to us. (James 4:8)

What a blessing it is to stay 'hooked up' to Heaven.

December 1st ~ Blind Disciples

Jeff Walker, our wonderful pastor at Victory Christian

Center in Rancho Mirage, gave the best teaching I have ever heard about blind Bartimaeus from Mark 10:46-52. He began by showing us that the disciples were as blind as Bartimaeus and that we are all blind in certain areas of our lives. The disciples actually told the beggar to be quiet and quit calling on Jesus. Sometimes people try to tell us to quit asking Jesus for help, too. (Compassionate, eh?)

Thankfully, Bartimaeus kept calling for Jesus to have mercy on him. Jesus stood still and commanded the disciples to bring the blind man to him. Then they acted like it was their idea. We read that Bartimaeus threw off his cloak and came to Jesus. This was very significant as he needed his beggar's cloak to be able to beg and now he would have to be completely dependent on Jesus.

Jesus asked him, "What do you want Me to do for you?" (He asks us this question, too.) Pastor Jeff was the funniest ever as he acted out the disciples' surprise at the question asked since the beggar was obviously blind. Pastor Jeff would point to his eyes or act like he was coughing and saying 'blind, blind' thinking Jesus needed help in recognizing the problem. (We sometimes put our own spin on what we think others need, too, when Jesus just wants them to admit their problem.)

We love the end of the story when Bartimaeus asked to receive his sight and immediately was healed. Jesus told him that his faith made him well.

I think we need to pray often to receive our sight in areas where we are blind. We need to be humble enough to admit that we have a need and then have faith in Him to meet that need. Lord, please give me eyes to see, ears to hear and a believing heart. Amen

December 2nd ~ "God's in His Heaven, All's Right with the World"

I've always loved hearing this statement because it means that God is sovereign and we need have no worries since He is in total control. I find this thought extremely comforting. I looked up where the quote originally came from and learned that is attributed to the poet, Robert Browning. (I am always amazed at what I can discover on the internet.)

It is so nice to know that He is in control of everything and, consequently, He will never allow anything to happen to us that will not be in our best interests.

Romans 8:28 says, "All things work together for good for those who love the Lord and are called according to His purpose." The Amplified Bible says it this way, "We are assured and know that (God being a partner in their labor), all things work together and are (fitting into a plan) for good to those who love God and are called according to (His) design and purpose."

I am sure I will never live long enough to stop be amazed at how God brought something good out of two terrible tragedies. These occurred within six months of each other; the premature deaths of William Burke Patterson and Ann Bridges Payne, leaving eight children between them. In truly miraculous fashion, He brought their grieving spouses, Clara Hurst Patterson and William Brant Payne, together to form a new family. Since the marriage was definitely created by Him, it has been a blessed one from start to finish with all members of the family drawing together in supernatural love.

We give God all the glory and continue to say "God's in His heaven, all's right with the world" as we trust Him with all our tomorrows.

December 3rd ~ Greatly Blessed, Highly Favored, Deeply Loved

I learned to speak this great confession of faith coupled with "I am the righteousness of God in Christ Jesus" from Joseph Prince who is one of my new favorite pastors/authors. I have read two of his books, *Destined to Reign* and

Unmerited Favor, and both greatly blessed me. Bill and I read a page from the *Destined to Reign Devotional* book each night and this really lifts our faith. (We need our faith lifted as we pray nightly for our huge family with a myriad of problems.)

When we speak forth the word of God into our own lives, we are GREATLY BLESSESD – Hebrews 6:13-14. We can go to the bank with the promise that He WILL bless us.

We are HIGHLY FAVORED – Ephesians 1:6. The word "accepted" in the original Greek text is *charitoo* which means "highly favored." Psalm 5:12

We are DEEPLY LOVED – John 3:16 sure ought to convince us that God didn't just love us, He SO loved the world that He gave His only begotten Son. He demonstrated His love for us when He sent Jesus to die on the cross for us.

We are the RIGHTEOUSNESS OF GOD IN CHRIST JESUS. 1 Corinthians 1:30 says, "Because of Jesus' perfect work on the cross, we are righteous by His blood."

So we can look into the mirror every morning and boldly declare, "Because of Jesus' perfect work on the cross, I am righteous by His blood, and I am greatly blessed, highly favored and deeply loved. I expect good things to come my way. I expect good success and I have a confident expectation of good!"

December 4th ~ The Secret Place, by Julie Setzer, Daughter

Is God afraid to ask you to do the Hard Thing? The Impossible Thing? The thing that causes you to say, "Oh no, Lord, please, not THAT thing." No, God is not afraid of anything.

One summer, a loved one of mine and I were at tremendous odds with each other. I knew that changes had to be made; hard, horrible changes. God specifically asked me to "let go" of my loved and cherished one, to place this priceless gift of mine in what I considered an unsafe zone, a danger zone.

"Lord, I cannot do that," I replied. "You've gone too far - You're asking too much. What if my loved one dies while apart from me? I could not bear it, Lord."

His reply to me, while gentle, stung to the core of my soul and caused a stillness in me. "I will be with YOU no matter what happens to your precious one. I will carry you through whatever pain awaits you. I will never leave you. I will be there for you. I will show you who I AM."

Although I didn't realize it until much later, I had just stepped into The Secret Place. The fact that there was no promise of my loved one's safety did not escape my notice, however, so I inquired of my Lord, "How do You expect me to handle this situation?"

"We are going to go through this together, just you and Me," He replied. "No one else is allowed in Here with us. You will talk only to Me about your pain, you will allow only Me to meet your every need, you will turn to Me for every answer. You will allow Me to wipe away every tear. You will climb into My lap and find rest there. I will become your Source. Watch what I am going to do and be amazed."

My life in The Secret Place had begun. I loved it from the moment I arrived there. It's a beautiful place, full of hope, compassion and strength; and sorrow, but sorrow that is extremely different from despair. There is no despair in the Secret Place, it's very quiet and safe. Jesus, the lover of my soul, ministered to me and showed me who He is. He gave Himself to me completely. He offered new revelations to me almost daily that silenced and calmed me and made me know beyond any doubt that He was taking care of the one I love. I still miss The Secret Place even though that experience was one of the most difficult times of my life. I tell Him that I loved it, would go again if He invites me, and am grateful He allowed me to go there with Him.

How do you get to The Secret Place? The road that leads to it is called "The Hard Road." It is also known as "The Road I Would Not Have Chosen For Myself." And how is my loved one? He is loved, and alive and so very, very precious to me and to the One who died for him. (Psalm 91:1)

December 5th ~ Great is Thy Faithfulness

This grand old hymn has such wonderful promises: "Great is Thy faithfulness, O God, my Father;" "Pardon for sin and a peace that endureth;" "Thine own dear presence to cheer and to guide;" "Strength for today and bright hope for tomorrow;" "Blessings all mine and 10,000 beside." Wow. Great promises and I receive them all. Just think about His presence "to cheer and to guide" us.

I used to think the Israelites were more blessed because they had the cloud to guide them by day and the fire by night. But I now realize that we are more blessed to have His Holy Spirit always living in us.

It took me a long time to figure out that the cloud guided but also protected them by hiding them from the enemy. And the fire at night was a wall between them and their foes. What a marvelous God we serve. He is so great and so good. I am constantly amazed by His unfailing care for His own. He never leaves us nor forsakes us.

I love the song "Move With the Cloud." The Israelites did just that. They had to wait each day to see if the cloud moved or stayed where it was. We, too, need to wait till the Spirit moves us.

John chapters 14-16 tell us all the advantages we now have because of the Spirit living in us. The Amplified Bible says in John 14:26, "But the Comforter (Counselor, Helper, Advocate, Intercessor, Strengthener, Standby), the Holy Spirit, Whom the Father will send in My name (in My place, to represent Me and act on My behalf), He will teach you all things. And He will cause you to recall, will remind you of and bring to your remembrance, everything I have told you." (This sounds especially good to me now that I am getting older and seem more forgetful. I can stop and call on my Helper to bring to my mind what I need to know.)

This Scripture promises His guidance and support in all our undertakings for Him—even our witnessing.

Praise God for His precious Holy Spirit who faithfully leads and guides us each day and points us to our blessed Savior.

December 6th ~ Grace of God

When I was a baby Christian, and even before, I thought of God as an all- benevolent Father who loved me so much that He yearned to give me everything to make me happy. Then I began to be taught a lot of do's and don'ts, rules, laws, and ways I was supposed to behave to become more like Jesus. Well, after being a Christian 40 years, I've come back to my original belief in the all-benevolent Father. I was right all the time, but well-meaning people caused me to focus on my own sins and unworthiness instead of the grace of God, and the sacrifice of Jesus, who died so that I could receive forgiveness for all my sins - past, present and future.

Since there is no way that I can possibly become worthy of God's love, I just have to believe in the shed blood of Jesus and personally receive His sacrifice for me — believe and receive.

We must remember we are not under law, but under grace, and that God is love and has perfect love toward us all.

I have found that when I focus on His love for me, then I don't want to displease Him by sinning. My desire becomes to fellowship daily with Him, learn from Him, and do His will more and more. Then, the world begins to lose its charm.

I think of the line from the hymn, "Turn Your Eyes Upon Jesus." It goes like this: "Turn your eyes upon Jesus look full in His wonderful face and the things of the world will grow strangely dim in the light of His glory and grace." So true!

In the Amplified, 2 Corinthians 13:12 says, "The grace

(favor and spiritual blessing) of the Lord Jesus Christ and the love of God and the presence and fellowship (the communion and sharing together, and participation) in the Holy Spirit be with you all." Amen. So be it.

December 7th ~ I Am Free, by Will Payne, Grandson

I was tired of waking up on a daily basis with the remorse and pain that comes with the life I was living. When I looked in the mirror, the man I saw wasn't even close to the man I wanted to be. My drinking was out of control and, as a result, so was my marriage. Alcohol had become so prolific in my life that I couldn't do anything without it. I couldn't even watch TV without a drink in my hand.

My wife Amber had warned me that if I didn't stop drinking, she was going to leave. I didn't even think I cared. That is how caught up I was in the grip of drinking. It was so bad that my work, family and even God came second to "King Alcohol." I was on a total path of self-destruction and didn't realize the pain and misery that I was causing others. I thought that I was just hurting myself and I was OK with that, but was in denial of the chaos I was causing the people around me, the people who loved me.

During all that time, God was trying to show that this wasn't the way that He wanted me living my life, but I wouldn't listen. That is, until I started to get into trouble with the law.

Now my freedom was on the table, but I couldn't stop. The crazy thing is that I wanted to stop. But I felt trapped. I didn't want to lose the woman God was so gracious to bless me with. I didn't want to lose the job or wonderful life I had on the rare days I didn't use alcohol.

On one cold day in December, I remember very clearly being alone in my house. I had pushed Amber away and she was staying elsewhere because she couldn't put up with my drinking any longer. I had just ended a drinking binge and woke up alone in bed. I had never before experienced the loneliness I felt that day.

God instantly came to me in that room and reminded me that I wasn't alone. He was there! Even though I hadn't been living for Him, He still loved me and was willing to forgive me if I would humbly ask. I got on my knees that instant and CRIED OUT to God. I started crying and praying for God to give me the willingness to turn my life around. I asked him to take control; I was tired of trying to do it on my own.

That same evening, I went to a place where God led me to get help with my alcoholism. Within time, I received that help and soon thereafter my marriage was restored as He had promised it would be. All desire to drink had been removed. I had renewed my commitment to my life, wife, job and most importantly God.

The level of freedom I started to feel was nothing like I had ever felt before. The Lord put this Scripture 1 Corinthians 10:13 on my heart, "There is no temptation taken you but such is common to man: but God is faithful, who will not allow you to be tempted more than you are able; but also with the temptation will make the way of escape, that you will be able to bear it." I have held it in my heart ever since.

Now I enjoy a life free from the bondage that held me in its grip so many years. I haven't picked up a drink since that December day and I will never have to live my life that way again. I now look forward to the days and years to come. My wife has the husband she always wanted and knew he could be. As long as I remember to keep God first, there isn't anything to fear and there is everything to look forward to. Thank you Jesus, I am trapped no more, I am FREE!

December 8th ~ Goodness of God

King David not only knew about the goodness of God,

He had seen it work in his own life. He rehearsed his victories. I love what David said in 1 Samuel 17:37 about fighting Goliath, "The Lord that delivered me out of the paw of the lion, and out of the paw of the bear, He will deliver me out of the hand of this Philistine."

Until we settle the fact that God is good and we like David can trust Him with our lives, our faith is never going to be great because we will always draw back in fear. Declare boldly, "I believe that I will see the goodness of the Lord in the land of the living" (Psalm 27:13). The more deeply you understand the truth of these words, the more you will be able to trust God in every circumstance of life. Your confidence in Him will make you bold when others are timid.

Of course, traditional religion has made people think they can't depend on the goodness of God. Religion has taught that one day God may make you sick or poor or whatever; even preaching that God gives you sickness and poverty to bless you. What a lie of the enemy. God is not confused about what's good and what's evil. He knows the definition of a blessing and a curse. Deuteronomy 28 spells out the difference between them. He names every sickness and lack and calls them a curse. And He promises in Galatians 3:13 that we are redeemed from the curse.

The Hebrew word *shalom* that the Lord uses so frequently to bless His people, means to have wholeness in your life: body, soul and spirit. It means there is nothing missing, nothing broken.

Psalm 145:7 says, "The Lord is good to all." He wants you to be able to say, "Look what the Lord has done; the Lord is good to all." And especially to me!

December 9th ~ Grace and Peace

2 Peter 1:2 says, "Grace and peace be multiplied to you IN THE KNOWLEDGE of God and Jesus our Lord." I guess this means that grace and peace are increased as we learn more about the Lord. That sounds good to me.

I really got carried away when I read 2 Peter 1:2 in the Amplified: "May grace (God's favor) and peace, (which is perfect well-being, all necessary good, all spiritual prosperity and freedom from fears and agitating passions and moral conflicts) be multiplied to you in (the full, PERSONAL, precise and correct) knowledge of God and of Jesus our Lord."

This means my own personal knowledge, not someone else's knowledge, of the Lord. We each need a personal knowledge of His grace, peace and favor, especially His love. Until we have this personal, precise, correct knowledge of Him, we will not be able to trust Him completely. We simply must know what a loving Father God He is and that He always wants the very best for us.

I have noticed how through the years His peace has matured in my life. I have so much more peace in times of turmoil or even crisis than I ever had before. I received His peace when I was born again and I love to say how the 'butterflies' in my stomach left. But I still would become agitated when things in my life were not going smoothly.

Recently it dawned on me that the things that used to bother me, now just roll off my back. I no longer 'sweat the small stuff.' And nearly everything that tries to come against me is 'small stuff' and of no eternal value, certainly not worth getting worked up about. What a blessing to truly know, "This, too, will pass." AND best of all that God is in control. AND I have His grace and peace multiplying in me to handle whatever comes in my life.

December 10th ~ God Had a Plan, by Payne Patterson, Grandson, Age 11, and His Daddy, Burke Patterson

My grandmother is a woman of great faith, but she hasn't always been that way. In fact, she spent her first 38 years mostly interested in her friends, social events, clothes, and having fun. She had a great husband, wonderful parents, and all the things of this world to make her happy. But the plan God had for her was much bigger than fancy parties and nice clothes.

He knew what it would take to bring her closer to Him and it came through a series of tragedies in her life.

The first tragedy occurred when her sister-in-law died of brain cancer. It happened right after my dad was born. If he would have been a girl, they were going to name her Jane. Aunt Jane was my grandmother's best friend in the world.

As sad as that was, nothing could prepare my grandmother for the shocking death of both of her parents a year later. They had spoiled her and she loved them dearly. They were very close and she talked to them every single day. When they passed away, she thought that she might not make it. However, she still had my grandfather, who was a good husband and was her strength. He carried her through this awful time and after a year and a half, things began to improve.

But just as things were getting better, the unthinkable happened. At only 38 years old, my grandfather – while jogging one afternoon right before Christmas – suffered a massive heart attack and died. That day, at age 37, my grandmother became a young widow with two teenage girls and my dad who would turn two years old on Christmas day. Her friends rallied to give her strength, but she couldn't see how she would make it on her own. She had never spent one night alone and felt helpless to take care of herself. She had never had to deal with any responsibility and was always surrounded by a support system. That had all but vanished in just a few month's time.

So over a period of less than two years, she had lost her best friend, both of her parents and now her husband. Her friends would take turns staying with her so she was with someone around the clock.

December 10th ~ God Had a Plan, Continued

She cried all the time. One day, she somehow worked up enough courage to tell her friends she was going to try to stay by herself in the house. No one thought she could make it, as she had always been an extremely fearful person. She thought she could do it on her own, but she couldn't. She was absolutely petrified and couldn't sleep.

In desperation, she cried out to God for help. She asked for strength and He heard her cry for help and He answered her just like it says in the Psalms. The next thing she remembers is waking up after a peaceful night's sleep and feeling full of hope. Although she had attended church and read the Bible, she truly became born again in Christ that night, alone in her bedroom.

Later on that year, she got a letter from her college roommate that one of their friends had died and left a husband widowed with five children. Walking from her mailbox to her house, she heard God tell her, "That will be your next husband."

God had a wonderful plan and they fell in love and married. But she wasn't sure how she was going to handle eight kids. Two separate families that both had been through tragedies were now united as one, put together by God's hand. We just celebrated their 37th wedding anniversary, all 57 of us.

My grandmother has taught numerous Bible studies, been a guest speaker on Radio and TV, authored a daily devotional book and has another on the way. She has ministered to countless people who have endured the loss of a loved one and has been a source of great inspiration to them. She always says that although God took away the people she loved the most, He gave her even more love than she could've ever imagined.

I was born their 21st grandchild, and am named after, and in honor of, the William Payne, the man my grandmother married. They now have 23 grandchildren, 11 great-grandchildren and we're still counting. I, of course, am their favorite.

December 11th ~ Who Could Ask For Anything More

Bill and I take communion on Saturday mornings and it is always a special time with each other and the Lord. Recently as Bill was praying, he was thanking the Lord for His salvation and His free grace. Then he prayed, "Who can ask for anything more?" Since then, the phrase has been going over and over in my mind. He's right - Jesus did it all. What more do we need? It is finished. He bought us everything we could possibly need. Salvation means wholeness and includes peace, prosperity, healing, comfort, and so forth.

"Who can ask for anything more?" is a line in the song "I've Got Rhythm" by George Gershwin, often sung by Ella Fitzgerald. I looked up the lyrics online and especially liked the verse: "Old man trouble; I don't mind him, you won't find him 'round my door. I've got starlight, I've got sweet dreams, I've got my man, who could ask for anything more?"

Doesn't that sound like people who have Jesus as Savior in their lives? They can tell 'old man trouble' (Satan) to leave in the name of Jesus. And believers do have starlight; the Light of the World. And all their dreams can be sweet because they have "The Man"—the Son of man—Jesus the Messiah—the Anointed One.

The chorus: "I got rhythm, I got music, I got my man, who could ask for anything more? I've got daises in green pastures, I've got my man, who could ask for anything more?" This time I noted that it said 'my' man. I love that. Jesus is 'my Man' who I depend on because in Him I have my life and breath and very being. And He makes us to lie down in green pastures. The Amplified says "fresh, tender green pastures." He also leads us beside the still and restful waters. (Psalm 23:2)

December 12th ~ Choked by Worry

One of the definitions of the Greek word for worry is "to choke." Jesus talks about how we can be choked by life's worries, riches and pleasures. Luke 8:14 says, "The seed that fell among thorns stands for those who hear, but as they go on their way they are choked by life's worries, riches and pleasures, and they do not mature."

Why is the Bible so adamant about us avoiding being choked by worldly fears and worries? Because God knows worry short-circuits our faith and relationship with Him. It fixes our eyes on our situation rather than our Savior.

Worry can become a habit, even a way of life, and it's not easy to let go of it. Unchecked, worry seeps into our thoughts, poisoning our joy, convincing us to give up on solutions before we've even tried them. Like Eeyore, the donkey in *Winnie the Pooh,* we can let our lives be consumed by negativity. So we say, "What's the use? It will never work." Instead of looking for the best through eyes of faith, we assume the worst. And we're not the least surprised when the worst finds us. That's how easy it can be to be choked by the world's ways of thinking.

Jesus is not telling us to live in denial. The truth is that every day we are surrounded by opportunities for fear, anxiety and worry. We may be facing relationships that are about to fail or situations that require wisdom and action on our part. But Jesus still tells us not to worry or fear.

When the Bible tells us not to worry, it isn't a suggestion; it's a command. Worry and/or anxiety are specifically mentioned 25 times in the New Testament alone as something we should avoid. And we can do it with the help of the Holy Spirit, so let's lean on Him and stay focused on the Lord's provision and care.

December 13th ~ Apple of My Eye

It is very exciting to think of us being the apple of God's

eye. He even says whoever touches us also touches Him. How scary is that for anyone who would try to harm us? I looked up "apple" in the Bible dictionary. It means the pupil of the eye; the most tender part.

The Promise - Zechariah 2:8, "For thus says the Lord of hosts, After glory He has sent me against the nations which plunder you, for he who touches you, touches the apple of His eye."

The Prayer - Psalm 17:8, "Keep me as the apple of the eye; Hide me in the shadow of Your wings."

The Fulfillment - Deuteronomy 32:10, "He found him in a desert land, and in the howling waste of a wilderness; He encircled him, He cared for him, He guarded him as the pupil of His eye."

That makes me feel wonderful knowing that if I am in a desert land, or in the howling waste of a wilderness, He encircles me, cares for me and guards me as the pupil of His eye.

It occurred to me that we strive to guard our eyes more than any other part of our bodies. They certainly are our most vulnerable part. How precious we are to Him.

Bill and I have laughed about when we were young, our parents always put apples, oranges and nuts in our Christmas stockings. We would just toss them out. We realized that it was a tradition with them because when they were growing up, fruit was more of a delicacy than in our day. Thankfully, the Lord never tosses us out as we are always valuable to Him. Isaiah 49:16 says, "Behold, I have inscribed you on the palms of My hands, My walls are continually before Me."

December 14th ~ Wait, Hope and Expect

We are told to wait on the Lord, but to wait expectantly and with hope for Him to act on our behalf; to patiently wait, but not without hope. And not just with resignation, but with expectant joy and knowing that He always answers our prayers in the best possible way. It is such freedom to trust His will in our lives; knowing that His will is always for our very best good.

The Lord does not want us to have a moment of worry. Once when son Burke was having a colonoscopy, I was concerned when the nurse told him that she had never seen a 40-year-old with such a low heart rate of 36. I was also concerned because Burke has had a heart murmur since he was a baby and his father died of a heart attack at 39.

The devil can really have a field day with me when there seems to be another problem related to Burke's heart. Once when worry really tried to come in, the Lord quickly gave me the perfect scripture that calmed all my fears. Psalm 27:14 in the New King James says, "Wait on the Lord, be of good courage, and He shall strengthen your (Burke's) heart, wait I say on the Lord." The footnotes say to "wait in faith." That is what I did and the test was fine and so was Burke. Praise the Lord! He is so faithful.

The Amplified, Psalm 27:14 says, "Wait and hope for and expect the Lord; be brave and of good courage and let your heart be stout and enduring. Yes, wait and hope for and expect the Lord."

Psalm 31:24 says, "Be of good courage and He shall strengthen your heart, all of you who hope in the Lord." Oh, I do hope in You, Lord. I notice I have Bill's and Burke's initials written beside this verse in my Bible and others that I have prayed for when they were suffering heart problems. "I wait for and hope for and expect You, Lord." (Psalm 25:21-Amplified)

December 15th ~ God Inside

2 Corinthians 6:16 says, "For you are the temple of the living God." God has said He will dwell within us. We should become God-inside minded. Say this aloud to yourself: "When I walk, God walks. His hands are my hands. I have the mind of Christ. God is not a million miles away.

He's inside me right now. He's my Father and I'm His very own child. I'm a joint heir with Jesus and my body is the temple of the Holy Ghost."

We can seal the deal of God's presence in our lives by continually confessing 1 John 4:4, "Greater is He - who is love - that is within me than he who is in the world." Cultivate within yourself the conscious awareness that God Himself, your very own heavenly Father, is walking with you and talking with you 24 hours a day, seven days a week.

When you begin to live in the light of that revelation, and begin to obey God's promise of His love inside you, you won't find yourself wandering around in the spiritual twilight or darkness trying to find your way.

He's INSIDE you! Believe it and you'll be walking in the light of heaven itself, hearing specific orders from headquarters at every turn. You'll be treading on the path of the righteous which is like the light of dawn that grows brighter and brighter every single day. (Proverbs 4:18) With this revelation that God is inside you, with you, around you, for you, you'll be His light to the dark world everywhere you go.

"Nor will people say, Look! Here it is! Or, see it is there! For behold, the kingdom of God is within you, in your hearts and among you, surrounding you." (Luke 17:21 - Amplified)

December 16th ~ Altar to God

Ezra 3:3 says, "Though fear had come upon them because of the people..." This phrase made me think: Isn't it always people that we are most afraid of? What will they think? What will they say? What will they do? Yes, I suppose most of our fears are based in fear of people.

Actually, I have heard it said that the fear of death is the foundation of all fears. But as Christians, we are no longer afraid to die. So it seems to me that fear of people now ranks highest. Especially to those of us who are people-pleaser types. We so desire that everyone loves and thinks well of us, when we should be more concerned about what God thinks of us.

But let's look at what they did in spite of fear: "...they set an altar on its bases and they offered burnt offerings on it to the Lord, both morning and evening." Glory! They built an altar to God even though they were afraid and offered praise to Him. What a marvelous way to combat fear. Praise always chases away the enemy.

Ezra and the other Israelites who had been taken away into captivity to Babylon, now had come back to Jerusalem to rebuild the temple. They were faced with many obstacles, but still took time to build an altar to God and offer sacrifices to Him. Even before the foundation of the temple had been laid, they set the altar on its bases or foundations. What a good picture of what we should do. Our foundation is Jesus and in His name we are to offer up our sacrifices of praise daily, both morning and evening.

I once heard it said that prayer is like an Oreo cookie - with prayer likened to the top and bottom that holds the middle together. Remember how children sometimes eat the middle out first? Well, we try to do that and our days fall apart without the base of prayer. I thought of a sandwich, too, as Jesus is the Bread of Life. Good to start and end our day with Him.

December 17th ~ ABUNDANCE

The best-known Scripture about ABUNDANCE is John 10:10 where Jesus tells us that He has come that we may have life and that we may have it more ABUNDANTLY. I never read that without getting excited. He wants us to have an ABUNDANT life in every way! The Amplified Bible says, "I came that they may have and enjoy life and have it in ABUNDANCE—to the full, till it overflows." Wow! Our lives can overflow with ABUNDANCE.

I was even reading in Psalm 37:11 that He wants us to

delight in the ABUNDANCE of peace. How good is that? And in Verse 19 that even in the day of famine, His people will have ABUNDANCE. Glory be to God. ABUNDANCE is God's heart for us.

Sometimes I have said to the Lord, "I don't feel as though I am having an ABUNDANCE in a certain area (finances right now)."

Of course, He answered me, "Well, you just need to trust Me in everything as ABUNDANCE is My solemn promise. And you will see the goodness of the Lord in the land of the living. Just wait on the Lord, expectantly and be of good courage and He shall strengthen your heart; wait, I say, on the Lord." (Psalm 27:13)

When we think of ABUNDANCE, we usually think of prosperity and He delights in our prosperity, too. (Psalm 35:27) ABUNDANCE means plenty, surplus, enough. But the best ABUNDANCE of all is the Lord's ABUNDANCE of forgiveness and loving-kindness to all who call on Him. (Psalm 86:5)

December 18th ~ The Wagons are Coming

The wagons are coming and they are filled with goods! That was so exciting for Jacob/Israel when he looked up and saw the wagons his son Joseph had sent from Egypt! Genesis 45:21-28. The wagons were filled with all kinds of good things and Joseph also sent 10 female donkeys loaded with grain and bread and sustenance for Jacob and his family for their journey to Egypt. (Verse 23) This was in a time of famine in Jacob's land and he had thought his son Joseph was dead. Instead, not only was Joseph alive, he had been made ruler of Egypt.

Have we ever needed to see some wagons filled with every good thing coming to us? Of course, we all have.

We are all on a journey and need daily provision. That's why we pray for our daily bread in the prayer Jesus taught His disciples and we call the Lord's Prayer. (Matthew 6:9-

18)

Can we trust the Lord to send wagons for us? Loaded with the best of every good thing? I believe that it is His nature to give us superabundantly more than we could desire or pray for. After all, Jesus said that He came to bring us the abundant life. (John 10:10) Every good and perfect gift is from the Father above. (James 1:17)

Certainly, we can trust God to send wagons - even overflowing ones! His desire above all things is that we prosper and are in good health even as our soul prospers. (3 John 2) So look up and see your wagons coming. They may be just over the horizon.

Author's note: Excerpts above from a sermon by Pastor Freddie Ward, Highland Park Assembly of God Church, Kilgore, TX.

December 19th ~ Communion

One of the biggest blessings I have is taking communion with the Lord early in the morning in our quiet time together. During that time, I like reading the passages in 1 Corinthians 10:16-17 and 11:23-26.

One morning, Bill's *Message Bible* was sitting on the table near me so I read those Scriptures for the first time in that translation. I was very excited when I read these words in chapter 1, "When we drink the cup of blessing, aren't we taking into ourselves the blood, the very life of Christ? And isn't it the same with the loaf of bread we break and eat? Don't we take into ourselves the body, the very life of Christ? Because there is one loaf, our any-ness becomes one-ness - Christ doesn't become fragmented in us. Rather, we become unified in Him. We don't reduce Christ to what we are; He raises us to what He is. That's basically what happened in old Israel, those who ate the sacrifices offered on God's altar entered into God's action at the altar." Wow!

In the next paragraph, we read of the futility of offering sacrifices to idols since idols are "nothing." Or worse than nothing, a minus, a demon! I began to think of what idols I sacrifice to. Surely I don't want to become part of something that reduces me to less than I am. As the saying goes, I can't have it both ways: banqueting with the Master one day and slumming with demons the next.

We don't hear the words 'idols' and 'demons' very much today, but that doesn't make them any less real. They are very serious words that we need to give thought to in our lives. For instance, I know that fear is a demon spirit that often tries to attack us. And an idol is simply something or someone that we put before God. Thankfully we have authority over both because of the Holy Spirit living in us.

December 20th ~ Locusts

Joel 2:25 says, "Then I will make up to you for the years that the swarming locust has eaten, the creeping locust, the stripping locust and gnawing locust...." Other versions mention hopping, crawling, consuming, chewing locusts—yuk. *The Message* calls them savage, deadly, fierce and even locusts of doom. I think we have seen them all in our lives at one time or another.

How about those chewing and gnawing locusts, the icky ones that keep pestering us. They chew on us, gnaw on us, creep up on us and strip us of our faith. They hop and crawl around then sneak up on us and try to consume the promise God has given us from His word.

Savage ones remind us of the old Western movies when the Indians were called savages and the pioneers greatly feared them. They would circle their wagons to protect themselves and shoot from a defensive position; or barricade themselves in their forts. (I'll never forget my prayer partner, Lee Ann Bratelli, reminding me not to let the Indians in the camp when I was starting back drinking just a little wine. This admonition has stuck with me for many years now.)

I think locusts are like that, too; they creep up on us

when we are least expecting them and often are deadly and bring about doom. Praise God, He promises to destroy those locusts and even restore to us the years they have already eaten. He even goes on to promise that His people will never be put to shame. (Joel 2:27)

Do you have any locusts gnawing on you right now? As we pray, believe and have faith in the Lord, He will keep the locusts away from our lives. Glory to His name.

December 21st ~ Lighten Up

In the Amplified Bible, John 14:27 says, "Stop allowing yourself to be agitated and disturbed; do not permit yourselves to be fearful and intimidated and cowardly and unsettled."

We can't worry and trust God at the same time. Peace should be a normal state for a believer. God's plan for our lives is that we would be filled with peace, joy and hope – no matter what the circumstances. He will set us free from worry, fear and frustration if we will only let Him.

God Almighty, Creator of the universe, cares intensely for you and is mindful of you. You are indelibly tattooed on the palms of His hands, and His thoughts about you and toward you are countless. So cast your cares on Him today. And whenever you feel anxious, run to Him in prayer. Exchange your anxiety for His peace. It really is OK to lighten up.

Proverbs 12:25 says, "Anxiety in the heart of man causes depression" or another version says "weighs it down." This is so true. Many people go through life upset, disturbed and tied in knots on the inside trying to carry the weight of the world on their shoulders.

Anxiety is being 'apprehensive or worried about what may happen, concern about a possible future event, worrying about things that haven't happened yet or things that have already been.'

To live in the fullness of the joy of the Lord, we must

find something to be glad about besides our current circumstances. We must learn to get joy from the Lord living inside us instead of what is happening outside us. Fullness of joy is found in His presence - not in His presents. (Psalm 16:11) So lighten up and rejoice!

December 22nd ~ Lavish

What a wonderful word! 'Lavish' means to bestow profusely. In the Amplified, Ephesians 1:7-8 says, "In Him we have redemption (deliverance and salvation) through His blood, the remission (forgiveness) of our offenses (shortcomings and trespasses), in accordance with the riches and the generosity of His gracious favor, which He LAVISHED upon us in every kind of wisdom and understanding (practical insight and prudence)."

Picture a king, possibly Solomon, sending out a caravan to retrieve his bride. The caravan would be filled with LAVISH, wildly extravagant gifts. Every conceivable thing to bless her; nothing held back. There would be gorgeous jewels, gold, spices, perfumes, choice foods, cloths beyond description, with special arrangements for her comfort during the journey. All this to be given before she arrives at the gorgeous palace built especially for her.

Doesn't this sound just like our God and how He yearns to bestow on us profusely, LAVISHLY, all we need or desire? He is the King of Kings and the Lord of Lords and we are His chosen bride. Not only has He prepared a mansion for us in Heaven with Him (John 14:2), but He wants us to be profusely blessed on our journey. He came that we may have an abundant life here on earth. (John 10:10)

I was thinking about how He has LAVISHED us with wisdom and practical insight.

Once when I was dressing, the Lord gave me a very practical idea and solution to something that was bothering me. It was a very little thing, but it showed me how very much He cares about even the smallest details of our lives.

I need to spend more time meditating on all His LAVISH gifts.

December 23rd ~ Magnify the Lord

Psalm 34:3 says, "Oh, MAGNIFY the Lord with me and let us exalt His name together." Psalm 69:30 says, "I will praise the name of God with a song, and will MAGNIFY Him with thanksgiving."

The Scriptures speak often of MAGNIFYING the Lord. One of my favorites is Psalm 35:27, "Let them shout for joy and be glad, who favor my righteous cause; and let them say CONTINUALLY, Let the Lord be MAGNIFIED who has pleasure in the prosperity of His servant." Continually? Wow. Of course, I had been majoring on the words about prosperity, but recently when I was meditating on it, I was convicted about not CONTINUALLY saying "the Lord be MAGNIFIED."

Then reading in Psalm 40:16, "Let all those who seek You rejoice and be glad in You; Let such as love Your salvation say CONTINUALLY, 'The Lord be MAGNIFIED'." The psalmist repeats it again in Psalm 70:3, "Let those who seek You rejoice and be glad in You, and let those who love Your salvation say CONTINUALLY, 'The Lord be MAGNIFIED'." And do we all love His salvation or what? We would be lost forever without it.

CONTINUALLY? How? Well, I guess the best way would be to pray in our prayer language, because in Acts 10:46 it says, "For they heard them speak with tongues and MAGNIFY God." I'm so grateful that when I speak in tongues, I am magnifying God, for I am not so sure that I am magnifying Him in my everyday life. Am I magnifying myself or Him? For instance showing His love in all situations? Or is my behavior showing the opposite? Important questions to dwell on and, in the meantime, I will try to SAY as often as possible: "Let the Lord be MAGNIFIED," the One who is worthy of all my praise all the day.

December 24th ~ Blessed, Not Stressed

When I asked the darling woman, who volunteers at the Victory Christian Center Church in Rancho Mirage, how she was doing, she replied, "I am blessed, not stressed." How cute was that? This is possible for all believers as we truly are blessed and knowledge of the blessing should keep us from being stressed. Of course, sometimes it doesn't work that way because we forget that God is always blessing us and we can lean on Him and totally trust Him with all our problems. When we try in our own strength, we tie his hands and He can't help us.

It seems at really busy times – especially holidays — we tend to get the most stressed. We probably bring a lot of it on ourselves. (My mother used to say for me to not get 'in a tizzy.') But we can do some things that will help us, for instance, spending more time in the Word. This always calms and strengthens us. God does not want us to have stress or distress in any way. The busier we are or the more we have situations of stress in our lives, the more we need to double up on prayer and Bible study.

Anxiety is certainly stress and the very first Scripture that I memorized still stands me in good stead when I start to feel the least bit anxious. Philippians 4:6-7 says, "Be anxious for nothing, but in everything by prayer and supplication, with thanksgiving, let your requests be made unto God and the peace of God which passes all understanding will keep your hearts and minds in Christ Jesus."

Also, I think I will remember the clever answer, "I'm blessed, not stressed." And when I begin to get stressed, I'll say like she did, "I'm entirely too blessed to be stressed."

December 25th ~ Merry Christmas

'Merry' means laughing, joyful, rejoicing and full of fun. Isn't it wonderful that this word is forever connected to the birth of Jesus? Yet it's not so amazing when you stop and consider what Christmas means.

The word Christ is the Greek Translation of the Hebrew word Messiah. (John 1:41; 4:25) Both the Hebrew and Greek words translate into English as 'anointing' or 'anointed.' To anoint means 'to pour over, rub into or smear over.' We know that Jesus is THE Anointed One, not just someone anointed with something.

The word 'mas' on the end of Christ in Christmas means 'to celebrate.' We certainly have enough to celebrate. No wonder the angels were so excited at Jesus' birth. (Luke 2:8-14) Good tidings of great joy, the Anointing is here. The Prince of Peace has come bringing reconciliation and good will between God and man. Jesus came that we may have life and that more abundantly. (John 10:10) That's something to celebrate – to shout about forever.

Early on the Christmas morning my son Burke was born, there was a hushed feeling of wonder and awe in the air – different than any other day of the year. How special I felt to be having a baby boy on Christ's birthday. I commented to Billy and Mother, "I feel like Mary must have felt." (I'm sure thankful I was in a nice Ford and not a donkey and going to a modern hospital instead of a stable.)

Burke feels special to have been born on Christmas Day.

Think about what 'Merry Christmas' means when you wish someone that greeting. 'Christ' is not His last name; it's His wonderful gift to us and to our loved ones – Himself!

December 26th ~ Lights

In the Sermon on the Mount in Matthew 5, Jesus says to His followers, "You are the light of the world." I have no trouble understanding that He is the Light of the world. (John 8:12) But to think that I have been called a light to the world, wow, my mind has a hard time accepting that thought. He goes on to remind us that a city set on a hill cannot be hidden, nor do they light a lamp and put it under a basket, but on a lamp stand and it gives light to all who are in the house. (I certainly pray that I am a light to my household.)

Jesus calls us to be lights in a dark world. Think of all the types of lights there are: candles, flashlights, lanterns, oil lamps, chandeliers, reading lamps, floor lamps, fluorescent lights, neon and on and on. From airport beacons to movie premieres. Strong lights or small bulbs, they are all lights.

But not all lights are a blessing. For instance, when we see flashing lights in our rear view mirror, or the strong light when a suspect is being interrogated. So consider what type of light we should be. Not harsh, glaring lights, but kindly lights; soft and sweet. (Remember the hymn, "Lead Kindly Light?" Jesus is a kindly light.)

Bill says I leave every light in every room in the house on and then open all the drapes for the sun to shine in. I admit that I do like everything bright. I notice the older I get, the more light I need to read or do handwork.

We are all different. One of my friends married for the second time and the hardest thing for her to become accustomed to was the very small wattage bulbs in her husband's home.

When I was growing up, we attended a church that had very high ceilings and huge chandeliers with sharp, pointed iron spears at the base. To a small girl, these were frightening as I could not help but think that if they fell, they could kill me or someone else. A light that could harm? O, my. Perhaps we should think of that. Even too much light from the sun is dangerous.

"Lights, camera, action," we all are on stage for the world, at least our own little world, with footlights showing our every move. We are to shine for Jesus, keeping our chimneys clean so we can glow for Him.

"Let your light shine before men." (Matthew 5:16)

December 27th ~ Talk to My Hand, My Ears Are Not Listening, by Rachel Rice, Friend

What cutting words; I couldn't believe my ears! My face turned red and my temperature skyrocketed. I suppressed my anger until I got to my car. "He's the last person I would have expected to not understand or care," I thought. "After all," I consoled myself, "he's old enough to be my father! What does he know about what I've been through, or how I feel?" I bawled and cried until my eyes were swollen and tired, and even my head ached. "Everywhere I turn, I have to deal with uncaring people!"

A couple of times I half-heartedly tried to make peace with a friend, to salve my conscience and smooth out my emotions, but I couldn't seem to get a handle on it. Many times over, I sorted through all the aspects and happenings. What had I done to deserve this? Depression and fatigue settled in, and that's when I went to counsel with my pastor. He would surely understand. He was gentle, firm and gracious, but still honest and forthright as he told me, "Depression is nothing but selfishness!" Wow!

"By Golly! It's not my fault. I've bent over backwards! They're the cause of all this hurt," I reasoned. Took me about nine months to realize my pastor had given me healing truth in his genuine love and courage by speaking directly to me for my own good. He was right! I needed to deal with my own soul and pull out those hideous weeds I'd watered and grown myself.

I learned the hard way that good seeds bring great gladness; bad seeds harvest weeds that sting, stick, and can leave prickles under the skin. Stubbornness, with selfishness, digs in unless given a determined yanking out for a clean and happy garden. Anyone else for pulling out weeds today?

"Create in me a clean heart, O God, and renew a right, persevering, and steadfast spirit within me" (Psalm 51:10).

December 28th ~ "Darkest Before the Dawn"

Psalm 46:5 in the Amplified says, "God is in the midst of her, she shall not be moved (shaken); God will help her just at the break of dawn or when the morning dawns (at the turning of the morning)."

This verse sounds like the old saying, "It is always darkest before the dawn," doesn't it? How many times have I quoted that to myself or other people for encouragement? And it is encouraging to think that no matter how bad things get, there will always be a dawning.

After the night, just when we are about to give up, here comes the dawn and everything is better. God is always just in time. The Amplified says, "God will help her right early (at the dawn of the morning)." This reminds me of "weeping may last for a night, but joy comes in the morning" (Psalm 30:5). I like the thought that "joy comes." We don't have to search for it – it comes.

Joy certainly came to me in the personal knowledge of Jesus as Savior and Lord after the deep sorrow of losing my beloved first husband. Because of my salvation experience, I was able to face my grief and realize that I mourned, but not without hope. As I began to study His Word, I learned that He Himself had sent His Comforter who would be by my side (in the midst of me) and I would not be shaken. I read in 1 Peter 5:10 that after I suffer for a little while, the God of all grace who called me to His eternal glory in Christ, will Himself perfect, confirm, strengthen and establish me. I clung to that promise and He proved it to be true. Talk about joy! He quickly brought me another precious husband and five more wonderful children.

God is in our midst – always with us and, after a night of trouble, He will bring us restoration and joy. With Him, all our dawns are joyful.

December 29th ~ Take My Pain, Lord

This was my plea and the Lord quickly answered, "Give it to Me." He can say something so profound in so few words. A truth – we have to GIVE Him all our pain for Him to be able to do something about it. He will not take away our free will and choice. We have to freely give it to Him. He is a Giver not a taker. And He always gives superabundantly more than we can desire or pray for. (Ephesians 3:20)

In remembering back to when I received this revelation from the Lord, I think it was my spirit that was grieving; it was not a physical pain. Sometimes that kind of grief is even harder to give up to Him. We want to hug our hurt feelings to us, dwell on them and think about how unfair a person or situation was. We can more quickly give up a physical pain.

Also, I began to think that we have to give up our bad habits to Him – He will not take them away from us. As we give them to Him, He will then take away our desire. In fact, it is only with the help of the Holy Spirit that we can hope to break a stronghold in our life. I guess a stronghold is anything that has a 'strong hold' on us.

Right now I fight overeating, especially sweets during the holidays. I console myself thinking that the Israelites had times of feasting. They did not continue for weeks like I do until all the Christmas goodies are gone. I must practice what I preach and give up to Him the tendency to overeat and really let Him break that stronghold in my life. (That is not the only sin I struggle with, but the current one of which He is convicting me.)

1 Corinthians 10:13 says, "No temptation has overtaken you except that which is common to man; but God is faithful, who will not allow you to be tempted beyond what you are able, but with the temptation will also make the way of escape, that you may be able to bear it."

December 30th ~ "Boy Hidee"

Bill and I laughed when I came out with that old expression. And then we began to wonder where in the world it came from. He pointed out that we never said "Girl Hidee," just "Boy Hidee." Talk about dredging up oldies, wow.

At the Hurst family Christmas party I said something about Burke having a "keen" cover on his truck bed, and Burke and the Hurst boys all laughed and teased me about my archaic saying. O dear, I must become conversant with the new lingo of the 21st century. I've never been very up to date, but now in my 70's I am really far behind. I think something being called 'neat' may be outdated, too.

The great thing about God is His Words never change. They never go out of style. The Word of God endures forever. (1Peter 1:25; Isaiah 40:6-8) Our God's Word stands firm. Fads and styles may come and go, but God's Word stays the same from age to age. The "thee's and thou's" are not in the more modern translations of the Bible, but their meaning remains the same.

Malachi 3:6 says, "I am the Lord, I change not." Our understanding of Him may change, but He does not. Jesus showed us how we could have a personal relationship with Father God and serve Him without the fear that the Israelites had for Him in the Old Testament. He has not changed, only our interpretation of Him.

He has always been a God of love because He is love and cannot be unloving. But He is also a God of justice and allows man to make his own choices, which sometimes cause unpleasant consequences. God did not cause sin to come into the world – man did.

But praise His name, He sent a Savior to save us from our sins if we will only accept Him and believe on His power to save us. Hebrews 13:8 says, "Jesus Christ is the same yesterday, today and forever." What security those words bring.

Boy Hidee!

December 31st ~ It is Finished

Every believer sincerely wants to change to be more like Christ but, for some, Godly fruit never seems to manifest. The reason may be that we believe Jesus was sent to deliver us from our sins, but not from the power of sin. (Romans 6:11) We are dead to sin because we were crucified with Christ.

Take a closer look at who we are in Christ, what we have in Christ and how we can be changed into His image. We can see this truth in a new way and the truth can set us free. Knowing who we are in Christ is the first step to receiving the benefits of the finished work of the cross. Each one of us is a spirit, we have a soul and we live in a body. When we are born again, our spirit becomes instantly and totally renewed, the very core of who we are becomes just like Jesus. (2 Corinthians 5:17)

The moment we accept Jesus as our Lord and Savior, who we are totally changes. The Divine Seed of God containing all the characteristics of His nature is deposited in our spirit, giving us a growing desire to do what is right.

It is very important that we see that we are not trying to become the righteousness of God but that we are the righteousness of God the instant we are saved. (2 Corinthians 5:21) We are not the same old person with 'Christian' stamped on our heads, but we are altogether new creatures. Although what we do may not have changed yet, who we are has. All we need to do is believe it.

Little by little, He changes us. (2 Corinthians 3:18) Our job is to cooperate with Him and yield to His promptings. Why doesn't He do it all at once? Because He wants us to lean on Him for the grace (strength) to overcome, not rely on our own strength. He wants us to remember that He finished the work on the cross.

About the Author

Clara (Sister) Hurst Payne, is a native of Longview, Texas, where she and her husband Bill attend the Longview Christian Fellowship. She has spoken to numerous Christian Women's groups in Texas, Oklahoma, and California, and has taught two weekly Bible Studies for more than 30 years.

More Morning by Morning and her first book *Morning by Morning* are primarily compilations of journals she has kept during her early morning quiet times of communion with the Lord as she prayed and listened for His voice.

Sister was born again after a series of tragedies in her life. In less than two years she lost her dear sister-in-law, adored mother and father, and her beloved husband who was 39, who left her with two teenage daughters and a two-year-old son. Thankfully the Lord blessed her with another wonderful husband and five more precious children.

Sister has since lost her brother at age 53 and beloved daughter-in-law at 42 and special mother and father-in-law. She has endured struggles with alcohol, cervical cancer and financial loss, but continues to radiate the joy of the Lord as she grows closer to Him daily through the indwelling of the Holy Spirit.

She and Bill now divide their time between Texas and Palm Springs, California, where they attend Victory Christian Center. A weekly bible study that began in their home has grown so large that it is now meeting at the church.

They are blessed with eight children, 23 grandchildren and 17 great grandchildren with number18 on the way.

For prayer requests or speaking engagements, contact: Clara (Sister) Hurst Payne, 106 Village Green Drive, Longview, TX 75605 or 1260 Avenida Caballeros, Palm Springs, CA 92262.

Her Longview telephone number is 903-758-4889 and her cell phone is 903-452-0783.

Her Email address is sispayne@aol.com

Other Exciting StoneGate Books

The Incredible Journey of a Mafia Soldier takes a look inside the *Mafia's* murder, treachery and intrigue and one's man's search for the true meaning of life.

That man is Frank Bower who grew up in the Gambino crime family of New York City and became the personal body guard for godfather John Gotti.

"Hence, I entered the inner circle of the most powerful *Mafia* family in America," Frank says. "But I never realized how dangerous it was to serve in John's underground empire…Being around John empowered all of us to believe we could conquer the word — at least the world of crime. We were so busy making money we didn't consider the fact that the last stop on the journey of crime is the cemetery."

During his 15 fateful, danger-filled years in organized crime, Frank was arrested on 14 attempted-murder and12 aggravated-battery charges. He served two prison sentences including nine months on death row.

The Incredible Journey also tells how Frank escaped from the *Mafia* and found the true meaning of life. He became a faithful servant of God and today he ministers to men in prison all across America.

Days of Anguish, Days of Hope is the heroic story of Chaplain Robert Preston Taylor who spent 42 months in Japanese prison camps during World War II.

On Dec. 7, 1941, the Japanese bombed Pearl Harbor and Manila, the Philippines, the next day. Taylor was caught in a maelstrom of war and the every-day fight for survival.

He ministered to the fighting men on the front lines during the Battle for Bataan and received the Silver Star for bravery. He endured the Bataan Death March - where thousands of American soldiers died - the Cabanatuan Prison Camp, and the so-called "hell ships" that were bombed by American pilots who did not know the American prisoners were on board.

After he was liberated in 1945, he returned home to learn that his wife Ione, who was told he had died on the "hell ships," had remarried. Although devastated by the sad news, he decided to remain in the military and years later President John F. Kennedy named him Air Force Chief of Chaplains with the rank of major general.

The Commissioner is the intriguing true story of death and deception and reveals a corrupt political battle during the 1970s that threatened Shreveport, Louisiana. The city's police commissioner – the most powerful lawman in the state – was behind multiple scandals including racism, payoffs, theft of city funds and tampering with a grand jury. He may also have been involved in the murder of an advertising executive who was scheduled to testify against him in court.

The Commissioner tells the story of how *Mafia* boss Carlos Marcello was in league with the commissioner to bring organized crime into the City of Shreveport. However, dedicated reporters at *The Shreveport Times* newspaper exposed the plan. (Available at www.billkeithbooks.com and your local book store).

The Magic Bullet is a novel about a scientist who discovers the secret of life extension. However, the discovery creates all kinds of problems for him. A recluse billionaire in Chicago – who is dying – wants to find the secret and sends his men to kidnap the scientist. Also, the Chinese government hires a New York City *Mafia don* to find the scientist and learn the secret. The scientist hides out in the Barataria swamps below New Orleans and joins a motorcycle gang en route to the biker's rally at Sturgis, South Dakota, where he is captured by the billionaire's men and taken to Chicago. The reader will laugh and cry but will never forget the dramatic climax.

The Prayer Bag and Other Stories that Warm the Heart takes the reader on a spiritual journey through the prayer lives of some of the greatest Christians the world has ever known... a missionary in the jungles of Sumatra who prayed for a nail and found one; a survivor of the dread Ravensbruck Concentration Camp in Germany who prayed for a sadistic guard who brutalized her sister while in the camp; an evangelist who witnessed to Emperor Hirohito of Japan after World War II; and a preacher who carried a cross around the world. "And you will read about my dear wife Vivian Marie who carries a prayer bag with her everywhere she goes." ~ The Author

Gettin' Old Ain't for Sissies is a road map to guide all you older guys and gals through the golden years and help you live a vigorous and exciting life into your 70s, 80s and even the 90s. So get ready for the greatest challenge of your life as this book takes you places you've never been, tells you a story you've never heard and inspires you with a hope you'll never forget.

The thesis of the book is that old age doesn't have to be the end of the line. It can be a bright new beginning."

W. A. Criswell/the Authorized Biography is the story of a man who was the pastor of the First Baptist Church in Dallas for nearly 50 years. Some believe he was the greatest preacher of the 20th century.

Evangelist Billy Graham called him "one of the greatest pulpiteers of our generation and through the years one of my closest personal friends."

Dr. Robert Jeffress, current pastor of the First Baptist Church in Dallas, called him the "Prince of Pastors."

The Rev. Rick Warren, author of *The Purpose Driven Life* and pastor of the Saddleback Church in California, said that Dr. Criswell "was my father in the ministry. He's been an incredible influence in my life."

Dr. Criswell served two terms as president of the Southern Baptist Convention and preached throughout the world.